ISBN 978-0-259-09882-9
PIBN 10596073

1 MONTH OF
FREE
READING

at
www.ForgottenBooks.com

By purchasing this book you are eligible for one month membership to ForgottenBooks.com, giving you unlimited access to our entire collection of over 700,000 titles via our web site and mobile apps.

To claim your free month visit:
www.forgottenbooks.com/free596073

quirement surprising in persons of their
tender years, and as uncommon by the too
prevailing mode of education.

With pleasure, with pride, I made the
remark; and felt only anxious to trace back
this exquisite singularity to its grand cause.
The task was easy. I found it to have an
origin in the fulfilment of every maternal
duty. From their infancy you, Madam, had
been a real mother, a friend, a companion.
With every soft embrace you instilled a
lesson of piety, of virtue, of honour. With
every recreation of infancy you wove a
principle of goodness, or of morality.—
Thus in a few precious years, having se-
cured the useful of education, you allowed
your children to seek for elegance; and
elegance was added, under the most lovely

of

of all appearances,—the gracefulness and majesty of virtue. .

To you, Madam, an example both as a Mother and a Peeress of the Realm, I request permission to dedicate this work; and those who have the happiness to know you will proudly acknowledge the justice (at least) of my wishes.

, With unfeigned respect,

I am, Madam,

Your Ladyship's faithful,

Obedient servant,

ELIZABETH APPLETON.

CONTENTS.

―――――――

ERRATA.

PRIVATE EDUCATION,

&c. &c.

ADDRESS TO PARENTS.

BEFORE I attempt to offer my thoughts upon the inconveniences and advantages attendant upon the private education of your Daughters, I must beg leave to say a few words on the subject of those by whom, under the superintendance of your maternal and watchful eye, this education is conducted.

It is allowed by all, that the fashion of engaging at a stipulated salary a female by the year, for the purpose of educating young ladies in the houses of their parents, is become very prevalent within the last forty years. This is a fact to be lamented for three reasons; the first is, that as the profession of a private governess is an honourable and genteel one, and carries with it an air of opulence and grandeur extremely dazzling to the eyes of young females in middle life, they are anxious to become so, and their heedless parents not considering the expense and exertions necessary to gratify them, and being entirely ignorant of the heavy requisites the situation de-

The fashion of engaging a private governess has gained ground;

and is to be regretted for three reasons,

B   mands,

because first, many totally unqualified are dazzled by appearances,

mands, readily agree to their daughter's wish, that she may be a governess, like Miss Jones or Miss White, who with her pupils, called one day in a carriage to make a few purchases at their shop. The young woman, who may have had a year or two of *schooling*, is then put to some seminary as under teacher or apprentice; where, having remained a short time exercising her ta-

and hasten to finish a superficial education.

lents, if she have any, in a very limited sphere, she is considered by herself and parents, as sufficiently prepared to enter into one of the most difficult situations in life. An advertisement is drawn up by some clever friend of the family (if Miss .. will allow of a helping hand!), and this being answered by some thoughtless persons, who conceive

They apply for situations asking very small salaries,

from its style that the applicant may do very well with the assistance of a master or two, and supposing also, that she cannot demand a *high* salary, they appoint a time for an interview. She is engaged. The unfortunate children, whose minds she is destined to improve, are put under

but are entirely ignorant of their duty, and perhaps ruin their pupils.

her care; and woe be to them, if they have any little obstinacy, ill temper, vanity, pride, or selfishness, on her introduction. She may be gentle, kind, or patient, but she is ignorant of her business, and this business is not to be ac-

Theory is nothing in education without practice.

quired by any means but practice. Theory may do much with practice, but without it, nothing. It may be asked, " if young women are thus stigmatized upon their first onset in the world, when

when are they to hope for encouragement ?" This question is natural, and deserves to be candidly answered.

Far be it from my wish, to damp the early efforts of a sensible and feeling mind. Every one must make a beginning; but the foundation of the future fabric must be laid with care, and it should be sufficiently solid to ensure the safety of its superstructure. From amongst the hundreds of young females who are parading London and its immediate vicinity, in search of places as governesses, many would be more suitably employed in attending to their parents' books; in nursing their young sisters and brothers, and in teaching them to read, write, and sew. Some are qualified, by nature and cultivation, to shine in one or two arts, in which the mind has little share. These might be advantageously apprenticed in the families of respectable professors, and with industry, they might themselves, in due time, give daily instruction in the favourite pursuit. Others are fitted for the more general duty of scholastic business ; in which youth is governed by rule and precedent ; wherein the grand stimuli to application, are comparison and emulation ; through which education is seen like a broad beaten track without turning or winding, where no one can lose himself who has the perfect use of his faculties. Thus, this class of females might be eligible teachers in schools, and would

Many females that aspire to be governesses would be more respectable in other stations.

B 2   pass

A few who are steady, and have been trained up to virtue and innocence, are fit subjects for preparatory governesses;

pass through life in an honourable manner. The residue of the throng we may find to be, first, those who, if not fashionably or expensively, have been carefully and piously instructed; who, if they have acquired little of accomplishment, have learnt less of prejudice and vice; who with bashfulness and timidity, have the more of innocence; whose minds, if they have not been highly cultivated, are not warped by error, and are open to conviction; and whose taste, if it be not fashionably delicate, has the less been corrupted by improper books and pursuits. With such a subject you may entrust your young children. Place in

but they must be requested to study the duties of their profession.

her hands the most useful books upon education; request her to extract, to read, to comment, and above all to reflect. Give her the theory, she will practice upon your children with success. Your good advice, which should be given with gentleness and persuasion, will take deep root in her mind, and the most promising appearances

At first, they should not rule alone.

will follow. By no means leave her to herself with your children; recollect, she is young and ignorant: teach your little daughters to respect and to love her, and she will love them. Sentiments of affection, esteem, respect, and gratitude, are generally reciprocal. If the tutor love

Children should be encouraged to love them.

his pupil, the pupil certainly has a regard for his preceptor; do not be fearful then, in allowing

Different sentiments of affection may

your daughter to love her governess. Her regard for the preceptress does not, in any degree, lessen

her

her love for you; besides, where there is no regard, there is no interest. Why does a parent take such pains to form the heart of his child? Because the strength of his affection gives rise to the uncommon interest he feels in its welfare. By this rule, if a governess find nothing in her pupil to excite her affection, her heart not being interested she will perform her bare duty; but the lively zeal, the animating smile, the patient ear, the beating heart, the watchful eye, are never to be looked for. The duty is a heavy duty; it is not the unwearied exertion of a person who sees a captivating prospect in perspective, and mounts the hill with panting steps and sparkling eye in the hope of soon reaching its summit.

Your daughters should be young if their governess is so. If she be eighteen, the age of your eldest child ought not to exceed eight. There should at least be ten years between them; so that by the time you shall have formed your governess (which may be in two or three years as she is more or less steady in adopting a system) you may insensibly commit them wholly to her care. If she deserve your confidence, prove it to her; study her happiness; promote her innocent amusements; liberally increase her salary, and raise her to a level with yourself. Gratify her little ambition, and, if she wish it, let her be a parlour guest after studies are over; and whenever your children are present why should she be ex-.

cluded?

exist in the same breast;

and the fostering of them is conducive to benevolence.

Reciprocal affection a great assistance in education.

There should always be a disparity of years between tutor and pupil.

The wishes of the governess must be consulted and gratified;

and she will feel herself bound by gratitude.

cluded? Is she not their companion, their adviser, their instructress, their friend, their second mother? Does she not stand in your place? Have not you yourselves invested her with the authority of a parent? Does she not practise that which it is your duty to teach? If you have time or inclination to do without, why do you employ her? Do you consider that example is more powerful than precept, and that your children's manners, opinions, ideas, will take their colouring from the person they are most with? And with whom are they in the study, in the bed-chamber, in the grove, or the square—You, or their governess? I should confidently answer the latter. Then if the governess is worthy of being a pattern of imitation to your second selves, she is surely entitled to a seat at your table and a place in your society.

The residue of young females who are in search of places as governesses, is chiefly composed of the daughters of naval and military officers, clergymen, barristers, physicians, and merchants. These professions, honourable, active, and even laborious as they sometimes are, and forming, as they do, a grand pillar of the constitution, depend greatly upon the chances of fortune to enrich their followers. The amiable wife of the captain or the naval lieutenant, may, in her husband's absence upon his noble duty, superintend her little domestic concerns. Order, economy,

Her duties are vast, and parental.

The child will in many respects greatly resemble her.

The last of the throng of young women seeking situations are the daughters of those who follow liberal professions;

economy, piety and industry prevail in her abode
of peace. Her daughters grow in innocence,
and blossom in the encouraging soil which gave
vigour to their first sprigs of virtue. The father
is incapacitated for service, or calamities of war
have terminated his existence. In the event of
the first circumstance, the officer returns to his
pleased, yet lamenting family, and subsists upon
half his late pay. In the second case, his widow
leans for support on the generosity of the state.
To neither is there an alternative. The young
girls are growing into women; they must depend
upon themselves for subsistence. Thus, with a
trembling hand, the mournful parent leads her
timid child from house to house in search of its
future home.

- The curate, who lives upon his hundred a year;
the barrister not yet in fashion, and whose emo-
luments are uncertain; the physician, whose name
is unknown to the great world, and whose prac-
tice scarcely affords support to a large family;
the merchant, of indefatigable industry, but
whose losses are overwhelming;—these men, as
fathers, may feel anxious to put aside a little
property for their children's use; but anxious
exertion, when opposed to insurmountable ob-
stacles, avails nothing. The hand of death ap-
proaches. Young men may struggle with the
world, but their delicate orphan sister shrinks
from its rude gaze; the idea of being a burthen

and are re-duced to the necessity of seeking a live-lihood.

to her relations is insupportable, and the probability is, that she has not the opportunity of modestly declining their offer of temporary protection. Of employments for women, there are none but the education of youth in which the mind has any share, and upon this she is neces- They are not however always calculated to practise tuition with success; sitated to rest her hopes. From amongst the number of females thus thrown into active life, a few may be found who pine in secret at their lot. These have an appearance of melancholy, and are constantly drawing comparisons between their present and former situations; they dread the frowns or cold looks of their late acquaintances, and when walking out always conduct their pupils through the most private walks in order to avoid them. Such are not, alas! calculated for governesses. I have met with several of this description, and have invariably found their minds too mortified and depressed to enter into the spirit of private tuition. We may sincerely pity them, but but a few of them are ornaments to their profession. pity will not teach them to educate the child. Others of the number, from having been liberally and carefully brought up, become, with little gentle advice and kind treatment on your part, and with reflection and attention on theirs, great acquisitions to the families in which they are engaged.

The portrait of a truly finished governess. Hitherto, I have only spoken of those governesses who have at first scarcely any claims, or of those who have none to the title. It remains for me to undertake the more difficult yet pleasing

task

task of representing to you the contrast, in the picture of a truly finished preceptress. By the word *finished*, I would not be understood to mean the elegant dancer, fine piano-forte player, charming painter, or learned French grammarian. Accomplishments are useful in their way, as resources against fashionable *ennui*, and as they help to furnish the young lady with real, or often supposititious attraction, made necessary on every occasion, in every society, under every circumstance, by the present rage for them. Thus my finished governess may, or may not, excel in painting, or on the piano-forte; she may even dance well: but she will not, assuredly, attach any importance to these accomplishments, if put in competition with the *useful* parts of education. Her age is from five and twenty to forty. She has been an instructress for some years, and has deeply studied the duties of her situation. Her countenance is open, mild, and prepossessing; not from the influence of beauty, but from the general character of conscious rectitude. Her dress is more handsome than fine; more neat than shewy; her clothes are made genteelly, but within extremes. Her whole air bespeaks the gentlewoman. Her language is correct, pure, and free from the slightest affectation, and her sentiments are naturally, cheerfully, and candidly delivered. To a strong and reflective mind are added a refined taste, correct judgment, good

She may be clever without being accomplished.

If she has accomplishments, she considers them as secondary requisites.

Her age is the prime of life, and her appearance is the integrity of virtue.

She is elegant in mind, and possesses whatever can give dignity to manners;

memory,

memory, watchful eye, and quick intellectual perception. She is pious, patient, and affectionate, and is without prejudice. Besides these qualifications, she has a mind well stored with the knowledge of nature; of history from the best authorities; of general geography, the manners and customs of nations, and of the grand outlines of astronomy; she is acquainted with the biography of her own and of other countries, and has a taste for literature. Music, French, drawing, may be taught by professors, but these also she has studied, although she values the acquisition of them only as they may be advantageous to her pupil·upon quitting London masters for the season.

and her knowledge is liberal and extensive, consisting more in noble outline, than in cramped particularity.

,Oh, fond Parents, who clasp your enquiring prattlers to your bosom, and look with extasy upon their opening reason, can you nip every generous and sweet sentiment in the bud? can you risk every promising charm? can you expose the weak side of your daughter's infant disposition to the batteries · of ignorance and superstition? can you endure the frightful idea that your sweet child's failings will grow into vice? can you run every risk, for (I blush to name it!) a little saving of money? Paltry consideration. What! can you place over your children a weak-minded, inexperienced, rash preceptress, and decline the strong recommendation of your friend, merely upon the ground of salary?

Whether it be a prudent economy to engage an ignorant, narrow-minded preceptress, who may require but little salary but who ruins the child.

Whether from a fortune of three, six, ten, or twenty thousand pounds per annum, a hundred and fifty or two hundred

Is

Is money then so great an object to you? Would fifty or a hundred guineas, more or less, make a sensible alteration in your yearly income? If so, I would presume, with respect, to advise your sending away the governess. Better that your children should take their chance with a master occasionally, than be made by example and pre-cept, or rather, from want of precept, prejudiced, frivolous, silly, ill-tempered women. On the other hand, if you can afford to give grand enter-tainments, to keep up a handsome establishment and fashionable equipages, you surely can give a deserving woman one hundred and fifty or two hundred guineas *per annum*, for dedicating her youth, abilities, strength, and mind to the service of your children! You should recollect, that however the profession of governess be pleasing to an amiable-minded woman, yet she must have other motives in following it than those of plea-sure. Every one must feel how very precarious is health, and a few may call to mind, that the duties of preceptors are arduous, and very trying to the constitution. At eight and thirty, or forty at most, a governess should retire upon her well-earned competency. Either her salary should have been such as to ensure a future indepen-dence, or a pension from the nobleman or gen-tleman's ample fortune, whose children she has faithfully served, should be allotted to her for life; and this in the most delicate manner, with-

pounds should be spared for a sensible pre-ceptress to the little girls.

Fifteen or twenty years of la-bour should ensure a com-petency;

which the governess ought to de-rive from the families she has served, that she may retire to her family circle, and honourably finish her days.

out a shadow of ostentation or parade. Thus, in the vale of years, when the mind relaxes its strength, and the well-tried faculties lose their keen power, the matron governess, respected in her own circle of friends, beloved by her liberally-educated pupils, happy in the recollection of an active and nobly-spent youth, thankful in the possession of the comforts, and perhaps of the little luxuries to which she has been long accustomed in the families of the great, sinks down at length in quiet hope, and grateful praise, upon the bosom of her God.*

The second reason why we may regret the increase of governesses.

I must now advance my second reason, for lamenting the vast increase of those numbers, who style themselves governesses.

Many are so unfit that they draw contempt on the whole profession;

Where the market is overstocked the commodity loses value. This is precisely the case with private governesses. So many advertisements swell the columns of the daily prints; so many names are exhibited at the principal booksellers in London; and so many are the enquiries made amongst friends, for governesses' situations, that as many are of an inferior cast, and of the description I first gave, they attach a feeling of ridi-
rule,

* The only family I know that has settled a pension on their governess is an Irish one. I wish I had the liberty to mention names; that of the Bishop of —— should receive the public tribute of praise which is so justly its due. This gentleman and his lady have allotted three hundred pounds per annum to Miss ——, the late preceptress of their accomplished and charming daughters.

cule, and perhaps of contempt, or something bordering upon it, on the whole profession. It is partly owing to this general sensation, that the most deserving women find themselves, at times, treated with a sort of unaccountable neglect or indifference; that their services are undervalued, and their salaries so limited; for the unthinking parent mentally exclaims, " I will give so much, and no more; and if Miss —— cannot come to me for that, some one else will." This is very true. A governess may be had for any salary, from twenty pounds a year to two hundred. I know of several who have thirty pounds a year, some forty, others fifty to eighty, and a few only who have above a hundred. One of the highest p—— s in the kingdom, I have been told on good authority, gives only sixty.

and they are to be had for any salary which unhappily is thought the greatest merit.

You will say, perhaps, if a female gain even a hundred a year, she may do very well; in ten years, there are a thousand pounds. Allow me, ladies, to explain. Those who give but a hundred per annum to a well qualified governess, engage her generally but for a couple of years, as finishing preceptress. She is then dismissed, as the young ladies are old enough to do without her care. She applies to a lady who has several little girls, and asks a hundred guineas—the lady replies, " your salary is too high; I should not choose to give so much, as my children are young; when they have attained the ages of fourteen, or

A governess however deserving, can never save a fortune,

for when children most require a sensible teacher, the fashion is to give them a cheap one, which in this sense means ignorant.

sixteen,

sixteen, then I may give them a finishing go-
verness; at present, a more inexperienced one
will suit me." The preceptress thinks it in vain
to enter into an argument upon the importance
of forming good, early impressions, and of the
probability there is, that in the first twelve years
of a child's life, its character will take all the
chief tints of its future shades; she salutes the
heedless parent, casts a look of pity upon the
unhappy little victims to a miserable economy,
and retires. If she have not any relations, or
should she not choose to be indebted to them,
she engages a small apartment, and having pro-
vided herself with necessaries, and paid every ex-
pense; after having for two or three months,
visited twenty parents, and received from every
one the same answer, she is again engaged as
finishing governess, for two or three years, and
is then again subject to the same loss of time
and of money, and is again a prey to the same
anxiety and uncertainty; consequently, and with
the deduction also of money for dress, no con-
siderable sums can be set apart for future plans
of ease, comfort, or independence.

To proceed to the third reason;—I will pre-
sume to assert, that from the numbers of young
people calling themselves governesses, who are
rambling in London for places, many are caught
up for families, whose children have no preten-
sions whatever to be educated by a private pre-
ceptress.

The finishing
governesses
only stay a
short time in
families,

and every
change is at-
tended with
expense.

The third
reason.

That people
in trade often
engage gover-
nesses for

ceptress. Even allowing her to be but an indifferent one; admitting her to know little more than a tolerably taught nursery-maid, which not unfrequently is the case,* yet the evil is not on these accounts in any degree lessened; for honourable, useful and admirable, as are the employments of the trading classes in our cities, and pleasing as must be, to every Briton, the sight of the shopkeeper, standing with honest and upright mien to display those goods, on the sale of which he depends for support,—so, on the contrary, that tradesman must excite ridicule, who will be

aping

their children, as they may have some upon any terms.

A shopkeeper is an honour to his country when he knows and does not launch out beyond his situation;

* In the Morning Post, Chronicle, Herald and Times papers, I have often read advertisements of governesses written worse than those of the servants in the last page. Many I have seen couched in these terms. " A young person (perhaps lady) wishes for a situation in a gentleman's family, as governess to two or three young ladies.; *and can* instruct in English and the *rudiments* of French and needle-work, or *would* have no objection to wait upon some young ladies or to attend to the nursery."

· Such advertisers, just finished at some petty boarding school, are, it seems, not determined, whether their abilities qualify them for conducting the education of a child, or for washing its feet, combing its hair, and making its bed. A curious dilemma. But fortune, or rather the cruel parsimony or rashness of parents favouring them, perhaps two people apply; if the advertiser can write, she styles herself in her character of governess, " Miss;" if she is wanted for a nursery-maid, she must give her name as plain Betty Jones or Mary Giles. To be sure, it is prettier to be called Miss, than Betty or Polly.

One of these ladies of such extraordinary modesty, addressed a friend of mine in her quality of governess, and said, by way of recommendation of herself, that she had lived in *a E?* family. I should be curious to see her pupils.

aping the fashions, and assuming the manners of those who are placed in a higher sphere than he is. Were ridicule the only consequence, it would signify little; but dangerous consequences follow, and rest chiefly upon points too tender to bear them. These acute sufferers are the rising generation. The young minds of girls, whose opportunities of instruction have been very limited, are left exposed to every assault; and vice assumes various pleasing shapes in the hope of attracting their attention. In that of vanity, she seldom assails such subjects in vain. The giddy girl teazes her father for new ribbons—new dresses—new ornaments. She says nothing concerning a *new governess;* but the father, in concert with, or over-persuaded by a weak-minded mother, fills up the omission: " I do not see why we should not educate our girls at home, as Mrs. Robe the milliner does." The governess is engaged. She *educates* her pupils; and her instructions are attended with such success, that at fifteen or sixteen they are quite finished. They visit watering places, the theatre and the opera; give balls; purchase fine clothes; receive compliments from the men, and drain their father's till.—The father goes to jail; the girls upon the town !—

Having premised these observations upon the choice of private teachers, I will endeavour to state, as they may occur to my mind, the principal

but by making fine ladies of his wife and children, he renders himself ridiculous, and hurls them on to ruin.

The advantages and defects of private education.

cipal advantages and defects in education con-
ducted at home.

It is the opinion of many people, that girls
cannot be educated in too much retirement and
seclusion from the world. This principle, if
acted upon, would, I conceive, be productive of
much mischief; as, on the other hand, its oppo-
site extreme might be, perhaps, equally fatal.
A medium is desirable; but so finely drawn
are those lines which terminate the boundaries
of extremes, that the intermediate space is often
scarcely perceptible.

There is to
be a medium
between total
seclusion and
entire publi-
city of life.

By way of illustrating my first remark, I shall
mention a family with which I am slightly ac-
quainted. The daughters of Mrs. .... are
fine young women, but such was the plan of re-
serve upon which their mother conducted their
education, that their innocence is bashfulness;
their timidity awkwardness; their delicacy the
confusion and horror of guilt. In company at
nineteen, for the first time in their lives, their
look is terrified and panic struck. Misery is
seated on their countenances, where modest as-
surance and candid innocence should be ever
seen. Such subjects are in danger from the arts
and deceptions of the world. The mind has no
confidence in itself, and at the same time it is
not aware of its own debility—reason has lost
her tone for want of exertion, as the body be-
comes weakened by a deprivation of food. Op-
posed

The defect of
the first ex-
treme,

and of the
second.

posed to these young ladies are the Misses ....,
who from their earliest years have been intro-
duced into company. They are bold, forward,
pert, smart at repartee, quick at a pun or double
entendre, and are, to use a gentleman's words
in speaking of them, "very clever fellows."

You, ladies, would be sorry that your daugh-
ters should resemble either description of girls
just alluded to; and yet you are not perhaps

No one is
amiable,
good, and cle-
ver, without
having caused
troubles and
anxiety to his
friends, be-
sides self
exertion.

aware of the struggles which they make to gain
the path of vice, or eccentricity, from which
they can scarcely be turned aside by the most
sensible preceptress. How difficult to your con-
ception, that the sweet girl, whose lips are inno-
cence and truth, should once have been strongly
disposed to falsehood. And you, happy mother,
who are clasping the hand of your sensible and
devoted child, can you remember that she was
born headstrong, obstinate, and perverse? To
rational education, which alone can so improve
and ennoble human nature, let us henceforth
render every tribute of gratitude and respect.

We should
educate girls
at home, first,
because long
separation
weakens af-
fection;

Two most weighty reasons present themselves
for educating young ladies at home. The first
is, that by constantly residing with parents, their
affection increases daily; whereas I am con-
vinced, that by separating parents and children,
the tenderness and lively regard of the latter,
and sometimes of both, are very materially dimi-
nished. Our affections, it is said, do not de-
pend

pend upon ourselves. Although I do not sub-
scribe to this sentiment in its full extent, I cer-
tainly conceive that nature is not, in her present
subdued state, possessed of sufficient strength to
unite, independent of social intercourse, in bonds
of love or duty, the parent and child, brother
and sister, uncle and nephew. We grow at-
tached to the people with whom we reside; and
with the sweet recollection of our infantine years
is connected the pleasing idea of those persons
with whom we passed them. How have the
greatest of men been affected at the sight of the
spot where they pursued every youthful plea-
sure, and where " every scene had charms to
please ?" How fondly has the man gazed on
the lofty tree, which he remembered to have
planted, when a boy, and to have cherished
with water from a neighbouring spring in
the crown of his hat? Has it disgraced the
eye of the hero, to be filled with a tear on re-
cognising the simple tombstone of his widowed
aunt, who received him to her arms an orphan,
and watched over his tender years with a parent's
fondness? And might not the feeling which
roused the tear be equally strong with that which
would urge such a tribute to a mother's memo-
ry? I am persuaded of it. A child loves its
parents because it receives ten thousand endear-
ing marks of affection from them, not by reason
of near relationship. If parents are harsh and
unkind,

and we tenderly love the sweet scenes and companions of childhood.

We best love those who love us.

Duty is se-
condary in
the opera-
tions of self-
love.

unkind, their children may fear, but will not
really love. How can affection subsist upon it-
self? There must be an object. It matters lit-
tle whether that be under the title of parent or
friend. Let the mother and a very young child
be separated. The child shall be for a dozen
years under the care and management of an
amiable woman, who spares neither exertion,
tenderness, nor solicitude in forming its heart
and mind. Let us imagine the mother returned

Man is a gre-
garious ani-
mal, and
grows attach-
ed to those
with whom
he resides.

to her daughter, a blooming girl. Is it neces-
sary to say whom of the two women the maiden
will love most ardently and affectionately during
the remainder of her life? The habit of residing
with a person or persons, independent of rela-
tionship, creates I know not what of regard and
interest; and when to these are added the op-
portunities parents have of gaining the hearts of
their sweet offspring, by daily offices of kind-

How vast,
then, may be
filial affec-
tion.

ness, what dependence may we not place upon
the solid filial affection that must grow upon
such a stock! Who would forego such happi-
ness, and what should induce a parent to send
his child from him, and thereby risk the loss of
its affection! The same rule holds good with

Neither
should bro-
thers and sis-
ters be sepa-
rated till their
adolescence;

brothers and sisters. Those of a family who
have been most separated during childhood, have
certainly least reciprocal attachment afterwards.
They are united in vain on coming to years of
maturity. With age arises, in men, a desire for
honour,

honour, preferment, riches, or pleasure. Women are as eager in the pursuit of riches, and pleasure often;—of a settlement, or (to speak in plain terms) of an eligible marriage, nearly always. These periods of ambition and hope, are not likely to be such, in which birth will be given to sentiments of disinterested and tender affection between two brothers or sisters, who, as running the same course, are competitors; and what is the attachment of candidates? Each being anxious for himself in proportion as he is careless or envious of his rival. Thus let me advise you, ladies; teach your children to love one another in their early youth. Adopt, for their sakes, the idea that they will have no time for forming such attachments after their first adolescence. I dare presume that, if you err, it will be on the right side.

for with adults fortune engrosses all attention.

Another inducement to instructing young ladies at home, is, that the mother, or guardian, may superintend the education, and adapt it to the capacity, temper, disposition, or talent of the child. Under the guidance of, and with the most respectful deference to the parent, the prudent governess, like a skilful gardener, crops the luxuriant yet wild branches which shoot from her blooming shrubs. With the most unremitting care, she watches every opening blossom of morality, and anxiously shields it from the scorching breath of error, till it bursts into maturity,

The second reason for home education is, that it may be adapted to the capacity of the child, as checks and encouragement may be alternately and seasonably applied.

turity, and is secure for the season of life. When the sweet plant is tardy in putting forth buds, and when, as if in despondence, it droops its tender head, the kind friend smiles with affectionate encouragement, and supports with the twigs of amusement and instruction interwoven, the tottering tree; whilst with a careful hand she removes every stone, clod, or worm which might injure the root, and then refreshes her lovely charge with illustrations from the pure fountain of truth.

Some of the inconveniences attending private education.

To quit the metaphor—We have to lament that amongst so many solid and brilliant advantages arising to your children from private education, there should be found any inconveniences. And yet there are a few. We may reckon of

The want of objects of emulation.

the number, the want of objects of emulation. These grand stimuli are, or ought to be, banished from private families. Who would dare to call in this powerful auxiliary to two sisters? Do not those run dreadful risks of sowing seeds of envy in the young breast, when they say to a child, (though not possibly in these words,) your sister is a good girl, but you are not; your sister is industrious, but you are idle; you would do this, or that, were you like your sister, and so on? What may pass in the mind of the child on such comparisons being drawn to its disadvantage? Either a desire of imitation, or wish of being superior to the other, or else (as might be expected)

pected) a consciousness of its own inferiority, a despondence in exertion, and a secret disgust to the happy and extolled sister. On this account, there should be extreme care in the choice and application of rewards and punishments in private families. Reasoning, mild, firm, plain, will nearly always answer in place of punishment of slight faults. On the approach of vice perhaps a stronger remedy must be sought for, but on all occasions we should avoid making comparisons; the practice is seldom productive of good, and is in general pregnant with mischief.

The difficulty of finding reward and punishment.

There are other disadvantages to be met with in private education. The child is in its own house, and do as you may, it will be sensible of its own power and importance. Its little vanities are excited by the indiscriminate praises of visitors; its attention is diverted by the various scenes that are passing from the points at which a prudent governess would rest; and it is apt, at all times, to presume too much upon mama's fondness and papa's affection. At school a child finds no tender parent to look mournfully upon it, and pettishly with the instructor, when it is in disgrace; no person to presume upon when it has been highly praised for an early proof of diligence or intellectual strength. No plea can it find to superiority but merit. At their respective schools, miss and my lady, master and my lord, sit promiscuously upon the same

The presumption of the child upon the consciousness of its importance ;

and on the weakness of parental fondness.

Its distraction from study.

School treatment generally impartial.

form,

form, eat at the same table, sleep in the same
room. The few who are pointed at are those
distinguished by merit, who are held up as examples to imitate; or are those who, being idle,
vicious, and headstrong, are named only as objects of pity or contempt. From this point of
view, emulation may be seen to rule triumphantly. No relationship interferes to counteract her
designs; all are agreed that such an one is the
most generous, or most mean; most attentive or
most idle; most quick or most sluggish: and
here I cannot help remarking how often I have
been surprised at the acuteness and perspicuity
with which young school boys or girls have
summed up the character of a companion or
teacher. Probably, had the same children been
educated in a private manner, they would not
have possessed half the discrimination. Whilst
public education is defective in many essential
points, it yet produces in young people a liberality and nobleness of sentiment, a quickness
of thought, an acuteness of judgment, and a
knowledge of human nature, which cannot but
call forth our admiration and applause.

The conclusion I would draw from what I
have advanced, is this: that private education is
strongly to be recommended under a steady parent or prudent governess; but that when parents cannot afford to engage an experienced
preceptress; will not train up an innocent unprejudiced

Merit is distinguished and applauded.

Worthlessness is selected and despised.

School the world in miniature,

and gives a deep insight into human nature.

Conclusion drawn.

A parent's tuition.

That of a good governess.

judiced female to the profession; and finally, will not be at any trouble themselves, that there are only two considerations left : the engaging of a half-bred nursery maid, to act as governess under masters, and so ourselves slaughter the unfortunate victim; or the sending it to school, where among the thirty thousand said to be in, and round London, and the hundreds in other parts of England, we may find some conducted upon principles of rectitude and piety.

That of a modest, well disposed young lady.

Or a good school.

TO PRIVATE GOVERNESSES.

IN the foregoing pages, I have endeavoured to point out those who assume the title of governess, without having the least pretension whatever. To such I do not now address myself. Them I advise, as a friend, to follow a mode of life in which they may meet with respect and success, which they never can hope to obtain by imposing themselves upon their employers for what they really are not. To you, my friends, (particularly young ones) and partners in our important concern, whose exertions tend to promote the comforts of the rising generation in this world, and to ensure the happiness of it in the next; to you, do I presume to offer a few scattered remarks, founded upon experience, on the particular station of life in which the Almighty has, of his divine will, been pleased to place you.

A few remarks offered to governesses.

Educated, as I must suppose you to have been, upon noble and generous principles; cultivated as must be your minds by the perpetual ebb and flow of erudition, which your pupil requires at command; delicate as must be your feelings, from the quickness of perception so necessary to you with children; and softened and humanized as must be your manners, from having a continual

Supposing they have either been well educated or are well disposed and prepared.

guard

guard over every impulse; yet, considering the difficulties with which you have to contend, I should be inclined to pronounce your situation the most peculiar of any among British females. *Their situation of life is peculiarly arduous.*

Although, by the very nature of your profession, you are more immediately called upon to set a watch over your temper and feelings, yet I will assert, that, in more than a common degree are they sometimes provoked to rebel.

It is now more customary than was formerly the case, for governesses to sit at table with the parents of their pupils. They have a seat, and *Their rank is raised,* mingle with the company of the house. It cannot but be satisfactory to see you thus raised a step higher, as it were, in society; as it shews the wish of the parent to place you upon the footing of gentlewomen, which some years ago, was certainly not the case. Excepting, however, people *but it is the duty of all acknowledg this;* who visit at the house will condescend to speak occasionally to the governess, to take off the embarrassment she may feel before criticism, or superiority of birth and fortune, very little enjoyment or satisfaction is for you. Surely you should be introduced to strangers, provided the doing so can be effected without making you appear unpleasantly conspicuous. In Ireland, where the rights of hospitality are so universally known, and where I passed in a gentleman's family several happy years of my life, the go- *and in Ireland it is always done.* verness is introduced to any stranger who may

visit; and she of course, according to the cus
toms of our country, may converse, or at least
attempt conversation. But if you are to eat
your food in silence and neglect, I suppose you
would rather dine or sup in your study; and I
am of opinion that you would make a happy ex-
change. I once declined a situation in Lady
H——S——'s family, because she did not per-
mit the governess to associate with her. How
different is the liberal plan of a noble family I
have since had so much reason to admire and
respect! but at that time, I had just quitted my
Irish friends, by whom I was affectionately and
more than kindly treated; and because I did my
duty to my pupil, my feelings were consulted, and
my happiness promoted by every possible effort.
To dine or not with the family, would be now a

A generous
mind feels
with delicacy
for others.

matter of indifference to me. If our neighbour
be a liberal minded person, he will never be
wanting in the delicate attentions of good breed-
ing and humanity. If he be proud, sullen, or
scornful, our remedy must be patience, till the
signal is given to withdraw.

Want of so-
ciety the
chief depriva-
tion of a go-
verness.

Society you are not to expect. This blessing
is never tasted by you, excepting at the firesides
of your own family and friends. The company
with whom you mix are all either your superiors,
or are those who consider themselves as such.
Of marriage and domestic comforts you should
banish every idea. You cannot expect offers
                                            from

from men of birth and fortune. I will not insult you by mentioning the only men you see in opposition to these; therefore make up your minds to the deprivation of two grand female considerations;—society and settlement. And let not these imaginary wants afflict or vex you. Look around you on the world, consider the selfishness of general associates, and the unhappiness of many married couples. Repine not at any slight which has not been caused by your own behaviour. *But consolations may be easily found under imaginary wants.* Upon the whole, the world is more ready to give us our deserts than we choose to allow. Let us not rate too highly our merits; but in all events, we well know that however others may neglect us, or even wound our self-love, we have no excuse for impropriety in our own conduct. You are well aware that every state, from the *All states have their difficulties.* regal to that of slavery, has its difficulties; to contend with them in the best possible manner is our duty. Disgrace cannot rest upon you for submitting patiently to that, for which you cannot be in any way accountable. The shame falls to those who forget the rules of good-breeding and hospitality. The place you fill does equal honour to your dispositions and abilities. On *Her situation is her best recommendation.* ntering the most brilliant drawing-room with your smiling pupils in either hand, you present the most satisfactory credentials. If the sovereign approve, and give you a sanction, trouble not yourselves with the contempt or indifference

of

of the minions that surround him. Remember
you will have an account to give, on your depar-
ture from these perplexed scenes, of the man-
ner in which you have acted your part. Let not

No bad ac-
tion can be
admitted as a
precedent.

wrong therefore intimidate, or distract you from
doing right. I lament the mortifications and trials
you endure, but I would have you sensible of the
many comforts you actually possess. Food, the
most excellent in its kind; wholesome and airy
apartments; good beds upon which you may en-
joy refreshing sleep, and the use of domestics,

Of actual com-
forts we are
often igno-
rant.

who, if you are gentle and kind, are generally
ready to oblige you. Add to these, a salary, of
which you are never deprived, regularly paid,
and with which you may purchase every article
of clothing, and still possess a little purse to-
wards a store. Think then, my friends, of these
blessings, and be grateful. Conjure not up
ideal misery, but strive to do your duty, and
cultivate a contented mind.

Hints as to
general Con-
duct.

And now give me leave to offer a few hints as
to your general conduct with your pupils. I do
not presume to inform you, but to submit to you
those observations which experience has suggest-
ed to me.

Confidence
in honour.

If governesses are allowed to make one in
every family party, they must necessarily see
and hear more of domestic scenes than others
can. No common acquaintance is able to judge
of the interior of a family; he must be at
breakfast,

breakfast, dinner and supper, for days, weeks, and months, before he can well determine its economy. If you gain this knowledge, keep it to yourselves; for it would be mean, ungenerous and ill-natured, to retail to those who visit at the house where you may be, stories of Mr. or Mrs., Sir John or my lady. A husband and wife may be perfectly amiable in other respects, and still dispute at times. Instead then, of your seeming a party concerned, or of endeavouring to catch every unkind word that may chance to fall, you should begin to talk to your pupil, or to do, if you can, what is preferable—go out of the room; not in a way to shew you have any anxiety in the business, but in an easy, natural manner. Spare the feelings of others, and they will perhaps spare your's.

Slander is mean and ungenerous,

and will procure us ill-will.

But if a parent would be hurt at your representations of himself, how much more so would he be, should you think proper to publish the faults of his children! I am acquainted with several preceptresses, who have fallen into this foolish, nay, unkind custom, of entertaining an aunt or cousin of the child with an account of its faults. This plan only hardens its heart, and proves a great disadvantage afterwards, when the child may be grown to a woman; for, as we are told, " our evil deeds are written on brass, and our good in water." But if you are not so unfortunate as to have a pupil whose mind and

Ill-natured representation of children.

Some have an unfortunate habit of exposing children's faults.

disposition

disposition have been too much neglected or perverted to give hope of reclaiming, you will love her; she must become dear to you, and when that is the case, I cannot suppose you would do violence to yourselves by lowering the child in the estimation of the world; it would neither do good to you nor your pupil, and would give unnecessary pain to parent and child. So far would be this publication of faults from my plan, that I should conceal them from every ear but that of the culprit;—excepting, however, I were questioned, and then my conscience would direct my answers. I know not how it is with others, but for myself I am always disposed to love my little charges from the instant I am placed over them. Poor innocent children! Look at their agitation, dread, and submission: mark their anxiety upon the arrival of a new governess (as they call us), till they are assured by several interviews that she looks *good-natured*. Think of the hours which a governess and pupil have to pass together; and consider how much happiness must depend upon you. How do the children of the nobility and gentry labour every day at the most difficult sciences (music for example); and how very seldom have they those amusements, in which their simplicity and childish ignorance teach them to find pleasure. You may, and ought to make children and their studies as easy and agreeable as possible; but do

what

Marginal notes:

but it does no good to any party.

Yet truth must answer to direct questions.

The mutual dependence for happiness of governess and pupil.

what you will, the playfellow or doll will be
sought for with more eagerness than the piano-
forte lesson or French exercise.

It is natural that children should love play.

Many and excellent are the works that have
appeared upon the profound and inexhaustible
subject—the education of man.   This lofty theme
is generally to be observed, swelling in the ma-
jesty of dignified numbers, or reposing on the
elegance of beautiful and ingenious theory.
Practice stands afar off, admiring, yet perplexed
—willing, yet unable.   He collects breath to
run his race.   The visionary points the road;
but reality is continually raising before him py-
ramids of stone, to intercept his progress.   No
amiable author has condescended to be so prac-
tical as Miss Edgworth.   She treats her subject
in a masterly style, and discovers in every chap-
ter the penetration of a mind which ranges at
will through every avenue to the human heart.
But mothers only have the power of acting upon
her plan.   A preceptress durst not, without the
perfect concurrence and assistance of the pa-
rents, and an absolute command and authority
over the pupils.   The last, I apprehend, are
never to be obtained; for the most discreet of
governesses never rule alone, nor is it desirable
that they should, for the parent is, or ought to be,
supreme over the child.   The young lady's mind
must have been prepared from infancy, to re-

Many fine works upon education;

but scarcely practicable.

Mothers alone can act upon Miss Edgworth's noble plan.

ceive

ceive the full advantages offered by Miss Edgeworth's mode of practice; and a governess, taking upon herself the education of one or two children of ten, twelve, or fourteen years of age, has no time to spare in making experiments, of which, perhaps, the parents themselves would not conceive the ultimate benefit. A preceptress, upon being introduced to a girl no longer in childhood, is to consider that, according to the present fashion, she must be ushered into the world, as it is termed, in a few years. This being understood, it remains to the instructress to try the foundation, and to build accordingly upon it. She should examine with care her young charge in her knowledge of her Creator, of his works, and of his divine word; of history, ancient and modern; of grammar, geography, &c. &c. The answers that are made should be carefully noted down, that every deficiency may be supplied to the best of the ability that directs the whole. The temper of the child, her inclinations, sentiments, ideas, principles, should be quietly and judiciously studied, that no auxiliary may be unsought for, whose touch could strengthen or beautify the mental edifice.

I now claim your indulgence, and that of the public, in the reception of a plan of education, which acknowledges for its base the received and understood mode of instruction in private families;

A governess has no time to spare in making experiments;

nor would the parents like them.

A preceptress has only time to finish or improve what is begun.

She cannot lay foundations.

This plan has for its base the understood mode of education.

lies; which has for its object the hope of being useful to governesses and pupils, by shewing how the business of the study may be conducted and arranged, for the comfort of teachers, and the general advantage of the children placed under their care.

CHAPTER I.

ON THE MANAGEMENT OF YOUNG LADIES.

IT is not my intention to impose on myself the task of enumerating every fault and imperfection, with its proper treatment, to which young ladies may be subject; but I am desirous of touching upon a few leading errors, which when children fall into, are likely to be extremely vexatious and trying to the governess:—perhaps upon this nice matter I may be able to offer a hint not altogether unworthy of notice.

From the hour that a governess enters a nobleman's or gentleman's family till she leaves it, her pupil is constantly in her company : at studies, at meals, at recreation, perhaps even at the time of rest, as it not unfrequently happens that the preceptress and pupil sleep in the same bed. No intimacy can exist without respect and esteem. Now the grand difficulty, where much intimacy exists, is in maintaining respect; and its influence is absolutely necessary over the child's mind ; but if there be a shadow of injustice, tyranny, or ill-nature on the part of the governess, it will be for ever lost : the confidence and respect of the pupil are irrecoverably gone. Thus, whilst a dignity of character is preserved, the manners and conduct of the preceptress must be

gentle,

gentle, kind, affable, and affectionate; and set-
ting aside, as much as possible, personality, she
should appear to have in view only the child's
happiness and welfare.   Yet even in this appear-
ance she must be cautious, or her charge will
flutter in fancied importance and disgusting sel-
fishness.

The child is the great ob-ject of solici-tude.

When a governess is first introduced to her
half-inquisitive and agitated pupil, the young
lady is all submission, timidity, and obedience.
In the course of two or three days, or perhaps
of a week, or month, as the child's temper is
more or less under controul, it begins to unfold
its character.   The governess has now lost her
novelty; she may be viewed at ease.   We be-
gin, say the pupils, to find her out; no longer
is she formidable and unknown : like the frogs
in the fable, they by degrees venture to approach
their king.   The panic is over; and this is the
decisive moment.   The pupil makes trial of her
strength, and judges by the issue of the person
with whom she has to engage.

She is at first all obedience, and we should pre-serve this disposition.

In the first struggle for power, extreme deli-
cacy and caution, extreme firmness tempered
with mildness, should be exercised by the elder
hand, or she will inevitably lose the cause; and
then, like the wooden king alluded to, she will
certainly be regarded with contempt.   But if the
little champion find itself defeated, it will pause,
and with increased respect and submission, tinc-
tured,

The first struggle for power should be delicately managed.

tured, perhaps, with a little vindictive emotion, it will cease hostilities for some time to come. To illustrate what I have advanced, I relate a contest which I once had with a pupil, when I had not been with her a fortnight.

Child. Here is my copy-book.

Governess. I see it, my dear. Have you brought your globe?

Child. I wanted to write my copy now.

Gov. Perhaps, my dear, you did not hear me tell you to fetch your globe; I wish to point out to you the country of which we have been reading.

Child. Oh, I know where it is; I would rather write first, and look at the globe afterwards.

Gov. And I, my dear, would rather shew you the place before you proceed to any other study; therefore I wish you to bring me the globe.

The young lady looked greatly disconcerted. I appeared perfectly unconcerned, looking over a book. The globe was at the other end of the room, and rested on the floor, so that it was entirely within reach. Of this I took care to be assured. Teachers should be particular in never requiring any thing of their pupils but that which they may perform with some degree of ease. My young friend struggled very hard. She threw a glance at me, at the copy-book, and at the globe, not any of which I appeared to observe. I was particular in keeping command
over

over my countenance, that it might not discover
any thing of impatience or severity. Presently
the young lady pushed her copy-book towards
me, in a manner to take me by surprise. I
quietly looked up, and said, " No, my dear, I
want the globe." Another struggle ensued. I
uttered not a syllable. In a short time, a slow
step towards the door proved to me I was to
conquer. The globe came, and was placed with
a sort of a thrust at my side. The fretful move-
ment was human nature itself: I forgave it, and
immediately turning round, began to explain
the point in question to the half sulky girl, who,
upon finding I took no notice of my victory, soon
regained her composure, carried back the globe,
and began briskly to write her copy. Now it
was not a matter of great importance that I
should have the globe lesson first, but it was of
infinite consequence that my pupil should not
find that she was to be mistress; and I believe
the plan I adopted to prove it was pretty good,
for it was long before we had any other trials.
The little girl yielded at once, and I have reason
to think I never abused the power with which I
was invested.

No person should dare to triumph in a victory over a child.

As I have hinted, it is my opinion that go-
vernesses would perhaps act judiciously in being
rather upon the reserve on first coming to their
pupils; otherwise they may shew off all their
goodnature, and the child know to the utmost

A little reserve is prudent at first between governess and pupil.

what

what it is to expect. Too much kindness cloys
the mind. We are more likely to respect those
whom we regard with a little awe, and whose
characters are not traced in extremely legible
lines, than we are those persons who display to
our view their whole stock of goodnature and
kindness. Human nature is so ungrateful and
capricious, that even of these good qualities it
may grow tired, and may be satiated with per-
petual soothings, as the eye is fatigued by conti-
nually gazing on the same beautiful picture.
Between children and teachers I should there-
fore recommend, in the beginning, a reserved
communication; perhaps a little formality. 'The
affectionate zeal which a well disposed woman
would feel towards her pupils should not be at
first discovered; she must produce it by degrees.
In time, the child will feel in its little tender
breast the movements of affection for a being,
whom reason says it ought to reverence and
love; she may then give acknowledgments of
her own.

At all times, yet without appearing to do so,
the governess should set every obstacle aside
to promote the happiness and comfort of her
charge, and should gratify her as much as she
consistently can with her own dignity, and with
the advantage of the child. Every encourage-
ment possible must be given to the little prattler
when it strives to reduce its ideas to form, its

Children should be en-couraged to speak and act, but not to exercise authority;

principles

principles to practice; and to effect these its un-limited confidence only is wanting.

By degrees, the different faults which are com-mon to all mankind strike forth in obnoxious shoots.   It is often difficult, and sometimes im-possible, for a governess to trace these wild branches to their respective stems.   If we do not desire weeds in a newly made garden, let us crush the seeds of some, and endeavour to dis-engage the root of all.   Prevention is better than cure.   If we are too late with the first, we are bound to act, but with caution.   The diseases of the school-room are, principally, indolence, carelessness, sluttishness of person, fits of gran-deur to which some children are subject, and which, if a remedy be not found they will produce pride and arrogance; perverseness, pertness, conceit, and inelegancies of many kinds.   These lightly shaded are faults; but some of them, if not properly treated, will spread into vices in maturer age.   I have not placed in my catalogue deceit, lying, and pilfering, or, in other words, stealing, because no parent would allow that their daughter could be guilty of such crimes.   But what distinction is to be made be-tween the man who steals a leg of mutton from a butcher's stall, and the young lady who pur-loins from another girl a penny bun, or an orange, for her private eating?—between the woman who declares she never touched the cup

that

we have a better view of the character thereby.

He who de-sires a good harvest should first well prepare the soil.

Whether vice is to be esti-mated ac-cording to our power of committing it, or by its opposition to morality and religion.

that she broke, and the young lady who pro-
nounces as her own, and unblushingly smiles at the
approbation of drawings of which she is conscious
not a dozen strokes are hers?—between the man
who, with a whitened face and bandaged leg, so-
licits support for exhausted nature, but when out
of sight of his benefactor walks undisguised to
the house of intemperate riot; and the young
lady who, with a countenance of pain, asks per-
mission to retire to her chamber to sleep, only
that she may clandestinely peruse a book or let-
ter which she was forbidden to touch, or which
belonged to another person? For my part, I
think the criminals nearly equal as to propensity
—circumstances only depress or raise the boun-
daries of their acts. Wherein is the use of pal-
liating or of equivocation? Let us look at vice
naked, stripped of every trapping of birth and
fashion, and we shall not only feel horror our-
selves at the sight, but communicate that feeling
to others. Yet a foolish weak person would thus
argue upon such allusions: " Dear, that is very
odd, to compare a young lady with a thief; a
man that has stolen a thing from a shop, for
which he may be transported, and a gentleman's
daughter who only just takes an orange, poor
thing!—and what is an orange or a bun? you
may get both for two-pence. And the young
lady who shews a drawing and says it is hers,
when her master did the most part; la! there

*Fine distinc-
tions are not
to be tole-
rated in vice.*

can't

can't be any harm in this, for it's what all girls
do—of course the master helps them, and they
need not say any thing about it; but if they
are asked, how queer it would be to say they
had no hand in their own performances; at best
it is a white lie, to gain a little praise, and they
hurt nobody by it: but the saucy creature who
breaks my china and says she never touched it,
is really a notorious liar, and ought to be turned
away from her place. As for the man who im-
poses upon me by flouring his face to look pale,
and by tying up his leg to appear lame, and
takes my sixpence to the next liquor-shop for a
dram, I consider him a cheat, who ought to be
put in the stocks—now there is no great harm in
a young lady pretending to be a little sick; dear,
its what all young folks do now and then; there
is no putting old heads on young shoulders;—
to be sure, she was desired not to touch such a
book, but then perhaps she was fond of reading
—and as for the letters, she only just opened her
cousin's box with her key to peep at one in par-
ticular, which she had been refused a sight of,
and if she leaves things as she found them, what
does it matter!"—How often have such argu-
ments been laid before us, upon our expressing
ourselves with earnestness respecting an appa-
rently trifling fault, but which drew after it a
complication of enormities?—It is easy to talk,
but not so to prove. If we choose to be de-
ceived,

ceived, we may readily find excuses. The thief who stole the mutton may say, " I was hungry, and possessed no money; the butcher was a rich man, his shop was filled with the carcasses of a dozen sheep; I *only* took one leg!" The woman says, " What signifies one cup, when there are so many left; besides, I declare, I did not break it, it was the broom in my hand that knocked it down." And for the beggar he may assert, " That other people cheat now and then, and that he is not worse than his companions; and what is it that he has gained, only a sixpence, and as the money is his, he has a right to do what he pleases with it." These six characters are all

No character safe without principle.

wanting in one and the same essential; they want *principle.* There is no one moral and religious point in their composition, upon which rests that strong notion of right and wrong, which alone has power to regulate every action; hence they are tossed on the ocean of life like vessels without a pilot; they are at the mercy of every blast of passion; and, always on search for present gratification, disdain to guard against the dreadful rocks upon which so many have been shattered and lost.

There are faults of some kind always to correct;

There are then many diseases to combat with in the study, diseases of the heart, the mind, the manners; or I may divide them into improprieties, faults, and crimes. Of whatever nature they may be we must notice them all. But where reproof or expostulation is often repeated the effect

effect diminishes. Neglect and apathy, resent-
ment and obduracy, follow ; and lamentable are
the consequences both to pupil and preceptor.

To remedy some of these evils I keep a book,
in which I write, every evening, the character of
the child during the day. By this means the
most trivial faults may be noticed ; but the style
of the writing should be very affectionate: the
writer must explain why a thing appears wrong
with clearness and precision, avoiding long tire-
some words and sentences, which only perplex,
and often disgust, a young reader. I advise such
addresses as these to be made to the affection and
reason. No eye but that of the pupil and parent
should examine them. I would not have chil-
dren appear more wicked, nor more amiable
than they really are. From this consideration
I should not produce this book of faults; nor
should I, as some people perpetually do, amuse
my friends for hours with anecdotes of the young
lady's wit, quickness, sagacity, or super-natural
talents. There are very few children who can
bear much praise, and that which is indiscrimi-
nately bestowed by visitors, generally by way of
pleasing the parent, is, of all other kinds, the
most dangerous; many a little girl's mind has
been spoiled by it. The character-book may be
shewn to the pupil every morning, or perhaps
once a week; but the governess will be guided
by circumstances, and influenced by the effect
produced

but too much talk fatigues; we may write them down for the pupil's observation.

It is cruel to give a child too much praise.

produced on the child, whom, on these occasions, she will see the necessity of particularly observing.

Reference to Miss Edgworth's Education for instructions in different points. Every library boasts Miss Edgworth's Practical Education. Surely no person can peruse this work without advantage to himself in his character of preceptor or parent. The chapters on Truth and Temper are in particular filled with fine sentiments and judicious illustration: but, alas! a governess cannot make practical essays upon other people's children; the parents themselves are the responsible people. The influence of a governess is light compared to that of the parents. No young lady has a governess till she has passed her eighth or tenth year; and is not her character, I mean the bent of her disposition, determined upon long before that time, even by those who are most capable of forming such a judgment? Does not a mother say sometimes to the preceptress, with an affectation of candour, on introducing her children, " You will, I hope, find these good girls; I have seldom complaints of them: to be sure Maria is a little naughty at times, but mamma hopes she will leave off all passionate airs now; and little Emily must not be obstinate again; but indeed, Miss ——, they are very good upon the whole, and I am sure you will think so." The governess may tremble when a mother owns so much. Whose is the fault that one of these is a little tyrant, the other, a perverse untoward child?—The parent's. From the tender

age

age of six months furious gusts of passion must
have been observed in the one, and in the other
fits of sullenness and obstinacy   Infancy was
the period for intense observation and exqui-
sitely judicious treatment.   These were neglect-
ed : behold now the consequences of habit of
ten years' growth !

It is possible, that the youth who grows up
under the dominion of some vice, may, at times,
reflect upon the fatal weakness or carelessness of
his parents, who either committed his infancy to
servants, or themselves overlooked what they
feared would give trouble to examine ; conse-
quences were distant and undetermined ; ease
was present and certain.   They preferred the
obvious enjoyment to latent good.   Bitterly does
the young man deplore their choice ; let him
look however to himself.   The faults of others
are not extenuations of our •own guilt.   The
thief at the gallows bit off his mother's ear, be-
cause she had not corrected him for pilfering
when a child : but by the action he did himself
no service ; on the contrary, he added to his
crimes.   The reproach to his mother was useless
as it was undutiful ; he could not live his life
over again, and she, being probably an old wo-
man, would never again have an opportunity of
altering her line of conduct with other children :
the neglect had been truly hers ; and for it she
would stand accountable in the presence of her
Maker ;

Infancy, the golden age of instruction.

Not in books, but in respect to character. It matters

nothing what others are, if we are wicked ourselves. No guilt can lessens ours.

Maker: the season for reparation was past, and the reproaches of a child to his parent, however merited they may appear, are indecent. If through the carelessness of a coachman I break my leg, what am I to do? Load him with reproaches? Of what use will they be? Not any. I am only further endangering my life, by agitating myself with passion; I have but to remedy, if possible, the misfortune. The bone must be set; I must be quiet, and I may perhaps recover sufficiently to be enabled to walk, though never so well as before the accident, and always liable to pains and uneasiness; against which my surgeon advises me to guard, by particular cautions. So let it be with the vices we have imbibed through the negligence or rash treatment of our parents; we must endeavour to cure them, and not amuse ourselves in laying the blame upon those whom we should reverence and love; let us resolve to be our own surgeons, and we may do wonders with the assistance of the prescriptions from religion.

We must correct our own faults notwithstanding we possess them from the negligence of tutors or friends.

But how much more lovely would be the youth, how infinitely happier the parent, if each were spared the anguish which precedes, and the gloom that follows repentance! Fond mother! at the birth of your little babe, when in delight you gaze on its beautiful limbs and engaging features; and you, proud father, standing near with lofty exultation in your promising infant, has either of

you

you formed any plan for the training up of this
child? Are you aware that, at your child's first
entrance into the world, two invisible powers
are attending on your right and left, struggling
for the possession of it. On its first cry they
rush to your couch, and contend for the prize;
but it is for you to decide to which it shall be
consigned. These powers are good and bad
habit, each attended by a hundred spies and ser-
vants devoted to their mistress, and at all times
alert in executing her commands. Confide your
child to the protection of good habit, but be at-
tentive to court her favours, and she will amply
repay you in her care of her charge. Do you wish
your son or daughter to be an early riser? When
it is but a month old you may dress it at six
o'clock in the morning, and unrobe it at six in the
evening; continue this for four or five days, and
be particular, for habit loves regularity; and on
the sixth, depend upon it, she will dispatch an
emissary to awaken the child at that hour, and to
lull it to sleep precisely twelve hours afterwards;
continue the practice, do your duty, and good
habit will perform hers, not in this point only, but
in all.

I have thus personified habit, to give it more
importance; or rather, to shew that we must ab-
solutely be under the influence of good or bad
from the first stage of infancy. How vast then

[marginal notes]
Habit is form-
ed from the
birth.

and usurps a
dominion
which is
maintained
during life.

We must
have good or
bad habits.

is the trust reposed in parents, since *they* are to make the decision !

Let us, however, be more particular in our inquiry into the nature of this trust entailed on parents. . It will be proved to consist in one grand duty—the formation of the heart, or in another word, the disposition of the child.

To begin, then, by a very natural question : What is the end or object of education ? Is it not the means of happiness ? Now it appears to me, that what is here called happiness, may

be divided into two branches, the gratification of religion and virtue, producing gladness in a good conscience; and the enjoyment of something which lulls or engages one or all of the five senses, creating more or less of impassioned feel-

ing, called pleasure. The first happiness is the sympathy of angels ; the last, the concordance of men. The pursuer of the first grasps only that which is substantial ; the follower of the last aims pertinaciously at all that is showy ; the hope of the one is to render himself worthy., the passion of the other is to make himself brilliant. The virgin who smiles in the first happiness, is beaming in every virtue ; she that laughs in the second, is blazing in every accomplishment. He

who would attain the first must trample on the blandishments of impulse ; he that rushes towards the second, offers his hand to temptation.
                                                            The

The road to both kinds of happiness begins at the same point, but immediately separates; that of the first is rough, uneven, yet firm, and terminates in the lovely prospect of heaven; that of the second is difficult for a short time, then smooth, level, delightful, presenting innumerable arbours, in which reserve is hushed asleep, and reason intoxicated; the passions then lead turbulently on the remainder of the road, which is replete with danger, and the unwary traveller stumbles to rise no more.

The second is dazzling in voluptuousness, [and transports us with passion.

Here let us rest and consider what is to be done. Solid instruction, it seems, takes one path and superficial another. Are we then to think only of the good in education, and to omit the elegant?—No; but let us secure the one, and endeavour afterwards for the other. For the first eight years of a child's life, let nothing be considered but religion, under the most beautiful colours, and virtue. The child may know how to read, but he need understand nothing besides of school labours. Why is his character to be neglected whilst he is being made ridiculous at five or six years of age under the fiddle of a dancing master? Why is that sweet girl not employed in bestowing charity on the hapless beggar at the door, or the poor old man in yonder cottage, instead of being induced to act the coquette at the piano-forte? Who wishes to hear such shocking discord? But what heart would

Cannot these two be united in one breast?

Let us ground the infant in virtue, and add elegance to the youth.

refuse a tribute of esteem on the understanding of a tender action performed and planned by an innocent child? Does the child who begins to learn writing, or music, or drawing at five years of age, draw, or write, or play better at fifteen than she who began at eight or nine, allowing each the same teacher and the same proportion of talent? I answer, with confidence, No; for many are the opportunities I have had of judging. Nature never intended the enquiring mind, the active limbs, the observing eye, the vigilant ear of infancy and childhood to be clogged, chained, disappointed, fatigued by rattling the keys of a harpsichord, watching, till the fine organ of sight is dimmed in tears, a number of black strokes, and in scrawling lines on a paper. A child who has not been checked and spoiled, is continually saying, what is this for? what is that? why is this? He is delighted chiefly with that to which nature herself is most partial. When the time arrives for taking a walk, how his little fingers tremble with eagerness to clasp the shoe, or tie the hat! The freshness of the pure air, the beauty of the light clouds flitting before the wind, the chirping of the pretty creatures that are hopping from tree to tree, the very trees themselves gracefully nodding at one another, the soft enamelled turf, with the saucy grasshopper buzzing his little song, the flower garden filled with sweets, the pond teeming with

fish,

Infancy is not the season for accomplishments.

A child loves to read the book of nature.

fish, and the little lamb with its mother sipping
from the edge.   These are the scenes that nature
colours so exquisitely for young eyes, as to
make a little heart swell with joy. " Why do
the clouds move so fast ?" says a child; " and
why is the grass always green ?"—" Oh, never
mind, never mind," replies the maid; " come,
run about, little children should'nt ask ques-
tions."   Prudent mother, be yourself on these, *The wonder-*
and on all occasions, if possible, with your *ful power of
nature over*
child; and when its heart is warmed with the *an infant's
mind.*
works of the Creator, pour into it instructions,
which to the day of its death will be remember-
ed.   I ask you only for eight years of your at-
tention, after which you may confide your girl
to a good governess, and your boy to school
or a tutor.   What opportunities does a walk
present for saying, after we have answered the
questions of the dear child, " only think, my dear
little girl, how good God Almighty is to send us
all these pretty and useful things; how much
obliged we ought to be for His kindness : if He
pleased he could take them away; but we will
try to be good, and then He will give us all that we
deserve, and a great deal more.   Take care, do
not put your foot upon that little worm, for the
poor thing would be hurt, and perhaps killed.—
(How tender are infant hearts when properly
cautioned!)—Every living thing can feel. See,
I will gently pull your hair; does it hurt ?"—
D 3   " Yes."

The opportu-
nities of in-
struction in
a walk are
not to be
enumerated.
" Yes."   " Then you can feel, so can a fly, or a
worm, or a bird, or any animal that swims, or
walks, or crawls on the ground, or that flies in
the air.   Hark! what is that noise?   It is a
poor child crying.   What is the matter with her?
Oh, she says she is hungry, and she has hardly
any clothes.   What can we do for her?   What
have you given your piece of bread and butter?
Good child.   Mama hopes her little girl will al-
ways think of people that are poor and unhappy,
and strive to be of some use to them.   Yes, my
dear, you shall try, if you wish it, to make a frock
for this poor child, and I will shew you how.   God
Almighty is always pleased with those that are
good-natured to the poor."

Such is the instruction, the only kind of in-
struction, that I recommend to parents during
the period of time which falls between the birth
of a child and its subjection to a private governess,
generally including eight or nine years.   In one
of the noble productions of a late author we are
told, that he who shall walk with vigour three hours
a day, will pass in seven years a space equal to
the circumference of the globe.   What may we
not expect from exertion and observation made on
the same object for eight years during twelve hours
a day?   Well must the child have traversed the
road to the better kind of happiness; he must be
deeply impressed with its importance, and fami-
liarised to its appearance.   He may now take a

guide

guide and travel, but with caution, through the path of minor happiness.   In his pursuit he has advantages which the unprepared have not; he has the liberty of passing certain barriers which lead by a short turn to the first road, so that he varies his walk at his own or his guide's will. —(Happy the child who has a guide ready to gratify this inclination!)   These barriers are defended by three virgins called the Graces.   How sweetly do they smile upon the favoured youth as he passes and repasses by them!

No talents are graceful without virtue.

Does this task for the parent appear very difficult?   It is more so in idea than in reality. Let him, or rather her (for it is the business of the mother) be but resolved to succeed, and she will meet with success.   If she have herself good principles, she will be desirous of planting such in the breast of her child; and if she desire theory, she has only to consult the best writers, and in practice to be extremely careful till she may have gained a little experience.   Good will leads to perseverance, perseverance opens to possibility.   Of what is an anxious mother not capable!

But before an infant can be taught it must be corrected—corrected in such a way as to win its heart by our gentleness, firmness, justice and mercy.   The first requisite then to a parent is discrimination.   To discriminate between the suffering and fretfulness, the hunger and greedi-

The great secret of education is discrimination.

ness,

ness, the sulkiness and gravity, the ignorance and
obstinacy, the art and simplicity, the gaiety and
impertinence, the playful raillery and malice of
an infant, or of a child, a few years old, is a
very nice point in the commencement and pro-
gress of education; but we are not sufficiently
aware of its importance. How often, by preci-
pitance of judgment or caprice, has an error been
punished as a crime! How often have I seen a
vice honoured by ignorance as a virtue. Alas!
how has a child been laughed at one day for do-
ing that, which on repetition the next, gains him
severe rebuke. How has he been indulged this
week, and chastised the following. What amaz-
ing contradictions does he see sometimes in the
same person; and when his little reason begins
to expand, how confused are his notions of right
and wrong! On some occasions he may sin with
impunity, on others he is punished for the
smallest trifle; hence originate cunning and de-
ceit. He can discriminate just enough to deter-
mine upon a cross face; he cannot guess why he
should, but he feels he ought to be immediately
upon his guard. Is it wonderful if this child
grow up to be inconsistent and artful?—No. If
we wish our child to be consistent, let us be so
ourselves. We must be vigilant and just, ever
careful in checking the wrong, and studious-
ly examining every relative circumstance; we
must dive for motives. No good motive can
justify

Caprice is the
ruin of a good
disposition.

justify a bad action; but I would rather' pardon
a child for having committed a reprehensible
action, having clearly perceived the motive to
have been a good one, than I would the bad mo-
tive, under specious appearances; the last seeks
to impose upon us, and has recourse to deceit to
wrest from us that praise or reward due only to
goodness. But in saying this, I hope it does not
appear that I approve of the first, for right and
wrong can never be tolerated together: right
ceases to be lovely when wrong approaches. It
is then our interest and our duty to keep them
asunder.

Thus the important care of first forming the
character of the child upon immoveable and no-
ble principles, falls with an endless chain of con-
sequences upon the head of the parent: tre-
mendous may be these consequences in aggra-
vated neglect; blissful they must be by the per-
formance of duty.

Nature gives the bias, and the parent principles to the future character.

Generous parent, do you acknowledge any
justice in these sentiments? Do you say you
wish to enquire further into the obligations you
are now anxious to fulfil? You will be gratified
then and improved by the perusal of the annexèd
books: may their contents assist you in your ar-
duous exertion and laudable hope!—[See the
conclusion of the volume.]

But before I conclude this chapter I must be per-
mitted to make one or two observations. I have

recommended to the parent the elementary parts
of education; I have endeavoured to shew the
importance of early habit, and that the duty of pa-
rents is to inculcate, from the age of infancy, only
that which is good, to correct all that may have
a tendency to the bad. I have said that such a
course of instruction, persisted in for eight years,
must make a deep impression upon the heart of
a child, and will operate strongly in the deve-
lopment of his character : but I have not said,
because it is not my opinion, that the critical pe-
riod of education is past. I imagine the follow-
ing five or six years to be of extreme import-
ance; and hence it is that I express myself so
earnestly upon a subject too little considered—

A good go-
verness fi-
nishes that
which a good
parent began.

the choice of a governess. If the child has been
well prepared, who would wish to see his work
injured : in this case I cannot say ruined, for no
work so well begun will ever be entirely destroy-
ed even by a weak ridiculous preceptress. If it
has not been attended to, it may be made better
by good instructions, but only worse by that of
the contrary. Besides, though we have taught
the child activity, and of course habits of industry
among other good ones, we have not tried him
with any study excepting reading. Difficult, vexa-
tious, and tiresome are the rudiments of art and
science to young people, and particularly so to the

Every trial
shews a new
point of cha-
racter.

very young. Every fresh trouble in life shews the
human character in another point of view : feel-
ings

ings that, but for a particular accident, would have lain for ever dormant in the breast, are now alarmed and in action. The trouble of childhood is opposition to its will. Children can draw but few conclusions, and such as they attempt are dictated by nature.—" If I eat that pudding my hunger will be satisfied; but if I study music for two hours every day, what good will it do me ?" So says the child in its mind, and so it would say and maintain if it durst. We ought to reply, " You learn music because your mama or papa is fond of it, and it is to please them ;" and not, " Why, child, your cousins learn, and Miss —— learns, and every young lady learns now, so you must; and then you know you may play to people, and how nice that will be: see how your cousin is praised for her playing." Children learn therefore, and require strictness, indulgence, punishment, reward, praise, expostulation; all employed occasionally to encourage them to exertion. These means are resorted to by the governess : her power is great, and so ought to be her judgment in the exercise of it, or a good-tempered little girl will grow peevish or perverse, and a child at first anxious to learn, will turn away, or struggle to do so, in complete disgust.

A sensible preceptress may improve a bad subject, but a silly one will only injure a good, and harden a naughty child.

I shall now consider those parts of education which are generally conducted by the private governess. As studies, they consist of the use-

In education there are three parts, The essential, —— useful, —— ornamental.

ful

ful and the ornamental; but I do not now include the essential, excepting in one or two points connected with the subject of the foregoing pages.

In my plan of studies I neither calculate for stupidity of intellect nor versatility of talent; I make easy arrangements which may be likely to suit moderate abilities. In the list of accomplishments I am guided by the fashions of the present day. Girls must attain them, so it is decreed. The teachers then must render their duties of the school-room as pleasant as possible; and I consider as the grand means of so doing, the establishment and the maintenance of regularity, method and order.

CHAPTER II.

ENGLISH READING.

Religion.
Definition. READING may be defined the act of examining and repeating that which has been written by others.

Division. The reading for children should be religion for duty; history for information; moral fiction, biography and select poetry, for instruction and gratification.

From the moment that an infant draws its first breath, it shews in an eminent degree its weakness

ness and entire inability to help itself; but al-
though it may be at first thus wretched, yet in a
few months it undergoes an amazing change.
That chaos which wrapped its intellectual powers
in a void, is now busily arranging itself into dis-
tinct faculty; the frame, once so overcharged
with the tottering weight that hung above it, has
now consistence to support the head in all its
movements ; the eyes no longer roll in vacancy,
nor seem lost to diversity of object; they open to
receive pleasing images, and the faithful retina
ushers those on to the imagination; strength is
added to the bones and muscles ; the feet no longer
refuse to measure space ; the gums partially con-
tract in order to form sockets for the hard sub-
stance they are destined to preserve and support ;
finally, the tongue is released from silence, and
waits the command only of its oral master.   And
by what astonishing power is this change effect-
ed?   Who is it that plans a work so wonderful,
and that conducts it by such fine and gradual
touches to perfection ?—It is God.   It is God
who in the majesty and magnificence of his idea
creates, and in the infinity of His wisdom and
goodness preserves and matures.   And shall we
teach the lisping tongue to sound every name
and forget that of its Maker?   Can we observe
the blooming faculties ripening for tuition, and
forget to teach our child to whom it is indebted
for them?   Can we kiss those sweet ruby lips
                                              when

when they are to close in sleep, and omit to tell the child to whose watchful care it will be indebted for a night's rest? Can we really refuse to offer our little one to Him who loves little children, and in an especial manner takes them under His protection?—Surely not. Surely there cannot be parents who. deliver their daughter to a governess, eight or nine years after she may have been in the world, who have left her in ignorance of the Being through whom she was placed there? Far should it be from our plan to fatigue a little child by long prayers and sermons; but, surely, we ought to teach it to beg the protection of Heaven in a few words suited to its comprehension; and we ought to take the opportunity, as has been observed, of exciting curiosity upon religious and moral subjects, to gratify which is the most delightful part of education.

. Children ask many questions : the information they receive in answer they are willing enough to believe, till they discover a palpable falsity in the person whom they have consulted; and then they feel less and less of interest, and perhaps some disgust towards him. After we have then, for five, six, or seven years, conversed upon what we imagine most important, how pleasant is it to stamp an authority on all we have advanced, by the choice of the most estimable little books, in which, when the child have learnt to read, he

Every verbal instruction receives weight from the authority of books.

may

may see a repetition of that which he already understands. " Why you told me all this, mama; this is just like what you said," observes the child, with increased tenderness and respect for his kind, his wise instructress. How bright is the mother's eye, as she smiles in soft pride and strokes down the hair of the little boy or girl, as he looks up to her in pleasing wonder at her vast knowledge!

The first, and, in my opinion, the most intelligible and useful reading books for children are, " Easy Lessons," by the late excellent Mrs. Trimmer, in several parts; " Mrs. Barbauld's First Books;" and a few very " Easy Stories, by Miss Edgeworth." Some of these works are written (as their authors say) for children of two or three years of age. A child need not begin them till five or six : but this is a question for the decision of parents. The perusal of these will lead the child to that engaging book of Mrs. Trimmer, called " The Introduction to the Knowledge of Nature ;" and this will be immediately succeeded by a small " Scripture History, with plates," by the same lady ; with- " The Footstep to Mrs. Trimmer's Sacred History for Little Children," (anonymous). These several works must be explained in the easiest language, and a reference must be made to pictures where there are any. This list will include all the infant studies, which

may

may be completed at seven or eight years of age.

As the young mind is now led through the only abridgment of the Old and New Testaments that I feel justified in recommending, we have to proceed immediately to the Bible itself: and in the choice of the book of God we should be particularly careful. A small confused print will fatigue the sight and weaken the attention : let us beware of creating unpleasant feelings on such an introduction. A plain calf binding, of large oc-

tavo size, with clear type, is the best description of Bible for a young person. I would present such a gift in an affectionate and serious manner, and in the title-page would write the little owner's name, with a line underneath expressive of my hope that it might be *well* used. The gift thus receives a desirable importance. From this period a few minutes are to be set apart every day (I would advise before breakfast) for the reading of a chapter, a half, or even a few verses. Suppose we first study the Gospels, proceeding slowly, and then the Acts. A child had then better not read any more of the New Testament, but be led to Genesis, having it explained, along

with other particulars, that Adam, the first man, was supposed to have been created four thousand years before our Saviour, Jesus Christ, was born. Question will succeed to reply; and every go-
verness

verness should be fully prepared with her subject; for much more may be taught by oral than by printed information.

Different historical chapters may then be chosen, and afterwards the New Testament again, and entirely, excepting the Revelations, to be reserved for maturer age. Once or twice a week the child might learn and repeat one of the Divine Songs for Children, by Dr. Watts; or a pretty and simple verse from among the Psalms as they stand in the Bible: the first Psalm, the four first verses of the 5th, the 8th, the two first of the 18th, the first and seven last of the 19th, the 23d, 24th, 25th, and the four first of the 41st, and many others are adapted to youthful feeling and capacity. As the child grows older and shews inclination for reading, she should be supplied with pleasing Sunday Books; in which, if fiction be resorted to, morality may be seen to spring from religion. But the parent will, of course, use his own discretion, and follow the dictates of his own conscience, as is his undoubted privilege, with regard to the religious authors he puts into his child's hands. Here it becomes me to stop: I have recommended the Bible, and am silent.

History will divide itself into the study of nature generally, and the study of man partially. We will first glance at the perusal of those memorials of kingdoms and states which have affected

History.

fected more or less the interests, and have accordingly depressed or exalted the character of man.

Civil History.

As this study demands the exercise of deep attention to embrace a grave subject, and the power of memory to retain it, let us call in every auxiliary. I do not consider an hour every day too much for this kind of reading, as every sentence is to be explained, every question it may

It is not the bare reading of words, but the consideration of the matters they describe that avails.

give rise to is to be encouraged and answered, and every country, town, river, or mountain mentioned, is to be sought for, in ancient or modern maps, which are to be regularly brought with the books, and lie open on the table for our purpose.

Perhaps in this hour we may not have turned over three pages. What then have we gained? A lesson in morality, in geography, in history, in biography, in chronology, in orthography, in pronunciation, in natural history, in etymology. Has the child added to her stock of knowledge a clear and perfect idea on any one of these subjects?—Yes. Anxious governess you may then be satisfied. " But the child yawns, and half an hour is not yet past." Really? Let us reflect a little. Did you rouse her sharply from an interesting play?—No. Is she going by and bye to make one in a young party?—No. Is she in pain?—No. Has she been poring over her lessons?—No. Does she appear to understand what she reads?—Yes. Perhaps you have given

an

an unsatisfactory answer to a question ?—I think
not. Is she seated comfortably ?—Yes. Still she
yawns : then shut the book and send her to take
a run in the garden, or the passages, for a quarter
of an hour ; afterwards make another trial.

Various are the present elementary books of   *Of the many plans for teaching history few answer.*
history, and as various the plans proposed to
implant it in the mind of youth ; the preferable
appears to me the most simple.

With deference to the opinions of others, I
must nevertheless 'assert, that the young girls of
our country are instructed in history, as in every
thing else, only upon points. Their education is
like a dissected map, scattered always over a
table ; every part has a dependence upon an-
other, but this is never shewn ; every piece would
join were it put by its proper neighbour, but the   *Perhaps be. cause the chain of events is so broken, and that no connection of historical science is maintained.*
trial is never made. A girl of fifteen will under-
stand the succession of kings, emperors, and
rulers of England, France, Rome, Greece, and
may perhaps know that such a king was born in
this year, reigned so many, and died in that ; but
ask her to give general information, nay help her
by familiar observations upon the state of Europe
in any century, upon the grand connection be-
tween kingdoms separated from others by a river,
a chain of mountains, a channel. Ask her whe-
ther one empire rose as another declined, and
why ? or, whether several flourished at the same
time ? Question her as to the probable and ac-
knowledged

History.

knowlédged *causes.* Ask her for *reasons,* for *principles* to ground her opinions upon : she looks confounded and is mute.

The minds of children should be expanded by every means.

In education, then, let us endeavour (I know the task is laborious) to give a grand and wide view of a lofty and noble subject; such is that of history. We begin with abridgments where the prominent features are collected. These are our object in early youth. We wish to imprint on the mind facts; when well remembered they make way for inferences, actual and supposititious. Without distorting historical facts how finely may we render them subservient to our particular purpose, and what sanction do they give to our own opinion and sentiment!

But they are depressed and tortured by long words and hard sentences.

But some abridgments are written in such high flown language; there are in them so many long words, and such unintelligible sentences, that the venerable works, which they profess to reduce and make easy to the youthful comprehension, are, in their own unaffected majesty of thought and simplicity of diction, infinitely more agreeable to the child's native principle of taste. But what can we do? We certainly have Mrs. Trimmer to help us a little; but when she stops, who continues in her innocent, playful, entertaining, yet always instructive, manner? I confess I do not know. We must continue, as well as we can, however, with the books we have, for we are not now to consider the theory but the practice.

The

The first abridgment of Mrs. Trimmer is that *History.* of Ancient History. This book comprises the four great ancient monarchies,—the Assyrian, Babylonish, Egyptian, Persian. This history is to be succeeded by that of Greece. These may be read, talked over, considered, three or four times. For dependence and dates we may refer to parts of the Old Testament, carefully remembering a little of chronology(this word is very hard sounding, we need not pronounce it) when we can conveniently do so. For example, "Well, Adam, you say, was created 1556 years before the deluge; and you have explained to me the meaning of this word, deluge, many times, yet I should like to hear it once more.—Very well, you are right. Now I will tell you how many years after the deluge, or if you like the word flood better, how many years after the flood this good (or naughty) prince (king, emperor, or lawgiver) was born, it was just ...., and our Saviour was not born till .... years afterwards." So much of chronology is enough for one lesson. At the next reading-hour we ask again, and, perhaps, are well answered; if not, we must have patience to repeat.—I wonder if you can tell me directly how many years ago our Saviour, Jesus Christ, was born? may add the preceptress "I know," answers the child with a smile, "one thousand eight hundred and fifteen, for that is this year."

Books are to be read and digested. Very few should be given to children, and never two at one time.

History is inseparable from chronology.

Is

History.

Upon first view education may appear in its minute parts very puerile.

These are not however so; and if we hope for success they must be attended to.

One principle of education is the teach-ing of youth to think.

Is this thought ridiculous and childish?—I can-not help it; for by this attention so minute, so monotonous, is the pupil advanced in her educa-tion. . I have known many girls, of ten, eleven, twelve, who could instantly name the date of the year, and who, nevertheless, were quite confused on being asked how many years since our Saviour was born. Why was it? For a very simple rea-son : these girls, with most others, had been taught many things, but one had been forgotten, how *to think*. These young ladies can tell you their opinions now and then; but if you say, " Why, my dear, do you judge so?" or, " What reason have you for that?" they open their eyes in astonishment; either they imagine the inquirer some extraordinary being, and are in-clined to laugh, or they summon up courage to say, " La! I don't know, one often says things without any particular reason. I heard, I believe, Mrs. Somebody say so, but I don't know exactly why. No, I saw it in some book." Do we wish our pupils to think? let us condescend to teach them.

My anxiety is to make myself clearly under-stood, even by the most dull of the well mean-ing, though inexperienced governesses alluded to in the first address; I shall, therefore, run every risk of being tiresome, inelegant, and un-interesting to general readers.—He who wishes to make himself generally useful should not be over solicitous to gratify his vanity.

Our

Our historical studies must seem to form a long piece of thread: we may tie a knot, and fasten one end, the other we keep in our hand unrolled; the ball is futurity; every succeeding day we unwind; the knot is the creation of man. A yard and half forwards is the deluge, four yards from the knot is a little crimson to mark the birth of Christ, and nearly two after it we may hold the present moment; these yards will represent thousands of years. *History.*

History should run in a chain.

Vast blanks occur, however, in the history of ages; surmise here takes place of fact, and posterity has regarded with respect, opinion, which antiquity has rendered illustrious, and distance incontrovertable. *The surmises of antiquity have repaired the chain which was broken by barbarism.*

Rome elevated her proud crest as Greece wept on faded glory and retired; Greece must, therefore, as I have said, be honoured by the first perusal. Mrs. Trimmer, I believe, has not helped us with an abridgment of the lovely testimonials to the merit of ancient Greece; and Goldsmith is above the capacity of a child of ten or twelve, at least those who desire their pupils to retain what they read, will think so. We are under the necessity of buying a duodecimo book, the price of which is about eighteen pence; it is written in tolerably suitable language, by whom I know not. I do not *recommend* this little work, nor others upon the same plan, by the same author, for there are

words

words of four, five, and six syllables in many parts, and passages which the scrupulously chaste and considerate Mrs. Trimmer would have scorned to extract from history, for the confusion of a governess and the puzzled inquiry of a little girl; but there is absolutely no other little book, excepting indeed Mavor's, and he is vastly inferior in my mind even to this.

The kind maternal friend to the young has, however, left a Roman History with plates; when this is finished we find a space in information—the preceptress must herself fill it up with a short

Conversation is the only means of information where infant books fail.

and easy description of the incursions of the barbarians, explaining who they were supposed to be, and pointing out on the map the tracts they are imagined to have marked with desolation and plunder. She has only for guide the sentiments of respected authors, expressed long after these dark and disgusting events took place, and these she may bend to the conception of her pupil. It matters not how short is the conversation upon this subject, a little tender heart shudders at the recital of the dreadful sufferings of outraged humanity.

When the Roman Empire began to sink under its own weight, the seat of government was removed from Rome to Byzantium. Constantine effected the removal in the year of our Lord 328; and thirty-six years afterwards the Roman Empire was divided into Eastern and Western, each governed

governed by a different emperor. At this epoch
we may rest to turn back to the birth of Christ
in the little history; and we may consider, in an
impressive manner, the constancy and fortitude
of the martyrs and primitive Christians.

Modern history now claims attention. At the
head of this ought to rank the respective country
of every student. Mrs. Trimmer has given one
abridgment, that of England; and with it finish
her historical labours for children. Will any
experienced person follow the plan she probably
traced, of making a complete course of history,
ancient and modern? will any one strive to adopt
her chearful and interesting style, her simplicity,
her innocent manner, in relating an *equivocal*
fact? If he, or she, (it seems fitted to the ma-
ternal delicacy of a female) would undertake the
task, inestimably great might be the advantages
to the young.

Modern History.

Let us give respect to the country of the pupil, and ever encourage a noble affection for it.

The want of such a work as this for children
under twelve years of age, must be severely felt
by preceptresses. What interesting little his-
tories might be made from the best writers of
France, Russia, Sweden, Turkey, Prussia, Spain,
and the other states of modern Europe; not to
be jumbled together, but to be bound separately,
with small engravings, without long words, or
aspiring to grand composition. The only book
that gives general hints of these particulars, but
in language infinitely too subtle for children, is

E   called

Mary. called " The Flowers of Modern History, by the Rev. John Adams." If we can skip over some pages, and make the learner understand the others, she will have a general idea of the governments of Europe.

A second course of larger abridgments is followed, and ends at fifteen.

Perhaps the young lady may conclude these studies at the age of twelve: she is then to begin the same course in larger works. Dr. Oliver Goldsmith has obliged us by abridgments of Rome, Greece, England; Rollin furnishes us with an ancient history; the Bible is always at hand. These occupy three years more, and here abridgments close.

Large works are introduced.

The taste of a young woman so formed will now be sensibly affected by the elegance of style, and noble simplicity of the most admired authors. Let it be gratified by perusing their historical compositions. Mark the indignation of her eye at an instance of perfidy; the sweet animation of her ingenuous countenance at the recording of an act of generosity; the tear that trembles as she struggles with delicacy to conceal it, at the misfortunes of the gentle, the brave, the virtuous; listen to her observations, expressed with doubtful modesty, and with caution unknown to saucy ignorance: she is devoid of prejudice; she dares to think for herself, and yet she is always ready to be corrected. Behold the fruits of seven years good instruction, even in reading!

Histories of the states of modern Asia and
            Africa

Africa may be severally found in the Encyclo- History.
pœdia.   Dr. Robertson is the elegant author of For retention.
a History of America, of Scotland, of Charles the
Fifth; Mr. Murphy has translated for our use
the Annals of Tacitus; Voltaire has written the
Life of Charles XII.; much of the History of Rus-
sia is included in the Life of Catherine II.;
Hume, Smollett, and Henry, represent England;
and Gibbon considers the Decline and Fall of the
Roman Empire.   From these celebrated works
the governess will select according as she may
think proper.   History of
Nature.

Natural History can only be rendered uninte-
resting to children by the assiduous ignorance of
those who pretend to write for them, and to be
judges of that extreme simplicity of taste, of which,
in truth, in their works they prove that they know
nothing.   With inexpressible satisfaction does a
little girl examine a curious animal, plant, or
mineral, whilst her preceptress is explaining, in
the easiest words, its history and properties.   A
delightful reward for good conduct is a plot of All children
are passion-
ground, with little garden utensils; further re- ately fond of
this pursuit.
wards are seeds, slips, shoots, plants.   Every tree,
shrub, or flower, has a name, which should be
named to the enquirer in Latin, according
to the plan of some introductions to botany.
Other rewards may be minerals—a bit of silver
or copper ore, different remarkable stones, or
shells, spars, &c.; and animals, a little dog,

E 2   a canary

Biography,
Fiction, &c.
———
when it is
properly in-
troduced and
considered.

therefore, an important study to youth; but in
the way it is generally taught, they reap no ad-
vantage whatever. A boy (or girl) is desired to
toil through a heterogeneous mass of information
concerning priests, soldiers, poets, sailors, law-
yers, and doctors; and when his book is finished,
he is sensible only of the weight of confusion
which dates, places, and names have left upon
his mind. We may pronounce him pretty well
disgusted by the time this task is finished.

Any regular biography, comprehensible to a
young person under sixteen, I have never met
with. If there be a work of this nature, it should
be kept, with other books of reference, upon the
study table, to be resorted to only upon the men-
tion of some celebrated person, of whom the
pupil is anxious to learn something; or upon the
introduction of the work of a deceased author
which he may be going to peruse. At any rate,
we have it always in our power to excite an in-
terest by conversation on any subject of biogra-
phy which we wish entirely to gratify. Works
upon this part of study abridged, or written for
youth, (according to their titles) are Lemprière's
Universal Biography; The Lives of the Poets,
abridged; Brown's Classical Dictionary, abridg-
ed from Lemprière; and Plutarch's Lives. Of
these I should prefer the dictionaries of Lem-
prière and Brown.

Well written   Books of travels, voyages, &c. rank next. A
man

man cannot separate himself from his discoveries; a small part of his life must necessarily be worked up with the descriptions he gives us. Here is then a portion of geography—Mr. Goldsmith's Grammar of Geography for Schools, would be a pretty book for young persons, though not for children, if the author would condescend to tear out of the copy for the next edition, different paragraphs which he may be ashamed to have written for children in a school room. An imaginary tour through Britain and Europe, undertaken by Juvenile Travellers, is published, I believe, by Miss Peacock. The Travels of Orlando, by Jauffret, in four volumes, have also an imaginary hero. Captain Cook's Voyages are abridged in two volumes, by an *abridger*; and there is Guthrie's Geographical Grammar for Schools; and to which may be added Cruttwell's Gazetteer.

A class of books has lately sprung up into a multitude, which professes to unite instruction and amusement. Of all others in the library, these may be the most pernicious in their effects; we cannot be too cautious in the choice of them. They are for the most part filled with scenes from actual life, or from celebrated romances, and are, in fact, little novels. As females have this trash in general, so, to please their vanity, girls are, according to their models, the general heroines of the piece. Little miss was the daugh-

ter

Biography, Fiction, &c.
travels are extremely useful.

Fiction.
The most dangerous of all books may be included in fiction.

Fiction.

ter of a lady and gentleman of *immense* property, and she was very *beautiful*, of course *good*; a young friend of hers was very *ugly*, and of course *naughty*. The good girl is acquainted with a young gentleman who makes love to her in miniature, and in time, he and his beauty are married. The ugly girl either falls sick with spite, and is killed at once by the amiable author, or she retires (always in poverty) behind the scenes. Such is the basis of the plots in these performances, which are devoured by children that are

We need not wonder at the airs of those children who have read every juvenile novel.

fond of reading; hence arise the thousand strange coquettish airs they sometimes practice. We may hear people say, I cannot think where the child imbibed such an idea; I wonder how she learnt such a thing; probably, from one of these books. But this is far from being the case with all of

A few of fictitious productions do honour to their authors.

them. - Evenings at Home; The Swallow; Keeper in Search of his Master; Mrs. Trimmer's excellent Fabulous Histories, and Servant's Friend; History of Carlo, the Dog; Sandford and Merton; Mental Improvement; Elements of Morality; (without the translator's preface), Visit for a Week; The Six Princesses of Babylon; Little Jack; the New Robinson Crusoe; Parents' Assistant, with other juvenile works by Miss Edgworth; the beautifully natural tales in Mrs. Leycester's School; The Blind Child;— are to children entertaining and instructive. This style of books for young women may be

found

found in Mrs. Palmerstone's Letters to her
Daughter; Agrippina, by Miss Hamilton; The
Cottagers of Glenburvie, by the same respected
and able author; Rasselas; Mrs. More's Essays
for Young Ladies; Dr. Gregory's Legacy to his
Daughters; Death of Abel; Zimmerman on So-
litude, abridged; Economy of Human Life.

The beautiful prose compositions of our perio-
dical writers children are utterly incapable of
admiring, or even of understanding; but a young
lady of seventeen would, if she had been well
educated, feel much pleasure in reading every *A well-taught*
day at breakfast to her parents, and sisters, one *girl must love*
and be im-
paper of the Spectator, Rambler, Guardian, Tat- *proved by*
the writings
ler, World, or Adventurer. Originally these pa- *of an Addi-*
son or a
pers were delivered out early, and were often *Johnson.*
perused at breakfast. Why may we not now sip
our tea, and read one, as it chances to follow the
other? It would be a pretty and edifying sub-
ject for conversation, and might promote har-
mony and chearfulness.

In order to understand poetic fiction we must *Mythology*
and poetry
have some idea of mythology. It will be then *combining.*
advisable not to pass over any celebrated hea-
then deity without explaining very briefly its at-
tributes, and the estimation in which it is sup-
posed to have been held with the ancients.
Brown's Classical Dictionary has been mention-
ed; it contains every information a preceptress
can

Fiction.

can require to convey again to the pupil in her own words.

Poesy is the touchstone to sensibility.

One reading lesson of poetry in the week is surely enough for children, to whom we give it as an exercise, principally upon tone and emphasis: but we must be careful in our choice of pieces. The versification of Gay's Fables is not difficult: the first part of them may be, I should think, easily explained. Tales of the Robin, and

But we must be content to fix principles before we cultivate taste.

addresses to, and descriptions of that sweet bird, form an innocent and pretty work. Original poetry is engaging from its simplicity; but let us not confound the rude with the simple, if we wish to lay the foundation for true taste. The Beggar's Petition may be useful; The Hermit, by Dr. Parnell, it is needless for me to say, is admirable, but requires much explanation; Edwin and Angelina is a beautiful ballad, but there is too much of love in it: one cannot put words in a child's mind without giving their meaning; if this is not to be done satisfactorily, let us withhold the piece altogether. Some passages in the Deserted Village could not fail of pleasing and instructing, particularly those concerning the clergyman. The Ode on Solitude, by Pope, children are delighted to read, or learn, because they observe that it was written when the author was a boy. John Gilpin may be read and laughed at; and a work which I have lately seen, called the

the First Book of Poetry, by W. F. Mylius, appears generally suited to the very young. All poetry for children should be selected as free from love descriptions and satire as possible; these form, indeed, the basis of poetic fiction, therefore we should be ever on our guard against them, if we do not wish to implant the seeds of affectation, romance, and ill-nature in our pupils.

Fiction.

Poetry treating too often of love or satire excites the most powerful feelings, and should be selected with the utmost care.

So circumscribed are the poetic studies for children. What shall we say for youth? From amongst the beauties, native and borrowed, of our poets, which are we to select for the instruction, the entertainment, the refinement of our young women? May I presume to offer to their consideration the stupendous Homer in his English dress; Virgil, supported by Dryden; and Milton, with more than the majesty of our native language? The Essays of Pope on Criticism, and on Man, and many other productions of the best poets, are collected in parts, prose and verse, in The Elegant Extracts, which work is well known and justly valued.

Nothing has been said of the drama. Some parents object to their daughters' perusal of tragic and comic authors; but where this objection does not exist, I imagine the most unexceptionable should be carefully sought for, yet not placed in a female's hands until she may be very far advanced in her education. The young lady

No dramatic reading should be permitted till a certain age.

E 6   should

should be requested to read them to her parents, or governess, aloud, that the lofty sentiments may act forcibly on the mind, as the impassioned images of tenderness inevitably will upon the heart. There is a work, called the Family Shakespeare, in which are collected the noblest of that author's plays; in it are omitted many unintelligible phrases, and exceptionable observations, which is a great recommendation, when we reflect upon the innocent eyes that are to peruse its pages. A collection of plays fitted for youth, made from the best poets and writers, would be a very interesting present to the public, and would save much trouble and time to a prudent parent or preceptress.

The matter has preceded : let us consider the manner in reading.

The principal points are pronunciation and tone. It is in vain that we are told by gentlemen, that there is no rule for pronouncing words which are changing perpetually, from the caprice and authority of the fashionable and the learned. Young ladies seldom mix in company, whatever may be their rank; and any improvement from the speakers in our parliament (as I have heard suggested), is absolutely out of the question, as females are not permitted to approach its august assemblies; we are, therefore, obliged to be satisfied with the information of a pronouncing dictionary, and that of Walker,

with

with his book of proper names, is, in my opinion, superior to some others for the study. If the purchase of Walker and Dr. Johnson's large dictionaries be considered too expensive, parents may be suited with the Union Dictionary, in which are united the productions of both of these indefatigable authors.

As to tone in reading we should always enforce an observance of that which is natural, still bearing in mind, however, the importance or insignificance of the subject, and being influenced by either. The tone of voice for the Bible should be grave, slow, impressive; that for history, energetic, distinct, precise; for fiction, easy, chearful, familiar; and that for poetry, clear, yet, in other respects, variable, according to the diversity of images represented

Nature and our subject are to regulate the tone of voice.

———————

CHAPTER III.

GRAMMAR AND THE ENGLISH LANGUAGE.

It is presumed, that, to a youth, no language will be considered so important in its acquisition as that of his own country. As a regular study in a British family, English grammar then holds the first rank. Let us proceed to the slight examination

amination of this useful branch of knowledge ; which for convenience, we may arrange under three heads, theoretical grammar, practical grammar, and composition.

Theoretical grammar.—This name may be given to the study in general, which treats of words, their derivation, signification, and use.

The study of grammar is in itself a dry one, and is particularly so to very young people, with-

out great care be used in its introduction and pursuit. A very small portion at a time might be taught by conversation, with reference to books. If, however, the child have a task from it to learn, it should be a very short one; every word having been previously explained, and the sense of the whole bent to the dullest capacity.

The first and best work of the kind for children, in my opinion, is a little one called The Mother's Grammar ; the next is Murray abridged ; from this we proceed to Murray's large grammar.

Articles are, generally, the first parts of speech in the arrangements of grammarians : with them the little girl must stay until she is fully acquainted with their use, and then advance to the

substantive. In the course of a walk a thousand objects present themselves.—When the little heart is bounding in gaiety and health we may insinuate instruction without ever damping enjoyment : we might at such a time endeavour

to

to draw out theory for practical use. The pa- *Theory.*
rent or preceptress can say, " There is a fine
horse grazing in the meadow : will you tell me
what is the word horse in grammar ?" The pupil
will instantly answer, " Horse is a substantive."
" Why ?"—" Because you can see him. Frock
is a substantive, I can feel it ; flower, I can
smell ; birds, I can hear whistle ; so horse, and
flower, and birds, are substantives. Oh, and
fruit I can taste, so fruit is a substantive." · Thus
might a child prattle as it skipped along the
green fields, and pleased with fancied discoveries,
repeat a lesson of grammar.

When the little girl has been judiciously led
through the first book, she may have the abridg-
ment of Mr. Murray, and proceed no further till
she has attained her twelfth year. She may
learn short lessons, and go through the book half
a-dozen times ; so much the better, there is time
enough for the large work.

But we are never to relax in our examinations The first ob-
ject of the
builder is to
of the learner's knowledge in the little she does lay a solid
foundation ,
understand ; every part of speech must be named
in a general manner. The noun, common or and the first
endeavour of
proper, its gender and number ; the article and the teacher
is to implant
its kind ; pronouns, personal, possessive, and the proper
elements.
conjunctive ; verbs, regular and irregular ; ad-
jectives and their degrees ; prepositions, the case
they govern ; adverbs, conjunctions, and inter-
jections, &c. Examples are to be given in all
these,

these, which, when understood, will prepare for syntax, or the art of placing words in a sentence according to certain established rules.

Mr. Murray's works are now to be consulted; they consist of the Grammar, Exercises, and Key. The last is for the use of the teacher, who may be sometimes in doubt. · They lead to

Practical grammar—by which is meant the reducing of the art to practice : synonomysing exercises, and parsing are here included.

According to the allotted time for each, the young lady must parse and synonomise, which she may do from the same book. For this purpose an easy, entertaining and instructive one should be chosen. Mrs. Trimmer's Introduction to the Knowledge of Nature; or, The Evenings at Home, for Young Girls; and The British Travellers, for the Elder, are extremely well calculated. · In parsing the whole grammar comes into action. In "An Introduction to the Knowledge of Nature" the student will say "*An*," the indefinite article; *an* is used before words beginning with a vowel, or h mute. "*Introduction*" is a common substantive in the singular number of the third person; "*to*," ·a preposition; "*the*," the article definite; "*Knowledge*," substantive, singular number; "*of*," preposition, as it is prepositive to some word which it governs; or in more childish language, as it goes before some word which it governs in the

objective

objective case; " *Nature*," a substantive in the
singular number, and of the third person and
nominative case.

Two or three lines will be sufficient at one
lesson of parsing; the same number will be proper
also for synonomising, which is the art of sub-
stituting one word for another; the ready appli-
cation of which is particularly useful to youth synonomys-
ing are ex-
tremely ne-
cessary.
in conversation as well as in writing. Its merit
is in giving an easy flow of words, and render-
ing a language delicate and perspicuous, by a
nice appropriation of sense to subject.

Ours is not a barren language; we are not un-
der the necessity of putting half a dozen of dif-
ferent marks upon the same word, in order to ex-
press half a dozen different objects, as is the case
in neighbouring countries; on the contrary, we
find many synonimous words expressive of one
quality. It cannot be denied that some of the
number have not the force or beauty of others,
and for this reason it is that we are to direct
young judgments in their selection.

At first, however, we are only to expect one Nature will
never submit
to be urged
with violence;
Those who
know least,
are such as
have been
taught every
thing at once
meaning of the word. We must not be fasti-
dious with mere children, especially when we
see that they are doing as well as they can : let
us be kind and patient; every thing will come in
its turn. No skilful gardener forces with vio-
lence the little plant he would rear to maturity;
he

Practice.

he may assist, but he dare not attempt to rival, much less overthrow, nature.

In synonomysing this sentence, " Many people were surprized that the youthful Maria seemed not gay; but there was one in the crowd who guessed the reason; and this was her injured friend, who imagined rightly that she was suffering from the stings of conscience:"—we may see it thus:

Many   people were surprised that Maria
Numerous persons   astonished
   Divers   •

seemed not gay ; but there was one, in the
appeared   lively yet

crowd   who guessed the reason, and this was
multitude that divined   cause

her injured friend,   who imagined rightly that
   wronged confidant, that conjectured justly

she was suffering   much   from the stings of
            enduring a great deal   wounds
conscience.
   reason.

It is allowed that the words as they stand here altered do not improve the sentence; but on many occasions the transposing of words of the same meaning gives energy or sweetness to composition.

Next

Next to synonomysing is a little exercise, to *Practice.* which I cannot affix a name. It consists in finding out opposites : as good, bad; handy, awkward; industrious, idle; virtuous, vicious; generous, avaricious; fortunate, unlucky; &c. We must not, however, permit any *uns* before the same word; as lucky, unlucky; happy, unhappy; this would be trifling.

English exercises remain to be spoken of; but *Exercises.* their utility is so well explained, and the manner of writing them so well described in Murray, that no comment is necessary from me. I therefore merely advise, that the learner write but very little at a lesson, on her slate; that, after reading it carefully over, and comparing it with the rule, she may shew it the governess, who will correct it before her, pointing out every fault; or perhaps by putting a + over Never should principle be severed from practice. the top, after which the child may correct the whole by herself. When finished, the exercise must be entered in a copy-book, but never ought rule and example to be separated. A very wide margin should be ruled in every page. In this margin we are to require the rule, or the greatest part of it. Every rule is numbered for clearness, and a reference is made to the page in the grammar; perhaps one side of the margin may be filled up by rule. We are to match the page with examples, and begin fresh rules and fresh examples in the next page, and so on.

As

As in this style :

Orthography.	*Examples.*
Rule 1. Monosyllables ending with *f;* or *s*, or *l*, preceded by a single vowel, double the final consonant. The exceptions are, *of, if, as,* &c. &c. (*see Gram. p.* 37.) *Rule 2,* &c.	It is no great merit to spel*l* properly, but a great defect to do it incorrectly. Jacob worshipped his Creator, leaning on the top of his staf*f*.

Syntax.	*Examples.*
Rule 1. A verb must agree with its nominative case in number and person, as, I learn, &c. (*see Gram. p.* 139.) *Rule 2,* &c.	Disappointments sin*k* the heart of man. The smiles that encourage severity of judgment, hid*e* malice and insincerity. He dare*s* not act contrary to his inclinations. Fifty pounds of wheat contai*n* forty pounds of flour.

In the appendix to the Grammar are some excellent rules for punctuation, with a list of the figures of speech. These will be attended to in the study of

Composition.—Youthful composition may be divided in three parts: letter-writing, narrative, and theme or essay.

What

·· What can be more interesting than the perusal of an elegant and unaffected letter, which is equally free from bombast as meanness, pedantry as ignorance, fastidiousness as vulgarity? and yet how rarely do we·see such! Nature and simplicity, without any violation of grammatical form, should be our ambition. It is in vain to tell a child, that the letter which he writes once a week, or fortnight, is to be in an easy, familiar style, and in "his own way," if, after he have poured out his little heart to an absent playfellow, we scrutinize, scratch out, interlard, with high wrought sentences and long words, his epistle, till the young writer, in despair, upon re-examining his slate, finds an unintelligible, and to him uninteresting, jargon. " Well," he says, " I am glad my letter is written. I know I shall never write letters properly; I am sure I never should have thought of that word." Poor child! instead of damping his early efforts, we should almost fall into the opposite extreme—even allow a paragraph to pass which is discordant to the ear, provided there be no flagrant breach of rule in it, rather than discourage his first attempts. " Suppose, my dear, your little friend, or cousin, were in the next house to you, and that you were not permitted to visit each other in snowy or wet weather, for fear of taking cold; suppose, also, that if you spoke loudly in your chamber your friend

Practice.
Letter-writing.

The perfection of letters is in the graceful ease with which they are written; so that we be doubtful, as it were, whether we read, or actually hear, the language of the writer.

friend could hear you, what would you say?" a governess might ask her pupil, who sits with her pencil in her hand. "Oh," the young lady answers, "I should have plenty to say. I would say, my dear Mary Anne, I am very sorry I cannot have the pleasure of seeing you, for it appears a long time since I had that pleasure."

"Very well, that will do for the beginning of your letter; you may write just what you would say, excepting in that word: you see there are two *pleasures* in a sentence; you must think of a word which will do instead of pleasure.

"*Child.* Why, I should be *happy* if I saw my cousin, therefore I may say "*happiness.*"

"*Gov.* Yes, you may.

"*Child.* But I thought letters should be like the writings of grown-up people, and that they should begin with "I take up my pen to inform you," or "I take the opportunity of writing to you." Should there not be *I* always at the beginning? *

"*Gov.* It is not at all necessary: in writing a letter, you may suppose you are speaking to a person, and you may begin with any words you like; only remember, that in a letter your friend's business is to be spoken of first, and your own last. You would not think it thoughtful or kind in your friend to tell you that she

had

Children are
often checked
in their pro-
gress by some
extraordinary
conception,
which we
should gently
eradicate.

* The question of a very sensible little girl.

had been to this or that place, had seen such
and such and such people lately, sign herself
" your's very affectionately," and then write in
a postscript, that she was very sorry to hear you
had had so severe an illness, but hoped you
were getting better; or that she was shocked to
hear of your accident.

" *Pupil.* No; it would seem as if she did not
care very much about my illness, or my acci-
dent. I shall write fast enough if I may say
what I would if I spoke."

There is some truth in this imaginary conver-
sation; but I shall, in order to set the matter in
a clearer light, insert two copies of letters in
my possession. One is written by a school go-
verness for her pupil; the other is the genuine
production of a little girl, who was encouraged
to write only that which she thought and under-
stood.

First Letter.

" My dear Mama,

" No doubt you anticipate the purport
" of this epistle, which is to remind you of a
" delightful period, which the revolving sun has
" again brought round; and with it also its
" joys, as you may suppose, when I say the va-
" cation commences on the 19th of this month,
" when I hope to meet you all in good health;
" and should you find me improved, it will
" greatly

" greatly add to the enlargement of my hap-
" piness.

" Believe me to remain,"
&c. &c. &c.

Second Letter.

" My dear Miss ———,

       " As I wish to become your correspon-
" dent, I now sit down to address a few lines
" to you. I am very sorry it rains, as I fear it
" will not be in our power to go out, but I hope
" it will be fine to-morrow, that I may be able
" to go to Mrs. E——'s, as I wish to have a
" tour to read. I like the one I have from the
" library very much. I suppose the little robin
" that flew in the breakfast room was very glad
" of its liberty; indeed it would have been a
" pity to have confined it to a cage, as it is so
" much used to range the fields. I was so sorry
" when Mary Anne's linnet died, and I think
" she was too, but we are very unlucky with all
" our pets; but I hope we shall be more lucky
" this year. I am very fond of writing and re-
" ceiving long letters, and I hope you will ho-
" nour me with one, and I shall keep it to look
" at, and lock it up in my writing desk. I must
" now conclude, having nothing more to say.

       " I am your affectionate pupil,
" L—— B——.

" P. S. I hope you will answer this letter and
" correct

" correct it, as I am conscious there are many
" faults in it."

Which of these letters is most to be admired,
the pedantic production calculated to create dis-
gust in a young mind to letter writing, or the
artless sentiments of childhood, expressed with-
out restraint ? It would be ridiculous to doubt.

When the pupil can with propriety and ease
express her own feelings, she may be taught to
represent in correct, though unconstrained lan-
guage, the sentiments and anecdotes of others ;
and to this species of study, in general, may be
given the name of

Narrative. No method can be better than that
recommended in Walker's Teacher's Assistant,
for the writing of narratives. The preceptor is
to take a short story from history or biography,
and to read it once or twice to the student, who
should be directed to write immediately after-
wards upon his slate, in his own words, as much
as he can recollect. The whole is then to be
corrected, and copied off. It would be also of
advantage if he were taught to relate the anec-
dote orally. Few, especially young people, for
want of attention to their expression, can describe
any event that they have heard or read in easy,
natural language; they often either appear pe-
dantic and bold, or ignorant and embarrassed,
when perhaps there is no truth whatever in these
appearances.

Many who
can write a
good story
cannot relate,
for want of
practice, a
simple inci-
dent.

P   After

Practice.

Theme.

After Narrative, Mr. Walker proposes the attempting of themes and essays. He begins with a regular essay; but, with deference to his opinion, I would advise theme composition at once. A theme requires closeness of thought, as he observes; but his rules are so plain, with a good knowledge of history and a few general good writers, examples and quotations are so comparatively easy to produce, that the pupil, with encouragement, finds no great difficulty in making them, after the second or third trial; at least it has happened so with all my pupils. Walker's book is almost indispensably necessary to private teachers of English · composition; it contains such simple rules and appropriate examples, as cannot but facilitate the means of improvement to both pupil and preceptor.

A teacher must shew that he understands principles and practice, before he can excite respect or inspire confidence in his pupils.

It surely is not necessary for me to say, that although we possess the book of examples, we are not to resort to it upon every occasion, and to model the pupil's opinion exactly upon Mr. Walker's. A dozen people may write upon the danger of delay, but they are not bound to write alike: nay, I am persuaded, in the dozen of productions there would not be found two sentences expressed in the same style, and very few sentiments would have any resemblance; yet the proposition might be ably supported by the different writers. Besides, we run the risk of being thought meanly of by our pupils. "Ah," think they,

Practice.
Theme.

they, " she gives us a thing to write which she cannot correct or explain without hunting all through Walker; and instead of putting what we say in good sense, she scratches it all out and puts in from the book; and how should we be ever able to guess what Mr. Walker says ?" This passes in a young mind in defiance of all we may affirm, for youth is a more correct judge of human actions than we in general choose to allow.

Themes should be written first upon the slate: a margin drawn off, and the heads arranged in paragraphs. The proposition or narrative comes first. The learner writes, in the margin, first, *prop.* or *narr.*, and then the sentence; secondly, *reason*, and then explain it; thirdly, the *confirmation*, &c. &c.

Lessons.

English lessons. Children, besides learning by heart grammar, generally are expected to study particularly that branch of it called orthography, or spelling. We have, indeed, a numerous collection of spelling books, and it is difficult to pronounce which may be the least useful. Some are too fine, and some are too gross; others profess to teach every thing, and they plunge into the deepest science, and lie uninteresting and repugnant amidst " words of learned length and thundering sound." If we wish the child not *merely* to learn spelling, it would be bet-

There are no good spelling books for children.

F 2   ter,

Practice.

Lessons.

ter, as I have always found, to give a few lines of some really useful reading book—one by Mrs. Barbauld, Mrs. Trimmer, or Miss Edgeworth, and let her have the short and long words as a lesson. Instead of confining a girl or boy to such unmeaning instruction as r, a, - k, i, s, h, ra-kish; i, n, - v, o, i, c, e, in-voice; l, a, c, k, - i, n, g, lack-ing; g, e, w, - g, a, w, gew-gaw; c, h, u, c, - k, l, e, chuc-kle; b, u, m, p, - k, i, n, bump-kin; t, r, u, c, - k, l, e, truc-kle; z, a, - n, y, za-ny, &.* we should give her something that will tend to improve the heart. In the little works above mentioned, the child may be suited according to his knowledge. If he is beginning to read tolerably, cannot he spell every word of such a sentence as this? "Do not pull the cat's tail, Charles, you will hurt her; you should stroak puss." Are these unmeaning words? No: they contain a proper lesson of humanity; a lesson that a boy will love to learn, and try to remember. What will he benefit by learning to spell rakish, and chuckle, and gewgaw? Nothing.

. A little sixpenny book with cuts, containing the alphabet, and a few divided syllables, might be used as a first introduction. It is called the First Step to Knowledge. After this, I see no use

No words should be learnt that are unworthy of an explanation.

* Vide Mavor's Spelling-Book.

use in the professed spelling books. As the pupil grows older, she may spell from various reading books, small and large words, and improve at once, her heart and her head.

Many girls of a more advanced age have tasks to learn from a small dictionary. This plan I do not condemn, but I never practice it. I prefer some useful book, as Mental Improvement; or a history, in which my pupils may read down a few lines, or half a page, and be prepared with the spelling, and with different definitions of words promiscuously asked them : but this is undoubtedly troublesome to the teacher, though very advantageous to the scholars; for whilst they are supposed to glance only at the orthography, they are steadily surveying good sentiments, and are acquiring real knowledge.

CHAPTER IV.

WRITING AND ARITHMETIC.

WITH the attainment of some knowledge in our native language, we are to consider the means of representing it on paper; and this we effectually do, by the formation and conjunction of certain characters, called writing

I have given my opinion on the practice of

F 3   teaching

It is a folly
to seek after
ornamenting
before the
edifice is
erected.

teaching, too. soon, those branches of education not immediately affecting the infant heart. I have said, that it is always dangerous, because it is evidently repugnant to nature. For this reason, I conceive, and am supported by experience, that eight or nine years of age, is a period early enough to attempt the first lines of writing. The child who is properly and regularly instructed six days out of the week, or even four, will be in a fine bold text in six months, and in single lines by the expiration of twelve months.. What more can be desired? Then will· the prudent parent look back with pleasure to those hours which have been devoted to the study of the book of nature, and to the cultivation of reason and pure principles; hours which might have been wasted in following pursuits, for the early practice of which a child is not one step the forwarder at twelve years of age.

In the first writing lessons great care is necessary, in order to make the little girl sit in an easy, unconstrained position. She should have a desk rising about six inches; and be taught for, a short time, the motion of the pen, without touching the paper. The wrist should be pressed firmly down, and the two fore fingers straitened to clasp the pen on one side, whilst the thumb raises, or depresses it, on the other; the third, and little finger resting on the paper, are further supports to the wrist. The pen is now dipped

Much of success in art depends upon first instruction.

dipped in the ink, and now trails its first un- *Writing.*
steady course. From this moment, the teacher's
eye must be fixed on the child's fingers. She
may rely upon it, that if she neglect the holding
of the pen, innumerable difficulties will ensue.
The pen must be constantly watched. Slippery,
indeed, will be its hold in the beginning of trial;
but as it moves wrong, it must be set right; not
an up, nor down stroke should pass unnoticed.
The governess may assure herself, that the more
indefatigable she is in the commencement, the
more rapid will be the improvement of the child—
so rapid, that there has appeared with some lit-
tle pupils, from extreme attention to foundations
or beginnings, a progress, almost marvellous; so
true is the old homely saying, that " well begun
is half done."

. The young and the old are pleased with no-
velty. Both seize with avidity the engagement
recommended by variety, and illumined by
fancy: but novelty is a traitress. No sooner
has she allured than she disappoints; no sooner
touched than she is fled for ever; not more re-
pugnant is meridian light to darkness, than sen-
sible possession to novelty. Hope stands to offer
assistance, when conjecture is satisfied and pas-
sive. This assistance we are to accept or reject.
In education we are commanded by necessity,
not only to accept, but to encourage, to pay
homage to Hope, if we would not sink under

F 4   the

the weight which falls equally heavy on pupil and preceptor.—Thus then, a child rushes with impetuosity upon a new study, or upon a new play; but as a ball struck against a hard surface is repelled according to the degree of force which sent it forward, so does the learner turn more or less disgusted from his pursuit, according to the alacrity with which he engaged in it.

As novelty vanishes some spur must be found to exertion.

This is a very arduous moment for a preceptress. Little plans of encouragement must be formed. Just and steady praise should follow a fatiguing lesson of exertion, as different symptoms of sorrow, rather than of anger, should arise on the perceiving of an idle yawning effort. It is impossible to calculate for the easy temper of childhood; some children are only to be touched by praise; some instantly grow insolent upon receiving it; and others have so little sensibility, as to be careless of both praise and blame; but these are characters warped by improper management. We cannot form general plans for particular subjects, for such require peculiar treatment. It is the duty of the preceptor to begin by the simplest means, and to strengthen them as they fail, or to substitute others, as simple, but hitherto unpractised, in their stead.

In writing, the governess may have at hand a pencil, ever ready to make a little cross, or other mark of disapprobation, upon a carelessly formed letter, and an o upon every good one. These

marks

marks may be summed up at the bottom of the
page; if the number of crosses exceed twelve,
she might desire another copy to be written;
(this cannot happen often), and whether good
or bad, the character of the writing should be
inserted in the " character-book." Blots and
scribbling are certainly to be reckoned worthy of
crosses; but justice must lean to mercy, in all
our determinations of what are faults, and what
are not. Accidents will happen. Should we,
the preceptors, with all our experience and
supposed knowledge, commit mistakes, and
hush up in the presence of our pupils our own
blunders, when we cannot condescend to make
allowances for the little trembling fingers that
are trying to grasp in their best style an instru-
ment full of the black liquid, which unfortunate-
ly disperses itself in the wrong direction—much,
indeed, to the annoyance of the child that guides
it; who sees, with trepidation, that she filled
her pen too full? No, accidents we are always
to deplore with gravity of countenance. If we
look pleased, (of which there is certainly little
apprehension) we must expect a repetition for
fun or pleasantry; but we are not to punish for
them.

There is not, I believe, any new fashioned
way of teaching writing. Strait strokes, as they
are called, or rather sloping lines, are the first
copies. When the child can make these tolerably

Writing.

Justice
should be the
basis of every
regulation.

Let us never
punish acci-
dent as a wil-
ful fault.

Copies.

well,

well, and has some command of her pen, will
follow the character in the shape of pot-hooks,
to shew the pressure of the pen upon the up and
down stroke. These are succeeded by letters,
the easiest of the alphabet, and to these, words,
which are called joining-hand. So far we may
proceed according to established custom; but
when the pupil can join words, and requires a
variety of copies for practice in different short
sentences, I begin to vary from it. We do not
assist the mind of our little pupils by giving them
one fine long-word to write; as, yaletudinarian,
or commiseration, or transubstantiation, or an-
titrinitarians, or immateriality; nor by sentences
which, though *sometimes* offering a good moral,
are yet above youthful comprehension: as, "keep
your own counsel; beware of flattery; procras-
tination is the thief of time; charity begins at
home; avarice begets wealth; adversity is the
touchstone of friendship; idleness has no advo-
cate, but many friends; zeal in a good cause de-
mands applause; money makes the man; truths
are not to be spoken at all times; service is no
inheritance; a fair face is half a portion;" &c.
&c. &c. Without entering upon an argument to
prove the merit, or demerit, of this sort of copy,
I shall observe, that my own are principally
taken from geography or history. I add a
few hints of the plan, which it is hoped will be
found clearly enough expressed, to be acted upon.

Some pro-
verbs are too
subtle to be
apprehended
by childhood,
and others are
too gross to
afford instruc-
tion. A few
are wonder-
fully impres-
sive when ju-
diciously in-
troduced.

                                      For

For the large text hand, perhaps, I may chuse a county, or town, which begins with an H. In large letters I write " Hampshire;" over the word, in a fair neat hand, I add according to the Gazetteer, " is a county to the south of England"—(every child ought to know the cardinal points)—I explain what is a county; " that the county of Hampshire is watered by the sea; wood and corn are grown in this county, likewise that it is famous for fine cattle, wood, iron, and honey." This must be read twice to the little girl, and as she writes Hampshire, all through the page, its productions will occur to her mind. Here is a lesson in geography for ever stamped on her memory; it is suited to her capacity, and she feels an interest in recollecting it.

For small hand, or round text, a few easy lines from history may be chosen, as " Edward the Third," in the margin, " was the eighth king of England. He and his son, called the Black Prince, conquered the French army in the battles of Cressy and Poictiers. Edward died in 1377 :" or, by way of variety, a familiar sentence in English on one page, to be translated into French on the other; as, " Si mon exemple est bien écrit ma chère maman sera contente." In the next page, " If my copy is well written, my dear mama will be pleased."—" When I have done my writing I shall work at my needle."—" Quand j'aie finie d'écrire je travaillerai à l'aiguille."—" If my

friend

Writing.

friend should walk to day she will take me with her."—" Si mon amie se promène aujourd'hui elle me mènera avec elle," &c.

Many fine hands are spoiled by scribbling and imitating incorrect writing.

We may observe, that when young people begin to write running hand, they are scratching and scribbling upon every thing that will bear a mark. This foolish propensity must be checked, or the finest prospect may be blighted: and when this is the case, it is vexatious; for the next aim to expressing unaffected and virtuous sentiments should be, of an elegant woman, the dressing them in graceful characters. What a pity would it be then, to allow our pupils the liberty of following their own thoughtless pleasure, and so run the risk of spoiling the style of writing that we are satisfied is infinitely the most easy, gentlewomanly, and admired!

For copies, on one line the governess should write, in an easy style, some useful paragraph. Every word should be compared with the attempt of the learner, and every letter marked that appears misshapen, or otherwise carelessly written; the particular words in which are the unfortunate letters may be written ten, twenty, thirty times, till success begin to dawn. Suppose the word be " Emilia," she may write " Emilia" until she can do it with ease, and then try another syllable she has failed in, and so on. These trials successfully made, lead to the black-line paper, which is put under the plain leaf, and

all

all pencil assistance is set aside, excepting where
the transition may seem too sudden; and then it
will be advisable to rule an inch at each side in
horizonal lines, leaving a space in the middle.
These little lines will be some guide from the
right to the left.   When the writing is small and
cramped, the pupil should practise flourishing
and capital letters; when, on the contrary, it is
too bold or straggling, which, of the two, is the
lesser fault, we must bridle the hand, by giving a
long copy in a moderate sized copy book, and
should require that every word be inserted.   I
have remedied this defect by ruling perpendi-
cular lines from the top of the page to the bottom
after having written my own line, so that the
pupil could not exceed the boundary.

Example.

Harold|was|slain|in|the|battle|of|Hastings.
Harold|was|slain|in|the|battle|of|Hastings.
Harold|was|

Arithmetic.   Having premised writing, I shall
venture to proceed to its general companion,
arithmetic, or the science of numbers.

Parents may teach the very first rudiments of
arithmetic before a child is put to the study. The
operations of this branch (which should be chiefly
confined to numeration) are dependent on the
mind, and are consequently likely to be useful,
as they incite to its exertion. So far, however,
is

Arithmetic.

Calculations
expand the
mind,

is it necessary to prevent this from being a work of labour, that the little girl should not be permitted to write, excepting upon a slate, a single figure, until she is tolerably skilful in writing syllables.

Small sensible objects are most proper for giving an idea of numeration, perhaps of subtraction.

and are very
interesting to
children if
suited to their
capacities.

To a little girl of six years we may say, giving her peas, or gooseberries, or counters—(Suppose the latter): How many counters are there? She will count, and must be assisted, and led on by a few more every time, to a hundred. When she has learnt this lesson of numeration perfectly, (and it need not be hurried) she may try a little at addition. The counters may be put in small heaps, promiscuously, six at one end of the table, seven at the other, and four in the middle. · She must then reckon—Six and seven are thirteen, and four are seventeen, &c. · By degrees these exercises in addition may be made more difficult. Subtraction follows.—Here are nine counters, says the parent; if I take three away, how many will be left?—The child of course will reply, Six, &c.

Numbers.

So far we may go on very intelligibly without the use of figures; but when the pupil is sufficiently advanced, we should mark them on the slate from one to forty, fifty, or a hundred, and explain to the child, in the easiest language, that figures standing alone, or the last in a range, are

are called units; that the next row to the units
is called the tens.   Suppose we take 7, or 6, or 3:
the child will name the figures accurately: then
we may write another figure on the left side, or
an ought 0, which stands in the place of one, and
point out there are two rows of figures, that the
7 was written first, and when it stood alone it
was an unit, but the 0 marked on the other side
of it, being the last figure, is therefore the unit,
the 7. is in the ten row, therefore we read seven-
ty; or ten; 6 and 0 are six-ty, or tens, &c. &c.

All this must be thoroughly understood.   The
little girl may, during six months or a year, try
some such simple exercises in numeration, and
if she seem extremely quick, may proceed to ad-
dition on the slate, and afterwards to subtraction;
but by gradual progress.   We say, if you take
six from nine, how many will be left?—"Three,"
answers the pupil.   " Seven from eight?"—
" One."   " Take eight from six ?"—" I cannot,"
she replies.   " Borrow ten, and add them to the
six: ten and six are sixteen.   Eight from six-
teen, how many will be left?"—" Eight."   " As
you have borrowed you must pay your debt,
therefore carry the ten you borrowed to the next
row; one and two are three.   Three from four?"
—" There will remain one."

$$4689$$
$$2876$$
$$\overline{}$$
$$1813.$$

Arithmetic.   However simple this may appear, it is much more advantageous to give easy figures at first; for when a child meets with difficulty in the beginning, she soon tires and dreads to proceed.

The governess will now practise with the multiplication, pence, and shilling tables.. These, in short lessons, are learnt by heart, and are useful in sums in different rules of addition, addition of money, subtraction, simple and compound, multi- *Division.* plication, and compound multiplication, division and long division. These branches of arithmetic, learnt and practised again and again, are sufficiently difficult to employ a girl, at times, till she is twelve years of age; after which she may be conducted as far as vulgar fractions, if it be considered *necessary* to the future convenience or pleasure of a female; but I would recommend that the taste and disposition of the learner be consulted, and would, especially, plead for moderation in the cyphering tasks.

Butler's Arithmetical Questions form a very useful book for young people. To every progressive lesson in arithmetic there is prefixed an account or description of some object in art or nature, or an instructive piece of history. This sort of two-fold exercise for the mind in studies, which, from their opposition need not confound idea, is extremely advantageous. I cannot do otherwise than recommend it, from having so

often

often witnessed its good effects. In the first part of the book is, I recollect, a good description of the battle of Marathon, with a question in subtraction of how long ago, from the year then mentioned, it was fought? The answer is certainly given, but the exercise in the sum, and the proof, are to be drawn up by the student, and to be presented for correction previous to his entering the whole subject of the question, with the answer, in his cyphering book.

CHAPTER V.

FOREIGN LANGUAGES.

THE French and Italian are, generally speaking, the only languages taught to young ladies besides their own.

Every writer upon education observes and deplores the prevailing custom of making every girl, in high and middle life, acquainted, however superficially, with these beautiful branches of study. My own opinion is favourable to the pursuit of knowledge in any language, provided that the nobleman's or gentleman's daughter consider

It is honourable to possess ornament if we have secured utility.

der

der it, with all other accomplishments, as subordinate to the grand considerations of humanity, religion and virtue. For the daughters of other ranks, as I do not now write, it is useless to express ideas unconnected with my subject.

Some children are so unfortunate as to be required to begin a foreign language before they understand any thing of their native tongue. To study at one lesson two grammars must be no easy task; and slow indeed, I should apprehend, would be the progress of labours so conducted.

The French is invariably the first foreign language that we introduce to our little girls in the British Islands : never ought it to be attempted till a pretty extensive knowledge of English is acquired by means of spelling, reading, reciting, and parsing. At ten years of age, a young lady who has been well prepared, is far advanced in the understanding of her own, and may, therefore, begin the study of the language of another country.

But the study of grammatical rules is very different from the repetition of a phrase in conversation ; by the practice of which much advantage is undoubtedly to be gained. A mother may accustom her child from its tenderest years to little sentences in French, and without appearing to attach any importance to them : the child will endeavour to answer with assistance. The plan may be pursued by the governess, for much will

be

be learnt by speaking; but the moment that an indiscreet parent is anxious to have it " shew off," and says, " Now, my dear, let that lady hear how prettily you can speak French. Now, M'am, listen to Fanny; she is going to ask you how you do in French." That very moment Miss Fanny will lose all interest in speaking, excepting when prompted by vanity, and even then caprice may overrule her.

French.

We should beware of exciting wrong motives.

A young lady, who commences the study of the French language at ten years, may continue it, by easy lessons several times in the week, during the next five : she is then perfect in the grammar, and nearly so in the idiom. The three next years will afford opportunity for the Italian, yet without relinquishing altogther the practice of other studies of this nature, which have cost her time and labour to understand.

This branch of education may be divided into, first, reading, which necessarily includes pronunciation; secondly, reciting, which embraces whatever is learnt by heart and repeated; thirdly, composition, under which I shall take the liberty of placing translations. The two former of these heads will constitute

Practical Grammar. It is acknowledged that the learner can derive so little from rule, in the pronunciation of the French language, that it is better, and less perplexing, to present to beginners words promiscuously in all their variety,

Grammar.

than

than to select some as authority for the rest. Were custom less arbitrary, or could grammarians prescribe the bounds to a living language, we might succeed, even by multiplied precedent; as the case is however we proceed in a different manner.

Some would not teach a child the French alphabet; this is, I think, flying to extremes. The first letter which we find so often standing alone, as an *a*, has; *à*, at, to; and in the beginning of words that are continually wanted, as *avoit, avoir, après, âgé, avancer*, &c. cannot be in the least formed if the alphabet is not known, or at least the vowels; these must be understood, and we may then venture to proceed.

The easiest and plainest books are most proper for beginners.

Of Mr. Porny's grammar my opinion is unnecessary, as Chambaud and Wanostrocht are the general and deserved favourites of all French teachers; but his *Syllabaire François* (French Spelling Book) is superior in some points to any of the kind perhaps for children. Here are the verbs in the four great conjugations arranged, and relieved from the multiplicity of tenses, with which some philologists have swelled their pages. A few easy dialogues in which, if there be not found elegance, there is that of more importance to children, plainness; a few fables with literal translations; a small selection of grammar rules; a vocabulary of things in common use; and some words of different syllables, arranged in their
respective

respective order. From this little work much
may be collected in the way of preparation; but
the governess will probably disapprove of many
parts, and particularly in the division of the syl-
lables, or rather in the classing of them. Surely,
such words as these are not monosyllables, for
they will, in spelling, admit of two impulses of
the voice, and should. be written, whether they
are to be spelt or not with a hyphen, *cieux, bien,
chien, buis, cuir, fier, hier, lier, mieux, nuit, pied,
rien,* and some others, ought to be divided and
spelt (if spelling be necessary) *ci-eux, bi-en, chi-
en, fi-er,* &c. and pronounced afterwards quick.
In this matter we are not to be influenced by
those English words which bear a strong affinity
to the French, *pâle, rose, drôle, dangereuse, tour-
mente, caressante, fontaine,* &c. : the three first
are evidently words of two syllables, *ro-se, pâ-le,
drô-le;* in English they are of one, as rose, pale,
droll. In English, torments, of the third person
feminine, is of two syllables; in French it is of
three, as *tour-men-te*: the feminine adjective *ca-
ressante* is in English three syllables, caressing,
in French of four, as *ca-res-san-te;* dangerous,
dan-ge-reu-se; fountain, *fon-tai-ne,* &c. The
first examples of monosyllables, as they are call-
ed in Porny (but improperly, I imagine), are no
where divided, that I can learn, in any spelling
book. Certainly, it would be a great assistance to
a learner, if his book shewed him this natural
distinction

French.

distinction of sounds: from the want of atten
tion to it young people are often puzzled in pro
nunciation, and confounded with orthography.
A young lady will spell the English words lame
and same; if she is asked the French *même*, she
very likely takes it in the four letters off at once,
and as she knows not the distinct sounds of *mê-
me*, she possibly may pronounce it like the ame
in tame, which is very different from the sound of
the lengthened *é* in the first syllable and the *e*
mute in the second. It is, therefore, of infinite
importance to give the child the words that it is
to read, or learn, properly divided; and where
there is a want of hyphens, as signs of division,
we must supply them by a dot, or other mark,
over the particular syllable.

Such words are now to be pronounced by the
governess one by one, the little girl repeating
them after her, according as they are in page 9.*
This lesson may be continued from time to time,
during a week or fortnight, by way of encou-
raging the learner; for we gain nothing by load-
ing her memory with instructions. "Look at
that word, it is pronounced thus; try to repeat
it after me," is all we need at first say to our
pupil, when she begins to read. Afterwards,
we gradually bring forward whatever proof we
can find to illustrate remarks upon pronuncia-
· tion

---

* See Porny's Spelling Book,

tion or orthography; we tell the child, that as there are not in the French language words enough to express every thing by a different name, marks called accents are used, and that these alter the pronunciation of a word, and cause it to mean something else. We must make ourselves understood: therefore a governess may write "*matin,*" morning. Now the same word, with the circumflex accent upon it, will be the French for mastiff dog, "*mâtin*." "*Coté,*" with an accent (which when it turns this way is called acute, from allowing a sharp sound, and when the other grave, from the relative power), is the French for side; when written "*côte,*" it means coast.—"*Tache*" is spot, "*tâche*" task; "*ferme*" firm, "*fermé*" shut; "*la*" the, "*là*" there; "*des*" some, "*dès*" as soon as; "*a*" has, "*à*" at, to. It is easy to procure more examples, but these may be perhaps sufficient.

By way of trying whether the child understand a little what she is doing, we may tell her to name different words as they are in the first French reading books: Mrs. Barbauld translated, Porny's Fables in his *Syllabaire,* or Perrin's Fables. Our great object is to give, at first, a good pronunciation; the meaning of the sentences in English is of no consequence to beginners compared to that. To those children, however, who are soon disgusted with the mere sounds of the language, we may give, as a reading

ing lesson, some easy dialogue or little fable, with its annexed nearly literal translation, as an encouragement to proceed with some degree of pleasure.

I shall not follow my little student through every page of her first books; yet I know of scarcely any unexceptionable ones by which they can be succeeded.

There are, in truth, but few French books for children of from eleven to fourteen years of age; of the few, the greater part has been written by French people, who are likely undoubtedly to preserve the idiom; but their descriptions are full of levity, as their sentiments are sparkling in the glare of passion. There must be scenes, and these so highly wrought, that the work becomes food only fit to vitiate pure and uncorrupted taste. If the language be easy and natural, children are satisfied with a very tranquil catastrophe ; and, as a lady extremely capable of judging observes, they are even content to read the same story many times over.

The most popular French work has been *l'Ami des Enfans*, by M. Berquin. Some of the subjects of this collection are very pretty and instructive; others fail, not so much in general effect as in particular causes. These tales must then be read by the governess first, and any, of course, may be marked for the child, which offer a good moral, by honest means; but vice that is

punished

punished by means of vice, or goodness that turns aside from its path in order to detect artifice by fraud, are dangerous as examples, and revolting as pictures of truth. *Les Veillées du Château*, by Madame de Genlis, were expressly written, I believe, for young people, but only a few of the tales should be bound up for children, or at least read by them. *Olympe et Théophile* is indeed affecting and pretty; *le Palais de la Vérité* extremely ingenious; *Daphnis et Pandrose* lively; but I would lay them all aside with *les Deux Réputations*, which is a good story for grown up persons, but perfectly incomprehensible to young people. *Le Recueil choisi*, by Dr. Wanostrocht, is happy in some of its pieces; *Le nouveau Robinson Crusoe* has much merit; as it encourages children to think correctly and act well. The Abbé Gaultier has published a *Cours de Lecture*, in several parts, and it has been well received; Mr. Bouilly has also obliged the public with his *Contes à ma Fille*, but his daughter was fifteen. The French books for young women are also too lively, generally speaking; yet some are exquisitely beautiful in sentiments on simplicity and honour. *Elizabeth, ou les Exiles de Sibérie; le Souterrain, ou les deux Sœurs; Numa Pompilius; Estelle; Galatée;* (the two last are pastorals) *Gonzalve de Cordoue; Bélisaire*, by Madame de Genlis, from Marmontel; *Paul et Virginie; Adèle et Théodore; Télémaque;*

G

Cyrus;

French,

Cyrus; les Incas de Pérou—are all in the style of tales. Of another cast are the works called *Abrégé du Voyage du Jeune Anacharsis en Grèce, Charles douze, Rollin sur les Belles Lettres,* &c. To these may be added a few select plays from Racine, Corneille, Molière, or other elegant writers.

A book should improve heart or head, or both.

When we give a child a book to peruse, we ought to have two objects in view : the improvement of her heart, and of her mind. The first is to be gained, we expect, by the virtuous sentiments of the author (with them we are undoubtedly acquainted); the second, by means of the purity and ease with which they are expressed. Whether the book be French or English, we trust the learner is the better for having read it. If, however, the young lady passes on from page to page through a language, of which she can understand only general words, or extremely simple sentences, and must then shut her book and walk away, we may suppose that her pronunciation is possibly improved by the lesson, but that she has reaped no other advantage. For a few weeks or months, for the sake of the pronunciation, we must make some sacrifice; but afterwards this cannot be endured, or the mind

We are not benefited if we read that which we cannot comprehend.

will suffer in disgust. In general terms, we like only that which we comprehend; and all imposed obligation creates repugnance. When we begin to learn a foreign language we cannot

comprehend

comprehend it, and yet we are forced by parents or teachers to continue the study. Here are two causes which should be stripped of power. Teachers counteract their effects by making the French lessons in reading as interesting as possible. Period by period must be translated in familiar language, first by the governess, then by her and the pupil; and in the course of several years, by the latter alone. By this translation, which immediately follows the reading, the young mind is kept awake, and it will meet with gratification for exertion.

But in translating, as in every other pursuit, we are to be steady in our endeavours to assist industrious effort, and not tolerate passive indolence. In judging this nice matter concerning children, let us however sum up their giddiness, ignorance, and tender age; and we may find much to excuse, much to prevent them from recollecting words, rules, directions, and events, which even we who have seen perhaps twice their number of years, find difficulty in remembering. We are to distinguish between *cannot*, and *will not;* and a verb conjugated wrong to day, which has been many times repeated; or a noun several times translated which is to be waited for, is no proof of the latter, which is partly known by the shuffling feet, pouting lip, impatient or sullen brow, and the muttering tongue: but even these are not infallible signs. A thorough knowledge

only

French. only of the child's character and manner will be the means of leading us to judge accurately whether ignorance or not be the real cause of her silence, inaccuracy, or hesitation.

Learning for repetition is necessary. *Reciting.* Children commit to memory what they afterwards recite to their instructor. The first object is to make them secure upon elementary knowledge, as without it no art or science can be acquired. Thus rules are incorporated with the very ideas, and by degrees strengthen into principles; and from these all practical influence is in time derived. We should therefore be particularly careful to present these rules in such forms as that little confusion may arise in the mind. Some there will be; as human systems are all imperfect, and as language is inadequate to convey precise meaning from man to man, much more is it from man to child.

We should hide the difficulties and shew to the learner only the pleasures of study. Such rules as we have must be given and learnt. We need not frighten by talking of the exceptions, which are tacked to every one separately; we are to shew the flowers, and to hide the bolts of science, till strength, or art, shall give ability to flatten or resist.

In foreign languages, (but we are now speaking of the French) the verbs are generally the first parts of grammar recommended to be learnt by heart. Of these are the auxiliaries, *avoir* and *être*, and four in the principal conjugations of regular verbs in Porny's Syllabaire. They are divided

vided into simple tenses, that they may be the more easily understood. At this part I should stay with my pupil six months, that she might be able to conjugate every verb, composing it, and know beginning, ending, middle, and any person or tense she might be questioned upon: that not only she could have it in her power to answer instantly to the verbs asked interrogatively, simply, negatively, as, I shall give; shall I give; I shall not give; he received; she shall receive; shall you not receive, &c. And, to, " what is the second person plural of the present tense, of the indicative mood, belonging to the verb *avoir* or *être*, or *donner*, &c. &c. but that she might go through any other verbs regular, and conjugate by her four rules, without having toiled in any extraordinary manner; nay, with only a little lesson every morning; but this lesson well learnt, and perfectly understood; consequently from having been admirably explained.

The verbs, in the book of which I have been speaking, have the old terminations in their tenses, *oit, ois,* instead of, *ait, ais, aient;* as, *il parlait, je parlais,* which is the orthography of most modern authors. Upon the propriety, or convenience of this alteration, it is not for me to decide.

When the verbs are pretty well studied, the articles must be explained with the change they

undergo

undergo on being placed before nouns that begin with a vowel, or *h* mute: this part of speech is to be well declined with the noun. English grammar has told what is a French noun, but practice alone can conquer difficulty, in the gender of it. Adjectives follow. They, as in the English, are expressive of quality; but they submit to be governed by the noun, and are masculine or feminine, singular or plural, as may best agree with their masters, &c. The other parts of speech are to be afterwards separately considered; but Mr. Porny's grammatical pages are very few in number, yet might be sufficient, perhaps, for beginners, if the explanations were more suitable to youthful comprehension.

It is a great step to make from Porny's French Spelling Book to Chambaud's Grammar, but this must be done a year or even two after the child has studied the language, according to the progress she makes. The method proposed by Chambaud is excellent; I must refer the inquiring teacher to his preface, page 10, for particular instruction.

In one point, however, I presume to differ from him. As I understand he advises the learner to get by heart (at stated times of course) the first ninety-eight pages upon pronunciation and orthography, which would be more than enough to sicken girl or boy. Reading half a page at a time, previous to the regular reading lesson, till the whole is tolerably

tolerably understood by dint of repetition, will be as much as we could wish, or at most, as we durst venture to try.

The following paragraph I shall copy from Chambaud, for the benefit of those who may not have the advantage of his excellent remarks and advice upon the subject which he treats.

" I make my scholars begin with the adverbs " instead of the common nouns, that they may " have the indeclinable parts of speech, the ad- " verbs, prepositions and conjunctions, treasured " up in their memory against the time they will " be capable of construing French. This is the " most difficult and necessary part of the voca- " bulary; and, when once learnt, the scholar " will meet with nothing to stop him in constru- " ing, but the signification of the nouns, ad- " nouns and verbs, which he will learn, of course, " by dint of translating and construing, besides " his usual task out of the vocabulary."

The vocabulary is the next thing to be consi- dered. His own I cannot recommend for a young lady's library; it is entitled " The Treasure of " the French and English Languages; contain- " ing Nouns, Dialogues and Maxims." The nouns are often most indelicate; the dialogues sometimes coarse; and many of the common say- ings, as Chambaud terms them, too common to pass the lip of innocence. Mr. Vivier has writ- ten some natural, yet elegant and useful, dia-

G 4   logues,

logues, expressly for young ladies ; and the Ele-
ments of Mr. Perrin consist of short questions
and replies. A work upon idioms, in the form
of dialogues, is a necessary though late study,
as may be sentences from historical writings, or
select poetry. The *Bibliothèque portative*, or
French Elegant Extracts, are for this purpose,
and indeed for that of reading, admirably calcu-
lated.

Translation.   *Composition.* Translation is a sort of minor
composition when it is literal; but when we dress
our author in the noble appendages of style, and
animate by native heat, we deserve a higher
rank; for, surely, his taste must equal the writer's,

We are to
endeavour
after the au-
thor's sense,
and after-
wards his
elegance.

who can apprehend, to the finest delicacy, what
the other conceived and penned. Thus merit
cannot be discovered and appreciated without
merit.

This enchanting power of perception is only
to be secured by years of study ; we are to rest
satisfied with the gradual progress of the young
towards it.

Of two kinds of translation, the easier to chil-
dren is the rendering of a foreign language into
their own, as they have many words at com-
mand, and understand a little the arrangement of
them.

Whatever be the subject, the child should first
peruse it carefully, and then seek the meaning
of words; afterwards she will write the whole

upon

upon a slate, take it up for corrections, standing by to hear them explained, and then insert the fair part in a book. Perrin's Fables are as proper as any work for young translators; there are very useful explanations and assistance at the end of them suited to every one separately. For the rendering of English into French we must give regular exercises, with their authorities prefixed. For children, Dr. Wanostrocht's are preferable, I think, to those of Chambaud. Here, as in the English exercises, not one example must be written without its rule in the margin. When this book is finished, Chambaud's Exercises may be attempted, beginning at the article; and the remarks, rules and exceptions are to be sought for in the grammar, and abridged, in the very large margin which is marked off according to the length of them. By degrees the grammarians withdraw the help they give on the commencement of these themes, and the learner translates with correctness. Ease and elegance are only now to be sought for, and the second branch of French composition will be introduced in order to lead to their attainment.

Letter Writing. Many people imagine the writing of a French letter an easy undertaking to a young lady who has studied the grammar. A mere dialogue letter may be; but if the idiom be nicely preserved, the sense and spirit sustained, and the language divided into natural

and

French.

No perfection can be looked for without

and graceful periods, the writer has studied well, performed with extreme attention, and deserves to be considered a scholar of great promise. Let us always enforce this observation to the young, that nothing can be done properly that is performed carelessly: This is not the age of prodigy. Genius or no genius, he alone shall be clever who is studious; for, as Pope says,

> " True ease in writing comes from art, not chance,
> " As those move easiest who have learnt to dance:"

and chance has as little to do with any other study as with writing.

We must have a standard of perfection.

Letter-writing.

A young person should not begin to write French letters until she is fourteen or fifteen, and has learnt the language, at least, four years; perhaps she would find benefit in the beginning, by turning a pretty unaffected English letter into French. We must then make choice of some of the best written French letters, and desire her to copy, upon her slate, the first paragraph and the conclusion; in other words, we provide with a beginning and ending, the middle she is to fill up according to her own ideas. Perhaps the preceptress may disapprove of this plan; she may plead the want of connection in style, with other objections; not one of which, probably, has escaped my notice : but those who will learn something, must make some sacrifice to experience; the advantage in this point will be comparatively great, and the concession small. We have the

ease,

ease, spirit and elegance of a polished writer, *French.* and this combination we ingraft on our young stock. For a season we can perceive no thriving blossom; on the contrary, the little stem is disfigured by the insertion: in time, however, the harsh and prominent lines of boundary wear away, excellence becomes incorporated with that which was worthless; and by its generous exertion and powerful influence, conquering nature herself, it springs forth as a blushing ornament or grateful aid.

Madame de Sévigné's Letters, arranged by Lévizac, are as well calculated as any for the purpose of extracting or ingrafting. Her expressions are truly lively, and even romantic, but they are delicately turned; and, after all, we run less danger in presenting to our pupils a strong picture of affection, subsisting between mother and daughter, than between mistress and lover.

This study pursued, as is now recommended, will be a great assistance to translation in its last stage of difficulty and perfection. Some elegant and useful English writer may be selected for this purpose; and from twenty to twenty-five lines may serve as a lesson to be turned into French. Dr. Johnson's Rasselas, or one of the beautiful tales in the Spectator, will be equally amusing and instructive.

G. 6   Boys,

French.

. Boys, when at public schools, are required to write verses in Latin, as occasional exercises,—-I see no reason why girls should be prevented from amusing themselves in the making of English or foreign poetry, provided they attend to every thing necessary in education, and that they appear to have a talent for so elegant an occupation; for often the drudgery of elementary knowledge is past every employment that can strengthen a taste for home, and for useful, elegant and innocent pursuits might be sought for, recommended and practised: but moderation here, and everywhere, is to be our guides. Disgust ever follows excess; and innocence herself will no longer give countenance when we rush to her own points of extremes.

I shall now offer an observation or two upon the speaking of French.

Conversation.

I have observed, with much concern, that many parents absolutely insist upon their children speaking French during the whole of the day. I conversed lately with a lady of rank, who has six little daughters, the eldest of whom is nine years of age; she, with three of her sisters, aged eight, seven, and six, are obliged to speak in this language constantly. I heard the governess enjoined to speak nothing else herself, and to allow of no expression in the English tongue : many a preceptress to my knowledge, has received the

Too many insist upon foreign languages, and neglect the pursuit of their own.

same

same sort of orders. What is to be said? Is a governess to expostulate, to argue, to act in opposition to the commands of a parent?—Never. If she dare not act according to her own principles she must retire—there is no alternative.

It is, certainly, a great pity to chain up thus the-sentiments and confidence of children; for how-can they be supposed to express themselves well in a foreign language, who are too young to have more than the very elementary knowledge of their own? A few sentences, occasionally, are very well; but, till the child is eleven or twelve, surely she need not be compelled to speak French regularly. But even at that period I should advise the confining of this language to some hours in the day; perhaps, from the time of rising, including one meal (breakfast) during the hours of study, until dinner; and then to give *carte blanche*, of which the little emancipated tongue will soon take advantage.

The lady, however, who will admit of no relaxation in this matter must be obeyed. We cannot then do better than to establish a little mark, made of a small counter of ivory or wood, which, with a ribbon passed through a hole bored for the purpose, may be thrown over the neck of the little girl who speaks English, and passed to her sister for the same deviation; and at the daily appointed hour when the preceptress inquires for the mark, if, by way of shewing her disapprobation,

French. disapprobation, she writes the name of the child who possesses it on the black side of the character book, I think it might be found a sufficient punishment.

In addressing her English or French governess I shall make some observations on the title by which the child ought to distinguish her. Madam, madame and m'am, are cold and formal; miss, mademoiselle and m'am'selle, disrespectfully familiar. There is a title, soft, endearing, and yet expressive of obedience, and by this I would teach my pupil to address me—" *Ma bonne.*" *Une bonne* is translated very improperly, I think, " A nurse." I imagine it rather to imply my friend, my companion, my instructress, or my good adviser. May our pupils consider us worthy of such a name in such a signification!

Italian. *Italian.*—This language is studied grammatically, as nearly as possible, according to the method proposed in that of the French.

Italian words are generally pronounced as they are written, and for this reason it is that they are so easily read, with, perhaps, a very slight knowledge of the grammar. The words have besides so much resemblance to the French, and some other southern languages, that few scholars, who are determined to learn the construction and meaning of sentences, find much difficulty in the *Grammars.* study. The grammars of the best masters are

by

Twelve.

No 7. G Minor. 2 Flats.

No 8. C Minor. 3 Flats.

No 9. F Minor. 4 Flats.

r.

r.

1 Sharp

r. 2 Sharps.

Example to mark off into Bars.

(La

by Santagnello and Veneroni. The first is well   *Italien.*
adapted to the capacities of youth, and has the
advantage of explanations in the English tongue:
the second is written in French and Italian, and
is calculated chiefly for those who have made
very considerable progress in the former lan-
guage. A useful companion for students will be
found in a work lately published, called " *The
Italian Reader,*" consisting of extracts from the
most eminent Italian writers in prose and verse.
Many of the Italian books are written in a style
elegant and harmonious; but we must remem-
ber, in selecting them, that the graces of diction
can never be truly charming unless they serve to
embellish a lesson of morality.

CHAPTER VI.

MUSIC.

In its general sense, music implies every thing   *Theory.*
that is subservient to, or susceptible of, the
powers of harmony. The word in female studies
simply means the theory and performance upon the
piano forte, (of late years) upon the pedal harp;
and, finally, the culture of melody in the voice.

It is not absolutely necessary, according to the
proposed plan of this work, to inquire for rea-
sons of the application of every young lady to
the same studies and accomplishment; other-
wise, upon this article we might, perhaps, fix one
of these: to gratify the musical fondness of pa-
rents;

rents; the unfolding taste of childhood; to avoid the shame of being outdone in fashion; to open another source of amusement; or to add to feminine attraction. Whichsoever may be the true cause matters nothing; the business of a governess is to consider the means of rendering this and other difficult studies, by regularity of method, more easy to the child, and less fatiguing to herself, than they sometimes are found to be.

I know not of any gentleman's or nobleman's daughter who has not attempted, at one period in her life, to learn music. So general a pursuit requires, and so elegant an accomplishment demands, our particular consideration.

Sooner than the age of eight years no little girl need begin this study; later she ought not, if we desire a finger for execution as well as a head for taste. In the art ladies seldom are, or wish to be, mistresses of the profound science of music. Of performing on the piano-forte, I shall merely examine the grand divisions, theory and practice.

It is the opinion of some professors that children should not touch the keys within less time than six or eight months from that in which they began the theory. To this plan one objection may be made, that the child will be wearied, and probably disgusted, with reading and learning from a large folio introduction for so long a period, sentences, or marks of explanation, of which she scarcely understands the separate words of reference. If we wish our pupil to succeed

ceed in any undertaking, we must be careful to give pleasing impressions of it from the first moment.—Music then introduced with a smile to the little eager girl, and gently, familiarly, cheerfully talked over and explained, during five minutes at first, then fifteen, then thirty, every day for two months, will completely prepare her for touching the piano-forte. But I shall enlarge upon these first principles. Of all introductoins, perhaps, that of Clementi is the best. The preceptress from this will gather her instructions; but she will do wrong in giving up the large book to the child, for what will a little child understand of an interval, for example, in the second page, explained thus· " An interval is the dis-" tance, or difference, between two sounds, in " point of gravity or acuteness ?" I advise her, therefore, not to frighten with much jumbled together, but to copy from Clementi merely what is absolutely necessary. One single half-sheet of music paper, filled on both sides, will contain all that is necessary, and all that I ever found to have been wanted for the elements of theory.*

This piece of music paper the preceptress may write bit by bit, as the child stands by admiring the odd marks and wondering what is to follow.

We begin to write (as the little one is earnestly gazing) the treble and bass cleffs: these, we surely

---

* See the Plate.

Theory. surely say, mark the upper and lower part of the
piano-forte. Simplicity itself must dictate our
language, and prudence exclude every explana-
tion which will not be imperiously demanded in
the first six months practice. We now tell the
Lines. child to count how many lines there are toge-
ther. She will think it a fine discovery when
she says, "Five." We further ask, how many
Spaces. little white spaces, or lines, there are between
the black ones?—"Four," she replies. We
Notes. next observe that every letter, or note, of music,
is said to belong to some line, or space; and in-
form her how many notes, or letters, are used in
music, and to impress her memory with the
number. She may begin at A. and count her
fingers till she stop at seven. We may then pro-
mise to tell her more about them on the fol-
lowing day.

"I wish to-morrow was come; I should like
to know how to find out those seven letters, or
notes, upon the lines and spaces," says the child
thus prepared. Not so she to whom is given a
huge book of introduction, with directions to
learn by heart the gamut in the first page, and
to come up and say her lesson when she knows
it. She will observe, "Oh! I do not like
music; I wish I might not learn it."

The next day, according to our promise, we
write the notes from C. on the first artificial line
to A. We must not go beyond the first lines;
if,

Theory.

The value of notes is difficult to young persons.

if, at the beginning, they drop in one by one, afterwards, with progressive lessons, they may be then explained. The value, or length, of notes follows; crotchet, quaver, &c. are to be explained. It is very difficult to make children understand how one minim can be equal to two crotchets, four quavers, eight semi-quavers, sixteen demi-semi quavers, &c. They learn, but they are puzzled for months in the value of notes. Perhaps, as good a way as any, might be to compare the change of money with that of musical notes: most children are allowed copper or silver, or have opportunities of knowing its worth. We may produce a shilling and say, " It is the pleasure of our good king, who is not too proud to be advised by some of his wisest subjects, that this silver shilling shall be worth as much as two silver sixpences; and two silver sixpences are worth twelve pennies or pence; and if you would like to change away twelve pence, you may have twenty-four half-pence; and for these you may get forty-eight farthings. Now it was the pleasure of the person who first made these little curious marks of music, that one semibreve should be worth as much as two minims, and two minims as much as four quavers, and so on."

All this may seem very trifling, but it is of greater importance than can be expressed, if time be reckoned a first point to a good performer.

No person can perform well upon any instrument without strict attention to time.

Indeed

Theory.

Indeed the person must play, at least correctly, who keeps regular and perfect time, for who can clear every bar to the precise moment, when he stumbles upon wrong notes, and hesitates upon occasional touches? The knowledge of dots and rests is fully of as much consequence. How few children do we see who raise up the hand from the piano-forte when a rest follows a note? They will tell you it is a rest, but how little *do* they know, or at least, are they taught to consider the meaning of the word: down remains the finger upon the last note, vibrating its discord. Cannot we appeal to the reason of a child in this as well as other plain cases; and teach her that she is to lift her hand very gently up, and keep it held up in readiness a little above the keys till it is to play again: if it is a quaver rest, to wait the length of a quaver; if a minim rest, the length of a minim, and so on according as the rest may require?

Dots and rests.

We are not to deal with a child as with a machine, but as a reasonable creature to whom we are accountable.

Bar.

The bar is next; and this leads to the marks to denote the measure. The C. is easy enough; it is the first letter in *common*, and means that we are to play in common time, which is where two minims, or four crotchets, &c. are in one bar. Now let us search for examples. We may open any music book. "Well, here is a C.; we will count and discover how many crotchets we can make out. One, and one crotchet rest, will make two; and four quavers will make up just four crotchets,

Measure.

crotchets, or, at least, what they are worth in a bar. Here are two figures, they are $\frac{2}{4}$, they mean two crotchets in a bar, for a 4 is put for the fourth part of the C. bar. Here are $\frac{3}{4}$; that must be three crotchets then in a bar. What do the 8s stand for?—For quavers, or the eighth part of the C. bar; so $\frac{3}{8}$ must be three quavers in a bar, &c. &c.

All this subject is to be extracted and compressed in terms simple as these for our pupil. She will, by her eagerness and attention, fully reward us for our pains; and when she grows up, will peruse her friend Clementi with pleasure and advantage.

The sharp, flat, and natural are written, but not described till we approach the piano; we then simply tell the child to strike any keys of C natural, which are white. She will put her finger upon A perhaps. Now the closest note to A, above it, is a black one, it is A sharp; the closest note below is a black one also, and is A flat. The note so very near is called a semitone, therefore, when I say, strike C, she touches C; I say, go a semitone higher, and you find C sharp; a semitone lower, you observe C flat. Now go back to C neither flat nor sharp, it will be natural.

. Let us beware of loading a child's mind with technical terms: the commanding principles only are to be first given; minor ones, and exceptions,

will

Theory.

will drop in one by one in the course of practice; and she will learn without being conscious how she acquires her knowledge. We have still,

Chord.

however, to acquaint the learner that the chord (as we of course write it) is several notes struck at once; we may strike our fingers bent for execution on the table. An octave, the eighth note from any one. E is on the first line in the treble; we may desire the pupil to begin at E, and count the lines and spaces—there is another E in the

Octave.

fourth space. " Tell me the octave for F on the fourth line in the bass ?"—" F, below the line," she replies. We then point out the mark which

Pause.

means a pause; also the one which is called a

Tie.

tie, and explain its meaning—that she is to keep her finger on the key, but not to let it sound, &c. &c.

When all this is thoroughly understood, we may dodge in every part of the second page thus :

We must cross-examine our young students.

" Can you shew me a quaver? How do you know it ?"—" Because it has but one tail." " What is the name of the little note with two tails, as you call them ?"—" A semiquaver." " Now shew me a rest; what rest is it, and how do you know it ?" &c. &c.

This theory, with the plainest capacity, will be mastered in two months. A charming little pupil of mine, of eight years and a half old, knew it completely in one. She could, besides, mark off with a pencil the notes into bars, according to

their

their time, with great accuracy. I put her to the piano-forte shortly afterwards, watched her like a lynx for fear of bad habits, during only one half hour every day, and in three months she played things in a manner, and picked out notes with a facility, that I have witnessed in few who have learnt even a whole twelvemonth.

Of this I am firmly persuaded, that more real benefit will be derived from the steady, though short, instructions of a governess, or inmate of a house, to very young performers, than can arise from that of a master calling two or three times a week to give perhaps double lessons. I have several reasons for saying so. In the first place, every one has his peculiar method; the master has his, the governess hers. One makes a point of pushing the execution, and exercises the finger; the other rather neglects the mastering of passages, and only considers the eye in reading. The one may not lay stress enough upon time; the other is too anxious concerning the graces in music. It is plain, therefore, there is a difference between them; and this difference is sensibly felt by the child. The very terms in which instruction is given are unlike, and confound the little learner; but if the terms are unlike, how much more so is the manner! Perhaps the one is severe, high, impatient; whilst the other is calm, considerate and attentive. The lady who is capable

pable

pable of it, should, therefore, have the child to
begin with; and, as all the credit will be hers,
so she will strive to deserve it: but it is ex-
tremely mortifying that an accomplished woman
should toil at the child's practice, and that all the
credit and honour should rest with the master.
" Who teaches your little girl music, madam?
she plays very correctly."—" Mr. So and So."
" He must be very clever," replies the lady.
The governess is present, and conscious that the
credit is mostly hers, but is silent. How different
has been my treatment in some generous families
that have given up their children to me; the
chiefs of whom, upon being asked this question,
would turn instantly, and with a smile observe,
" She has no other instructor than Miss——,
whom you here see, who has never spared pains
to make her a performer." How kind, how can-
did was this. Who would not feel anxious to
deserve honest applause that has once tasted its
sweets?

I must not, however, pass on without giving it
as my decided opinion, that, after the first two
or three years, it is of infinite advantage to en-
gage for the pupil not only the master who shall
have most ability, but most patience also: and,
if I have been rightly informed by the most emi-
nent professional gentlemen in London and other
cities, they prefer, in general, the pupil who is
                                        thoroughly

thoroughly grounded and prepared for their masterly finishing, to the labour of attending to a child from its very beginning.

Some masters I am acquainted with, who are gentle and patient in the extreme with young people whose study (and surely music is one of the most trying) they are superintending. I know a very excellent master, who will teach from eight o'clock in the morning till five in the afternoon, and in that space of time have not observed a frown, or heard one hasty expression, which I consider wonderful, as he was invariably extremely anxious and highly interested in the progress of his pupils. There are, I hope, besides, other patient and excellent masters; but females, in their native gentleness and tenderness, are the most proper to attend to the very young.

Let us now proceed to the practical part of music.

Practice.—To a lover of harmony what can be more charming than to hear a fine piece of music executed in a brilliant and correct style, to which the performer does complete justice, and in whom are found united delicacy and taste, precision of sight, and rapidity of finger? But when this performer is a young and lovely woman, whose modest eye turning from admiration, is intent only on the composition, with which, through her taste and judgment, every one is delighted; whose innocent features are tinged, not

H   by

Practice.

by the flush of vanity, but with the glow of in-
genuous feeling at the dead silence of surround-
ing auditors; or of anxiety to gratify the fond
and happy parent by whom she is desired to ex-
ercise this talent; the effect must be, indeed,
great and irresistable.

We are now to trace the steps by which, with
the assistance of nature, this excellence is to be
attained.

Position at
the instru-
ment is to be
attentively
observed.

The child is placed at the piano-forte oppo-
site to the middle C; the distance she keeps is
such as to allow of easy movements of the arms
from either end to the other. The arm, from the
bend to the knuckles of the hand, takes an hori-
zontal line (of course the wrist must not be suf-
fered to sink), and the fingers are gracefully
rounded to meet the keys. Having settled the
position, which is a very necessary preliminary,
the child may attempt the several notes that fill
up the octave of C natural; naming every one
separately, and taking care to have the second
note ready covered with the appointed finger be-
fore the first is dismissed, the third prepared be-
fore the second is lifted up, and so on with all
the keys, or notes, till progressive lessons intro-
duce rests, when the value of the note will direct
the duration of sound. This lesson should be
repeated several times; first with one hand, then
with the other, in the bass octave, till a little
steadiness is obtained. But the sheet of theory
is

is to be, nevertheless, continued every day; and
we may add an exercise or two, occasionally, up-
on the keys. The pupil may play F, F sharp;
G, G flat, or E, and point it out on the paper;
the octave to it, &c. &c.

I would now give the learner at once the little
air, No. 1 in Clementi, as a first lesson; for I
should not venture to keep her six months at the
introductory passages, some of which are so dif-
ficult as to require a brilliant finger to execute
them. It is absolutely necessary to find encou-
ragement for exertion in execution; and by giv-
ing something that can be learnt, and pretty well
liked, we are most likely to do so. The passages
may be practised, one by one, every week, and
they will in time be learnt.

I am not pleading for trifling tunes, and rondos
with variations, and songs, for they are as impro-
per, and as ill calculated, to form the taste to
good music, as common story books and novels
are to ennoble the style and to raise the mind to
dignified and generous views of general litera-
ture. I am anxious that children should be in-
dustrious, and not that they should be loaded so
as to depress their young minds, exhaust their
willing efforts, hurt an amiable temper, and per-
haps affect their tender health.

When the learner is so far advanced, we must
begin to establish a custom, which is not to be
relinquished for years, however perfectly its im-

Practice.

First lesson.

Children
should be
taught little,
but that little
thoroughly.

Two ques-
tions ought
constantly to
be asked the
learner con-
cerning the
time and
key.

port may be known, that of asking these two
questions : What key are you going to play in ?
and what is the time ? These questions we at
first explain and answer ourselves ; by degrees
our pupils will take the trouble from us.

The knowledge of keys is to be obtained by
what I shall call preludes. They may be prac-
tised ·every day, during five minutes ; and con-
sist merely in the major and minor scales. These
we all know, are twenty-four in number ; major
sharp and minor sharp, major flat and minor
flat. I should confine myself to one octave, as-
cending and descending. A little every day will
amount to something considerable at the end of
the year. Let us begin with C, and teach the
child to say (always aloud) the distinguishing
marks of every separate key just before she plays
it ; thus, for C—" C major has neither flat nor
sharp." Then may begin the right-hand, then
the left, a few times each, strictly observing the
fingering, &c. This should be repeated every
day for a fortnight, perhaps, with the little ex-
planation first. Repetition is the grand key to
memory ; without it, the volatility or indolence,
the distraction or perverseness of youth is not to
be combatted with ; and however tedious to those
who have recourse to it, they must submit as to
a necessary duty.

· After C major should come G major (never
forgetting the word major or minor), which has
one

one sharp, F. Sharps and flats are easily found, *Practice.*
as they are easily taught. The next key is D Major and minor keys are to be practised for years.
major, with two sharps, F and C. In three
months we shall have glided through the twelve
major keys; in three more, we shall conquer the
minor ones. The minor keys, certainly at first,
appear more difficult; but, if we tell the learner
to count the second note from the key note, the
third, fourth, fifth, sixth, seventh, and say, the
sixth and seventh are made (or turned into)
sharps going up the octave; but, in coming
down, are according to the beginning of the line,
she will not long be puzzled. Suppose she have
E minor sharp, count up to the sixth and seventh,
they are C and D; make those two sharp, or a
semi-tone higher; in descending, make them na-
turals.

These exercises strengthen the hand more than Progressive lessons.
could be imagined considering their shortness.
Clementi's Introduction will furnish us with ex-
cellent progressive lessons, from which we may
choose according to our judgment. The child
now sees her own progress; she begins to play
correctly several airs and passages; and we are
to bestow that just and generous praise which
will spur her on with fresh ardour.

From the time that the little girl can play her
first tune, it would be found advantageous to make
her occasionally repeat it in the drawing room
in presence of her relations, or any person whose

Practice.

We should
consider on
what account
praise is be-
stowed.

ears we could take the liberty of shocking during
a few minutes, for notwithstanding any thing
which their politeness or good-nature might in-
duce them to say, they would be shocked if they
understood music, and if they did not, it is not
likely that this sort of music would gratify them. It
may be however thought, that there is, to a good-
natured mind, much to interest in witnessing the
execution and artless agitation accompanying
this childish display.   Good-natured persons will
be pleased with observing the little efforts of the
child; but, that they can be interested in the
music, without being her parent or preceptor,
I can scarcely imagine.

But against what dangers have we to guard
in this matter, trifling as it may seem.   Our pu-
pil will be seriously injured, perhaps, by such
ill-judged exclamations as these —" The dear
creature! how well she plays! amazing! won-
derful!   Why, my love, you will excel your
master soon.   Oh! that I could play half as well.
I declare she plays better than Miss ——, who
has learnt so many years."   What is the least of
consequences attendant upon this injurious lo-
quacity?   The little girl, thus puffed up with
vanity and conceit, yawns disgusted and dispirit-
ed at the prospect of mental exertion; and at
her next music lesson, is either very careless, very
sullen, or very pert; whilst her governess is pro-
portionately vexed and alarmed.   Would not
                                                    such

such an evil be done away with, if the mother
would herself give her friends the tone of praise:
Cannot she say to her little girl aloud, "My
dear, Mr. or Lady —— has been so kind as to
ask you to play on the piano, therefore do as well
as you can, and he, or she, will have the goodness
to make excuses for a little girl that has not
learnt a great while. Your friends do not ex-
pect you to entertain them yet, but they will tell
you, I dare say, that you are a little improved;
and, I hope, they will think you more so when
they are so kind as to listen to you again."—
Surely, some such address as this, steadily spoken,
would prevent the burst of flattery which rolls
over the little one, whose finger has done its
childish best. People might then be awed into
the truth, if they found their disgusting adula-
tion would not, for once, succeed with the parent.
"Thank you, my dear; you have played your
little tune correctly: go on, be industrious, and
you will play well." This is the right sort of
praise, and by it (when deserved) the learner is
indeed benefitted. It is almost a pity to run any
risk of hearing the sort of flattery I have men-
tioned; but what misery is it to a young woman,
who has never played in company, to be even
asked to do so. Whatever may be her merit, she
approaches the instrument with dread and agita-
tion, that keep her auditors in constant pain for
her, as they hear passages stumbled over, notes

Parents
should be
firm them-
selves, if they
wish justice
towards their
children.

False shame
unnerves the
strongest
hand, and de-
prives excel-
lence of
power.

Practice. missed, sharps put for flats, and naturals for
sharps, slow movements played as jigs, and ron-
dos as minuets. At last she finishes, and rises to
hide her shame, vexation, and confusion; and
whilst the ill-natured praise with the lip, and ri-
dicule with the eye, the good are silent from mo-
tives of pity or weariness. Let us save our pupils
this tormenting sensation, as it is the fashion
for young parties to entertain their friends with
their talents when they mix in society, but not at
the expense of modesty, or any property that can
make them less amiable or lovely as a female.—
But it is to mothers I would speak, and recom-
mend them to spare the delicacy of their daughter,
particularly if she is young and promises to be
handsome; and not to stand by and witness,
without disdain and resentment, the poison which
enters the ears of their child, if they do not
wish to see her vain, proud, conceited, forward,
pert, a coquette. It is them who should silence
the dangerous flatterers who surround her chair,
and shew that they wish their child to feel herself
as a simple mortal, and not as if she were a goddess.

But to return.

Having now surmounted the very first difficulties
in music, let us consider what next must be done,
supposing several little lessons are finished, and
can be performed tolerably well. We must still
be extremely watchful: if the little girl is back-
ward in counting her time, we must help and en-
courage

courage her; if her wrist sinks, and her fingers
are straightened, we must support the one, and
our wishes with respect to the other point will be
gratified; if she shakes her hands, we can place
a sixpence on the back of each, and ask her if
she could play and keep them on for two or
three minutes, she will glory in keeping them
five or ten. Perhaps she does not look at the
notes, but bends her head to the keys—naturally
enough, poor thing. Of this she should be re-
minded and the book lowered, or something held
between the keys and book to lessen this propen-
sity. She is heedless in lifting up her hand be-
fore she has the next note ready; or she strikes
the bass note before the treble one is sought for;
or she strikes several at random, trusting to the
ear. All these faults must be corrected.

I think it, in general, wrong to play before-
hand to young students the air they are to learn.
If they have any ear, as it is called, they catch
the tune in the shortest way. We are all sparing
enough of our trouble: what can be expected
from children? But when they have picked out
the notes, are acquainted with the subject, and
can manage the time, it is useful to see the dif-
ferent style of performing. Of shakes, trills,
turns, and indeed of all graces, I should recom-
mend a very sparing application at first: all we
can expect is the air simply and correctly played;

and

and very well it may be thought when it is so.
If the piece be badly played, a tolerable shake
will not support it; if it be correctly performed,
the tolerable shake only spoils it. The graces
may be practised one by one at times, but not
intermixed with lessons, till they will stand a
chance of agreeing. We wish them to be friends,
not enemies. And till the learner is two years
older, I do not know whether I should not be
sorry to see the simplicity of young practitioners
lost in ornament. I should consider it like deck-
ing infancy in gorgeous apparel; besides which it
would be impossible to help a reflection upon
the time and labour which any such attainments
must have cost; great part of which would cer-
tainly have been better bestowed upon more ne-
cessary parts of education.

Much is often said of the genius and taste of
children for such and such things. To no study
are these terms more applied than to music;
whilst the subject of them is, perhaps, applying
hour after hour, when, after a prodigious expen-
diture of money and time, it is discovered that
the young lady is not so clever as others who
have had but few advantages. Why was the bent

We discover
the bent of a
child's taste
at a very ear-
ly age.

of her mind not consulted in infancy? It would
then have been seen, that her inclinations lay in
another direction. She was dragged from her
books, or her plants, which she loved, to study
music,

music, for which she never was once prepared by nature. To the piano-forte she went with reluctance, and from it she stepped with alacrity.

But I would not be understood to mean, that no child should be taught music but her who gives distinguishing and early proof of talent for it. There are some whom I have known rise to eminence in the art, who really have not been favoured with assistance from nature. Most powerful must have been the motive for such perseverance, for by amazing perseverance only could this ever have been accomplished; and according to the motive, so should be the credit to the student. On the other hand, how often do we see great abilities, confident in their power, disdaining the means by which perfection would be to them so much more easily attained. When this is the case, how can we be surprised on observing the plodding, persevering, steady, yet dull child, rise gradually above the indolent giddy darling of nature? Yet, as all those who possess great abilities are not idle, and as all those in whom they are not found are not industrious, I cannot imagine why professors, as I have heard them, should prefer having the latter for pupils; for it is, surely, more pleasant to teach a quick than a dull child, even if it be true, that the quick of intellect will apprehend and forget, and that the slow will bear and retain. It is a delightful encouragement to a preceptress to see the child's eye brighten as she hears explained an interesting passage, or a difficult term. . " Do you understand me, my dear ; tell me, in your own words, what have I been saying?" This question, well answered, is indeed an inexpressibly gratifying reward for our labour and exertion.

It is not difficult to determine an inclination to any pursuit. The parent, however, who thinks proper to make music a part of the education of every daughter, may soon determine from whom excellence is to be expected. If, after some months, there should appear the same general cheerfulness in going to the instrument, the same desire to improve, and that we find a visible progress, we may conclude that there will be a good performer, allowing for a fit of idleness occasionally. But if the pupil, whether of genius or not, go to this study with extreme reluctance; appear to have no pleasure, or satisfaction, or interest in it ; do not endeavour to follow instructions ; murmur at repeating passages ; if she play false notes, and knowing them to be so, is not distressed by the discordant sound,—then we may pronounce, that she is no subject for the science of harmony.

In three months from the time she has touched the keys, the learner will probably be equal to Purcell's Ground, arranged by Purcell. I am thus particular, as there are many in London arranged by inferior persons. The little girl, for

whom

whom I wished this piece, had touched the piano-forte during only two months. Of the ground, as an exercise, I taught her a little every day; and for recreation, she had a simple air besides. In three months she played both with spirit and correctness, as she also did some pages of a pretty duet of Kozeluch; the recreation to the last piece was an easy lesson. This is a plan I generally adopt, though with caution; a piece for study, and a piece for reading as an amusement: a few bars of the latter are sufficient. These studies cannot be confounded as some might. It would be injudicious to give, in a reading lesson, the history of England, and that of any other country; the events of the different countries would clash in the memory. In practical music the mind has little share; the notes are placed immediately before us, we have to read them, to consider their value and meaning. When this knowledge is attained the attention may be kept alive, but we are scarcely sensible of it; and when we have reached some perfection in executive music, even more is this the case. Our ear is indeed gratified, and the passions are soothed; interruption disappoints us; but the reason arises solely in imagination, which is busy in building schemes of felicity, or in gilding anew a worn idea, with which we have, in our joyous moments, loved to fondle. Hence we trace the luxury, the danger of this study, with

romantic

Music is a study which rouses the passions.

Practice. romantic or weak females, who will not plunge into the depth of the science and employ the strength of reason, but flutter on its borders, and submit to be subdued by sound, without making one effort to release themselves from its enervating dominion. But of these soft chimeras the child knows nothing. She jogs on from bar to bar, steadily playing first the lesson, then the slow movement, and the *vivace* at the end. The fingers go naturally to the right keys after a few trials of the piece; she thoroughly understands the value of the notes; and all that remains for her is to say one, two, three, four, or one, two, three; which she will repeat very soon as mechanically as a clock can tick. We need not fear, therefore, any confusion from the practice of two lessons in the same hour.

Lessons. Of printed music there is now so great a variety for all ages, that it is hardly possible to enumerate particular sets of lessons; but of the eminent professors who have condescended to write for the young, I must particularize Clementi and Dussek. The first of these gentlemen has favoured us with a complete course of fingered practice, from the gamut to some very beautiful and shewy sonatas. From these there is also a regular gradation to his finest compositions; but we must familiarize our pupil to the excellences of other musical classics in her progress to the temple of taste. . . . .

                                        Duets

Duets are serviceable as they teach the time;
but either part should be taught first perfectly as
a single lesson, or it will be learnt by ear, if it
be learnt at all. But it generally happens that
learners play them with the assistance and sup-
port of a good performer, or, at least, a better
than themselves. The pieces sound rather fine,
for the mistakes are hushed up, and well covered
by the exertions of the most experienced. This
is like strutting abroad in borrowed trappings,
though worse in the consequences. The child
receives the praise, dares not own her mistakes
and failings; and in suppressing the truth, im-
bibes the first notions for paltry meanness and
deceit.

Once or twice a week I should recommend the
reading of music, and the exercise, when girls
are getting forward. Any music book will do for
the first, opened at any page; and merely to say
the name and value of the notes in two lines.
The exercise is to be one or two lines of notes,
written promiscuously on a loose sheet, by the
student, and then marked off into bars. This
will teach her to write and measure music. It is
a simple operation of three minutes, with a very
little practice.

There is little to be added to the few hints
which I have thrown together on this subject for
the use of the governess. Thorough bass, which
is a study of great importance, will be taught,
with

with composition, by the master who finishes the scholar. With one observation, and the advice to which it gives rise, I shall quit this branch of music.

When young ladies are requested by their friends, or desired by their parents, to perform on the piano-forte, they immediately move, or ought to do so, to obey. As they are going to seat themselves, they enquire what piece their mother chooses to have; or, perhaps, the parent says, " Play such a thing, my dear." Now it happens, nineteen times out of twenty, that the daughter has to announce to the company, that she is out of practice with the favourite piece. " Well then," the mother observes, " play that concerto you learnt last month."—" Mama," the young lady stammers out, " I have not practised that lately." The parent looks vexed, but answers in a little confusion, " Well, child, play something."

It is not difficult to find the reasons why a mother is thus disappointed. Want of method and regularity are the only ones. I will suppose the young lady takes a lesson from her preceptress or master in the morning; of course she will play the new piece. One hour a day is quite sufficient for a new lesson ; and, if she is not to forget her old ones, or, in other words, if she is learning music as an amusement for herself and friends, another hour should be devoted to prac-
tice

tice the things which she has already learnt, taking them in rotation, one or two, every day, as there may be time. Not to make any confusion in the different lessons, the student might, upon a large sized card, or bit of thick paper, draw off three perpendicular lines, and take a list of them; putting sonatas in one row, concertos in the next, then small pieces, and lastly, duets: thus, the practice of every one would be kept up in its turn.

Example.

THE LADY AMELIA B—'s LIST OF MUSIC.

Concertos, &c.	Sonatas.	Airs, &c.	Duets.
Steibelt, Storm	Dussek, Op.	Sul Margine, La-	Clementi
Non plus ultra	Cramer, Op.	tour	Nicolai
Overtures, Handel	Clementi, Op. 12.	Lieber Augustin	Meyer's Accom-
Griffin, Op. 1.	Pleyel	La Colombe retiree	paniment for the
Handel	Sterkyl	Air, Mozart	Harp
Dussek, Op. 27.	Kozeluch	Air Russe, Dussek	Dussek
Cuckoo, Op.	Von Esch	Beethoven	Mozart
Viotti	Mazinghi	Serenade; Cramer	
Corelli's	Evance, Op.	Meyer's Airs, Harp	
Bach, Op.	Himmel	No. 4.	
Arne's Overtures	Haydn		
Zauberflöte, Overture			

The Harp.—This elegant and delightful instrument is often attempted to be practised by young people, who are only half way towards excellence upon the piano-forte. It is impossible to find time for both, consequently, neither is ever well understood.

If there be in one family several daughters, and they must all attend to music, would it not be infinitely better to distribute our musical instruments amongst them, and to allow of only one to either? Piano-forte, harp, guitar, or harmonica,* harp-lute, castanets, and tambourine. Many a girl is obliged to touch (I can hardly say practise) three, four, and five of these, with what advantage to her domestic character as a daughter, a female, a member of society, a friend to the poor, or to her character as a human being and a Christian, it is impossible for me to conceive. I certainly imagine, that if three, four or five musical instruments are to be played upon every day, that something essential must be neglected; and for what, except it be for renown.†

The harp is generally considered rather an

easy

* I am not recommending a society of musicians in every family; the custom is already pretty well established; I would only endeavour to divide the labours of harmony amongst the female group.

† I once asked a curious old painter, who was teaching a young friend, why he instructed her in so many different branches. He replied with surprise, " Why, to add to her fame."

easy instrument to learn; this is a mistaken notion, for, to be a good performer upon it, requires as much time as does the piano-forte.

The mere theory of music is for all instruments the same; the practice is essentially different.

There are so few preceptresses who are qualified to teach this accomplishment, that it is almost unnecessary, as well as presumptuous, in me to enlarge upon it, as the young lady will undoubtedly have the advantage of a master; I shall, therefore, only offer a few words upon the subject, and leave it to my superiors.

When the learner is placed to the harp, particular care should be taken that her position be easy, unconstrained, and regulated by elegant propriety; the left arm should be rounded and raised, so as to be above the right in playing; the elbow must be propped and kept from sinking into a square, and she should sit rather high and near the edge of the stool, to have the feet at liberty to touch the pedals.

The keys, or strings, of this instrument are soon learnt; the red are C, from octave to octave; the black are F. They take their rotation as the notes of the piano-forte.

To bring the tone from the strings requires some strength, and an attentive observance to withdraw the finger, and to clear the space from which we desire the vibration; but if the finger be not prepared for the next note, as a commanding

Harp. manding point; if it be spreading, and weakly fixed, we may make a noise, yet we produce no tone. Nearly every string should be possessed and in the power of the appointed finger, before we resign it for effect; and as the bow is more or less bent, previous to the discharge of the arrow, according to the velocity with which the latter is destined to travel, in the same degree do we grasp the strings and reject them when we desire the softness of pathos, or the pomp, majesty, and swell of energy.

It is the opinion of one of the most eminent harp professors now living, Mr. Phillip James Meyer (to whom I am grateful for whatever I know of this instrument) that the lessons should be, if possible, learnt off by heart, as it is not easy to play entirely without looking upon the strings. This may be accomplished with a tolerable memory. We first pick out the notes, one by one, and play a few bars over several times, then a few lines, till we can thoroughly understand them, and recollect the fingering; and then we may endeavour to play without the notes. Thus we may gain a little confidence, and be at liberty to give some attention to the finger, as well as to the paper, which will be of great assistance in the progress of the study.

Till very lately the natural key of the harp was E flat major; the instrument is now brought to such a pitch of excellence, that every modulation

lation of key is perfectly practicable. Every whole tone, every semi tone, is complete. The key of the harp is C natural, as in the piano-forte, and every note is susceptible of a natural, a flat, and a sharp; which, before this great improvement, was found impossible. Persons used to be entirely confined to a few keys of the minor and major scales; but, upon the harps of which I am speaking, they may play in any one of the twenty-four.

To mention here the indefatigable exertions of the gentleman, to whom all who practice the improved patent harp are so much indebted, is no more than common justice; and, I trust, that, should this page ever meet his observation, he will not disdain the trifling acknowledgment it offers to his merit. To Mr. Sebastian Erard, whose talents in architecture and mechanism have been so appreciated in his own country, the improvement of the harp is solely due.— After a very close application, and the most minute attention, he has succeeded in remedying the former defects of this instrument; and every friend of science and harmony cannot but unite in wishing him an ample remuneration for the pains he has taken, to the injury of his fortune and of his health, in accomplishing his views, and at length completely triumphing over every difficulty, and rendering to this instrument

Harp. instrument the excellence it at present is entitled to.

Singing. *Singing.*—Young singers should be generally confined to the *sol*, *fà*, as the vocal gamut is called. The notes are given in Italian to shew the different sounds of the vowels. A few minutes every day, merely to strengthen the tones and expand the chest, will be sufficient; for children should be taught to sit, or stand, upright, especially when they sing, that the sound may ascend and fill the room; otherwise, they will make a rattling noise in the throat, which will be hurtful to themselves and unpleasant to others. The single notes may be played first, very slowly, and then thirds; afterwards four notes may follow one another, and prepare the octave up and down: more difficult passages will follow, and the singing book of Carri, which is considered a very excellent work for young people, will present lessons in almost every variety.

The words are of more importance than music in songs. When the young lady is to sing songs, it is to be presumed some discreet person will rather look over the words than the music, as there are many verses highly discreditable, and such as should not be pronounced by the lips of any young woman who has a character for delicacy and purity to sustain. I have heard gentlemen (who are, in general, nice observers of modest and unaffected female dignity, and are ever oblig-
ed

ed to respect its influence) often speak with dis-
dain of many fashionable songs, and declare,
whilst the young lady is uttering the most impas-
sioned expressions as she warbles, that no daugh-
ter of theirs, or wife, should sing them; and
they have, when the music ceased, approached
the piano-forte to deliver in their quota of praise
with an irony and freedom, of which the lady
little suspects the real cause. Well were it if
she did, perhaps; she would be proudly indig-
nant, and keenly stung. But the lesson would
be one never to be effaced; and she might learn
to respect herself in the manner and conversation
of others with her; for nothing so much shews
us our degree of merit as the behaviour we meet
with in the world. Never can that man be wholly
destitute of virtue, who is treated by several with
unfeigned respect, fidelity, affection, esteem, con-
fidence and honour.

CHAPTER VII.

GEOGRAPHY AND ASTRONOMY.

THE knowledge of the principal divisions and
particular places in the earth, is understood by
simple geography. Universal geography, in its
wide range, takes a gigantic view of the labour

or

Geography. or pastime of nature, and of the accomplish-
ments or efforts of art. The easier branch of
study will be first considered in

Few children understand anything of geography by learning mere lessons.

Simple Geography. Set lessons in this are
generally given to children, who learn, repeat,
and remember not a syllable after the book is
closed;—thus, when they ought to be pretty far
advanced in the study, they scarcely know any
thing of it.

No writer upon geography for youth has suc-
ceeded equal (in my opinion) to Mr. Gaultier.
This gentleman has thrown his subject into grand
and inferior divisions, in a very clear and com-
prehensive style; and being sensible how lit-

Repetition the key to memory.

tle could be done without constant repetition
amongst young people, he has invented a game,
by which every thing that has been learnt in his
regular lessons may be rehearsed, and so im-
printed for ever upon the mind. The work to
which I allude forms a complete course of simple
geography, and this is the title by which it is
known.

It matters not when we begin this study with
children, supposing, however, that it is made
pleasing and interesting, which is very possible,
if the person who teaches will bend his, I should
say her, language to the capacity of the child.

We should first explain the words we use.

At first we may teach by conversation, and a
few examples upon a slate, the meaning of the
word geography, and the lines that mark the
divisions

divisions of countries, or of land from water. I
have taken a common white leather sixpenny
ball, and have pierced it through with a long
pin for an axis, whilst the little girl has stood
by, delighted with the process, which we may
explain in this manner :

"This little ball is in its shape extremely like
the world we live in ; but you may easily think
that the world is thousands and thousands of
times larger than so small a thing as a ball. I
will try to tell you something about it, and pray
ask me to repeat whatever you cannot under-
stand. Now I will go on very slowly.

"First, observe this large pin. See how easily The shape o
the ball turns round it. Well, our earth, or the the earth, and
world, turns once round in twenty-four hours. its motion.
Fancy my head the sun. Now this part of the
ball is opposite to me; if I were really the sun
I should shine upon it, and it would be as light
as day—but when I turn the same part round, it
is quite away from me, I do not shine upon it;
therefore it is dark, and this side is the light
one : so that the people on one side of the earth
have the light, whilst the people on the other
side are in darkness."

How eagerly does a child observe and listen Theory
to theory, playfully or cheerfully delivered, when should be as
accompanied by experiment. Let us proceed to sible enlight-
the second lesson. ened by expe-
riment.

"The top of the earth, where you see the

I   head

head of the pin, is called the North; and the
bottom of the ball is the South pole. Any top
part of a country is the North, the bottom is the
South, to the right part is the East, and on the
left is the West. On this side of the ball I am
going with my pen to mark out a pretty large
piece; this is for Europe, which is one quarter
of the world: just below it I make a long zig-
zag, or in-and-out line, for the top of another
quarter, called Africa. To the eastern side of
these two, I draw these marks, close to one side
of Europe, and this piece is for Asia; and be-
yond it I draw two large pieces, and join them
together in the middle, to make America."

It is absolutely necessary to begin in this way;
but when we have mentioned so far, we may
stop, and desire an account of all that we have
been saying. If the child have a clear idea of
these outlines, we may proceed thus:

" You understand that these four pieces are
the four great parts of the world: look at Eu-
rope—very well. Now at America; there is a
great space between the two, what do you think
that is? Water, salt-water, which is called sea;
all the spaces or pieces between the land that I
point to are called seas. So the world is part
land and part water. Large pieces of land have
a different name from little pieces; but every
drop of water in the world is not salt, like those
great seas, therefore pay attention to me, and I
will

will tell you the name, and draw upon the slate
the picture, or when we speak of countries, &c.
we say maps, of every one of them."

After this explanation, the learner may begin
Gaultier's Geography at the introduction, which
describes continents, islands, rivers, straits, &c.
drawing first the divisions of land, and after-
wards the marks for water, &c.

I appeal to any sensible mother, whether this
very simple manner of explaining the formation
of the earth, and its principal features, be not
preferable to the general practice of giving a
child all at once a piece to learn by heart, from
some elementary book, which begins thus: :

" Geography is that science which makes us *It is impossi-*
acquainted with the constituent parts of the *ble that chil-*
dren should
globe, and its distribution into land and water." *understand*
many sen-
This one sentence is yawned over, but by dint *tences in*
their books o
of perseverance is at length repeated, as a par- *geography.*
rot repeats a witticism. Ask the learner if she
can understand what she has just said, she will
answer no. Not one idea can she form of the
earth from the map of the two hemispheres as
the frontispiece to her book, and with other
maps she is perfectly confused. Consequently,
soon disgusted with what she cannot compre-
hend, she hurries over her lesson that she may
replace her book upon the shelf. •

Nothing is so proper to give young people *Artificial*
globes are of
strong and clear conceptions of the subject, as *very great*
use.

the being permitted and incited to turn round and examine a large artificial globe. We should encourage them to ask questions; any answer too difficult for them to understand we might reserve for a future time, merely saying, I will tell you that when you are a little older—ask me something else. Very well. Now do you shew me which way you would go from London to the island at the bottom, or south, of America. Now draw your finger over the way you would go from Ireland to Persia, &c.

I extremely approve of the pupil beginning in Gaultier, by learning concerning her own country; but I advise the preceptress to march at first by gigantic strides, entirely setting aside minute division, until the whole has been learnt once, and played through many times. I will explain this more particularly.

. The work is divided into lessons, which the child may learn in halves or quarters, at once. It begins with the seas of the British islands, next follow the divisions of the kingdom, and the counties of England. The instant that we have conquered the seas, the division, and the six northern English counties, we may prepare a bag for the game, which is to be played as an amusement, and a delightful one it is generally considered.* •

The game succeeds to the lessons.

We

---

* The geographical counters are put in the bag, and drawn by
all

We must play with the same counters every evening, till they are well, extremely well known; and then we may add a few more, never relinquishing one, but always adding. Our choice must be directed by lessons, that have been learnt, at different times, in the study.

I propose that the seas, the divisions, counties, great rivers, seaports, and mountains of England,

all who sit round the table. By turns each repeats the answer to what is asked on the counter, and this is a part of the morning lesson. The eldest girl is at first president, the next in age the second, and so on afterwards; they take places according to the number of reward counters gained, and the meritorious begins next time. So far Mr. Gaultier is right—but if a girl should draw a longer sentence than another, why is she to be paid several reward counters, and so gain the presidency? Is it not a matter of chance who has much and who little to say? and are we to reward her who has only been befriended by fortune? No: this is unjust, and no one can be sure of her place if merit alone do not secure it. She who draws a counter and cannot answer, may certainly pay to the governess one that she already possesses; but the president, or head player, ought not to find herself with fewer counters, after having laboured hard to maintain her place, than one who has lost a counter or two from negligence, but to whom chance has thrown half a dozen counters for a long reply. I wish this part were altered in the directions for playing the game, that every person who answered well might have one counter, and every one that answered badly might give up one. Strict justice would be thus established, and no appearance of the odious art of gambling would be observable. With my own pupils I always make this little alteration, and as we all play together, every one is satisfied and cheerful. It is ever to be considered a play, not a serious study.

land, Scotland, and Ireland, be first selected, learnt by degrees, played at night, and thoroughly understood. These belong to bag, No. 1. to be written upon—*British Islands*.

The next study should be Europe; its large seas, countries, great rivers, and islands. The counters for these will be gradually put into bag, No. 2, *Europe*.

The same grand outlines will be learnt in Asia, Africa, and North and South America, and the little bags for them will be marked accordingly, and figured Nos. 3, 4, 5, and 6.

The game should be regular when ten minutes will be sufficient for it. When these heads are understood one after the other, we must take the bags in rotation. On Monday the game of the British Islands, No. 1.—on Tuesday, Europe; Wednesday, Asia; Thursday, Africa; Friday, North America; Saturday, South America.

This may seem a vast work, but it is not in reality. By method and regularity, we may perform much greater wonders. A little pupil of mine had, in six months, learned and played with me every one of these divisions, and knew them perfectly; yet I continued the same counters, without adding more, although she had begun Gaultier's work a second time, and then attempted the small divisions. My object was, great and general principles only; and I waited till these should be irrevocably fixed; and I consider a few minutes in the evenings of one, two,

or

or three years, well employed in securing these
principles. The learner may go on with the les-
sons, she need not stand still to wait for the
game; but let us attain our end, and we may put
into the bags whatever we please.

Two or three times a week, we should have an
exercise on the globe. At first, this will consist
in merely finding out a dozen, or twenty places,
that are pretty far distant one from the other;
and it will be a good way to write a considerable
number in a small common-place book, that they
may be taken regularly, so many at a lesson.

The child should never read of any place, or
country, without searching for it on maps that
lie open before her. Of course, our assistance
must be given, and the explanation should be
ever ready, and pleasantly delivered. When a
map has a scale of miles, I am fond of giving
young persons a pair of compasses to measure
from one great town to another, and they are
universally delighted with such trials and in-
quiries, especially, if we ourselves appear in-
terested in them.

We can sel-
dom excite
an interest if
we ourselves
do not feel a
portion.

I invariably give ancient maps for companions
to ancient history. Young girls are never
frightened at the Latin words, if we introduce
them properly. These (we may say) are the
old divisions of the world, and the ancient names
for different countries; but many of them sound
so much like the present names, that they are

soon

soon found; whilst others would never be known at all on modern maps. This plan gives a little of classic elegance and correctness to our young students, who are generally shut out from the delicate simplicity, or sublime grandeur of the ancient original writers.

Geographia Antiqua, engraven from Cellarius, is the set often used in schools. I am no judge of its merit as a learned work, but I have found it extremely serviceable to me. Upon common paper, the price is half a guinea. I prefer the maps not coloured, because as the pupil reads by my side, she stops at the mention of a place, which, when we have found, I directly paint it, perhaps in vermilion, every thing lying before me ready for doing so. After the reading lesson, the rivers are traced in pale grey, as are the coasts and divisions of countries. It is wonderful the strong impression this makes upon the dullest memory, and I advise every anxious preceptress to adopt the practice for one month, and she will not only find her pupil instructed, but herself informed.

There is also a set of maps of large folio size. They have the ancient divisions and names on one side, and the modern names of a country on the opposite. These are undoubtedly extremely useful.

The modern Atlas is so various and excellent, that we scarcely know how to make a preference. These

These are of all sizes, at the principal geogra-
phers in London. Guthrie's maps for schools
are cheap, but rather small; Kirkwood's are
pretty. An Atlas of Faden, by the title of Geo-
graphical Exercises, with skeleton and coloured
engravings, are very good; especially, as it is
intended that the skeletons should be filled up by
the higher students. Drawing of maps is a use-
ful and pleasant employment, for such of youth
as can spare the time.

Universal Geography. It is the business in
simple geography, to point out boundaries and
local names; but that of universal geography
may be to consider the earth,

First, astronomically; as a planet of the hea-
venly system.

Secondly, mathematically; in its artificial lines,
as, equator, zone, tropic, &c.

Thirdly, minutely and extensively, in all its
grand and minor divisions of land and water;
as, continent, sea, town, &c.

Fourthly, politically; in the portions and
titles allotted by hereditary right, decisive treaty,
or conquest of war, to crowned descent, or elec-
tive choice; as, empire, kingdom, colony, re-
public, &c.

Fifthly, physically; in the variety of nature
exposed and concealed, as, animals, vegetable,
mineral, climate, &c.

Sixthly, nationally; in the inquiry after the

respective

respective inhabitants of a country; their genius, religion, customs, government, knowledge, &c.

Seventhly, chronologically; in the true arrangement of remarkable events that have happened in particular places since the creation.

The pupil having, at this point, arrived at her fifteenth year, holds out her hand to astronomy, which unites her for ever to geography.

We will now rapidly touch the seven steps to universal geography.

Astronomy is a science that strikes with awe.

First, the astronomical. No sooner do we draw aside the sacred veil of this sublime and awful science, than confounded, humiliated, subdued by the littleness of human nature, in comparison with the lofty grandeur and superb immensity of the power of the great God of eternity, we find words weak to express ideas, and ideas enfeebled by the mortal struggle of bounded apprehension.

In what language shall we speak to the innocent being who looks to us as her instructress, when we begin to open this universe of wonders? From the solemn extacy of our manner, she feels a sympathetic influence; and in the agitation of her unsophisticated heart, she feels the divine impress of an immortal architect. Her ear, faculty, homage, all are prepared. Shall we give a lesson, a map, a globe? Away with particles, barriers, limitation itself. Matter cannot aggregate in compass. The soul must have room for expanse.

We should respect the generous feelings that glow in the tender bosom of our pupil and not damp them by a drudgery of lessons.

expanse. We will have space, air, prospect. *Astronomy* The starry heavens, the universe shall be our canopy, the earth our carpet, the largest tele- scope our compasses, and the immortal part that is within us the monitor to apply every stupen- dous effect as it may rise, to the one great and everlasting cause.

The lovely evenings of summer are the best calculated for the unfolding of these beautiful truths. Defended by vestments from the slight influence of the soft dew, which rises to refresh a grateful vegetation, the sweet girl and her pre- ceptress traverse with hasty step, the short path to the spot on which the instrument is fixed for observation. Now and then they stop to exa- mine with the unassisted eye. Long are both si- lent. At length the instructress with a diffident voice and humble deportment thus attempts a beginning :—what I am now desirous of explain- ing to you is the science of astronomy, which is a history of the heavenly bodies, their motion, size, and distance.

As I proceed, you may be surprised how man could by his mightiest attention, even presume upon the calculation of distances and objects that seem immeasurable. I shall first endeavour to account for this.

The basis, or foundation for every science, is truth; which in this wide sense, means certain- ty. All knowledge is made up of parts. Now

as

Astronomy. ing in two roads that meet at the same point. Both philosophers are then respectable, each has his own system, and each has truth for his foundation.

Now and then, a great man rises amongst us. He chuses some particular science for his favourite study. He examines nicely, and perceives a weak part. This he seizes, considers, weighs, calculates, and at last is successful in working out proofs for a new one; which, when all are convinced is founded on truth, he is permitted to join to the science, and his name is ever after remembered with honour and gratitude; for, where he found a stone, he left a jewel, and that which only glimmered, now blazes in all the radiance of truth. Such men were Luther in religion; Harvey in the science of medicine; Linnæus in botany, and Sir Isaac Newton in mathematics and optics, &c

The science of astronomy, then, consists of many parts, of which every one might be a profound study. But I would not strain your young mind by dwelling on particulars however wonderful; I wish you at present to have only general ideas of this glorious subject.

The elements. It appears that before this world was made, the elements, air, fire, earth, and water, were struggling in a space, millions of times wider than you can see in the spangled plain above your head; for the first verse of the Bible tells

us,

us, " that God created the heavens and the earth, but that they were without form and void."

The Almighty having created the elements, commanded them to separate, and be arranged in the beautiful order we now see them. Water gathered upon water; land pressed close upon land; light rushed from darkness, and the earth opened her bosom to enfold every seed of vegetable life.

This was the heavenly work of three days. On the fourth, the Eternal said, " Let there be lights in the firmament of the heavens for signs, seasons, days and years, to give light upon the earth: there shall be a lesser light and larger; one to rule the day, the other the night—and stars also. And He set them in the heavens, to give light upon the earth."

The heavenly system framed by the Almighty for our use, after our earth was created.

Such was the birth of these wonders! Now let us attend to their powers.

I need not tell you that the large light is the sun—the other the moon.

The sun is an immense body of fire, by which we are supplied with warmth and light. It is the centre, or middle of the universe round it, at different distances are ranged all the heavenly bodies. These are fixed stars, planets, comets; the first are stars that never move from their places; the second are stars that are continually moving round a circle, at an equal distance from the sun; the third have a great communication

Astronomy. munication with the great globe of light, and from their long transparent tails are called blazing stars.

Now among the vast number, it would be rather difficult to remember every separate star in the heavens; therefore they are divided into con-
Constella-tions. stellations. One group is called the Bear, another the Ship, another the Serpent, because the number of stars seemed to fall into the figures of a bear, a ship, and a serpent. There are upwards of seventy constellations, and in every one are twelve, twenty, forty, or more of stars. The ancients only reckoned however twelve, which are now the signs of the Zodiac. They are painted round your globe, Aries, Taurus, Gemini, &c.

The planets. The seven great planets revolving regularly round the sun are, first, that called Mercury, which is the nearest to it; then Venus which is next, then our Earth; afterwards Mars, then Jupiter, then Saturn. The smaller ones, are some discovered by Dr. Herschel; and those called moons, one of which accompanies our earth in her journey round the sun.

These planets, as I have told you, move round the sun in their circles or orbits. Perhaps you do not understand this. Have you ever seen a target for shooting at? In it are circles within circle. Suppose then the middle, or eye, as it is called, to be the sun; upon the circles round

it

it you may imagine the planets incessantly
moving.

But the great wonder is, that these vast bodies
are continually rolling forward like a ball thrown
before us, and yet preserve their place, their
distance from the sun, and their regular mo-
tion. As a bird skims across the heavens and
appears independent of the earth, so the earth
moves in its course, and hangs upon nothing
for support. How shall I explain this to you?

There is a power in all matter called attrac-
tion. One thing has a disposition, or tendency
to move towards another, and every thing seems
to incline towards the centre of gravity, or
weight. I see you are puzzled. Stand for a
few minutes upon one leg. Your are uneasy.
How is this? You are off your centre: the
earth draws you on one side. Stand strait.
You are fixed in your centre. You feel her
attraction, but are guarded against its power.
Let us try still further to illustrate this point.

You understand very well the property of the
magnet. It attracts, or draws certain bodies to-
wards it. This you have distinctly seen. You
have also observed the steam from any thing
wet, which you have held to the fire. The fire
attracted, or drew out this moisture.—Now
something in this way does the sun draw all the
planets, and of course our earth, towards it.
Nearer to the sun than they are they cannot go;
because

because, from the weight of these spheres, they try to press another way. Our earth, with others, would seem to wish to roll on, in a strait line, but it is perpetually checked, and kept in its proper circle by the sun.

Suppose I had in my hand a ball of lead: it would fall if I loosed it; but if I tie round it a bit of packthread, and hold the string at a yard distance, the ball will try by its weight to fall, and my packthread, as long as I choose to hold it, will prevent it from falling. So is the influence of the sun on the planets; they would wander, or fall, but that the sun prevents them by his attraction.

But my lead does not go round and round. No; this wondrous power is given by the God of heaven, that both sides of our globe may feel the light and heat of the sun by turns.

Now reflect for a moment that this sun, this amazing body of fire, is 1,392,500 times larger than our earth, and that we are ninety-five millions of miles from it. A cannon ball shot from the sun to our earth, would be above twenty-two years travelling to us! Omnipotence, what dominions are thine!

Some have conjectured that the planets may be inhabited by a human race—I cannot think it. The stars, the moon, the sun, all were made for us, for our use: God himself tells us so. At the same time he made man; and after man's

fall,

fall, he promised his only Son for our redemp-
tion. We only, among the human of created
beings, have been spoken of. The heavenly bo-
dies have been made even to stop for us. " Sun,
stand thou still upon Gideon, and thou moon in
the valley of Ajalon." When has our earth ever
rested for either of the planets ?

Thus then, this inimitable and glorious uni-
verse was created for our use, happiness, com-
fort, and delight. Let us gaze upon the won-
ders of His hand, and adore; let us consider the
immensity of His goodness, and be thankful.

In this style may be our conversation when we
introduce astronomy. My anxiety is always,
first to impress a young mind with grand ideas;
to give mighty yet distinct, bold yet connected
theory; we can at any time descend to particu-
lars, when we consult authors. How sublime
are impressions raised upon the wonderful and
the superb! Majesty mingled with sweetness,
immensity with proportion, intermixtures with
harmony, and simplicity with elevation! Oh,
how near is this lofty and exquisite expanse of
soul to every generous inclination, every grate-
ful feeling, every virtuous hope! Discourage it
not, judicious preceptress; the noble enthusiasm
rises approved by heaven. It can exalt our
souls, purify our hearts from mean enjoyment,
teach us to appreciate the works of Providence,
and finally will give us a foretaste of heaven.

Faint are our hopes of the youth whose soul cannot be touched with the grandeur or simple love-liness of na-ture.

We

We proceed now to the second point in universal geography, the

Mathematical   The figure of the earth; its division into zones; the axis, poles, arctic and antarctic circles; the equator, ecliptic, or zodiac, horizon, meridian, degree, longitude, latitude, are all here to be understood. The lines are all imaginary, we are to acquaint our pupils, but their admittance is found necessary in calculating distances and measuring places, &c. The knowledge of them leads to the higher exercise of problems.

The local and extensive, in the understanding and application of large and small divisions of land and water. This is, in fact, simple geography.

The political, in the distinguishing of empire, kingdom, electorate, republic, duchy, &c. with the boundaries of each, titles of the supreme governors, nobility, laws, &c.

The physical, in the study and knowledge of the power and properties, and productions of nature, actual and existing in beast, fish, bird, insect, reptile, &c. belonging to a peculiar country; in plant, tree, shrub, &c. soil, air, mountain, &c.; or possible and discovered, in metal, fossil, stratum, &c.

The national, in which we ascertain the peculiar genius and number of inhabitants in a country; their religion; ancient and modern cus-

toms;

toms; their advancement in arts and science;
their edifices, manufactures, naval and military
strength, &c.

The chronological, in arranging the recorded
events of particular states in true and methodi-
cal order, under the respective century, year,
month, &c. which, in order to understand, we
must be acquainted with the method of computing
in our own and other countries.

This mass is to be reduced and digested by de-
grees, and not attempted all at once, or we
shall frighten and disgust instead of instructing.
Books that are assistants in the different branches
of this study are, Adams on the Globes; a Con-
cise Introduction to the Globes, by Mr. Moli-
neux; Exercises for the Globes, by Mr. Butler;
the Wonders of Nature and Art; the Grammar
of Philosophy; books of travels that have been
mentioned, and concise outlines of the histories
of nations—such as that of Dr. Priestley, ar-
ranged with a chart and references; of the Rev.
J. Adams, called Modern History; or of Mr.
Guthrie, &c.

The pupil with these studies must search out   *Exercises.*
every week places, countries, rivers, &c. on the
terrestrial, and constellations and stars on the
celestial globe. For example: I would advise
the preceptress to take a gazetteer, and name a
city. Whilst the young lady is fixing upon it,
the former might proceed to read the explana-
tion

tion and relative particulars; to all which the pupil listens, points to the spot, and instantly after gives its longitude and latitude. With the celestial globe, the governess may read the constellations regularly down, as they happen to be in Adams, or Molineux, thus: shew me the signs of the zodiac. Aries, the ram, which has forty-six stars; Taurus, the bull, one hundred and nine stars; Ursa major, the great bear, in the northern hemisphere, one hundred and five stars; Lyra, the harp, twenty-four, &c. &c.; and in the southern hemisphere, Argo, the ship, forty-eight stars; Canis major, the great dog, twenty-nine, &c. Eighteen or twenty of these will be sufficient to point out for one exercise. Next to this is the enumerating of the principal stars in their different degrees of magnitude, as they lie in their respective constellations.

The last kind of exercise in universal geography will be mentioned in Chapter IX.

CHAPTER VIII.

PAINTING.

Painting is the art of representing, on a flat surface, one or more objects finely proportioned, justly disposed, and naturally coloured.

Painting

Nº 1

nting may be executed with colours that
round up and mixed either with oil,
:, or distemper.

t before a person can paint, or attempt to
the colourings of nature, he must learn to
le the pencil, to trace lines, to sketch parts,
o apply the whole : in this is included the
imply of drawing. Drawing, therefore, is
alphabet, foundation, and introduction to its
e relative, painting.

'hen a picture then is outlined, or sketched
encil or chalk, it is a drawing. It is also
xd a drawing when shaded with lead, chalk,
rayons; but when the shadows are expressed
olours, laid on according to nature, diluted
il, water, or size, the performance is called
ainting.

Young ladies, for the most part, practise this
dy in crayons and water colours. I shall how-
r divide these, as an art, into three styles:—
it, the human figure; second, landscapes and
utes; third, flowers and shells.

But let us determine, before we rob our pupil
: so much time as is necessary to drawing,
hether her education be sufficiently advanced
) afford it; whether she have disposition or per-
everance to excel; whether we are resolved at
ny risk that she shall learn. If one of these
ositions be assented to, we have only to make

the

the trial. I trust it may not, however, be attempted until the thirteenth or fourteenth year, or at least till the hand writing is formed, for the pressure of the pen and pencil are so different, that if both are engaged in we find that one often suffers.

It rarely happens that a young person has a decided taste, I should rather say inclination, for more than one of these branches; we must therefore endeavour to ascertain which this is, but if we cannot trace any particular propensity, we should ourselves resolve upon the most noble, which is the study of the human figure.*

Materials. The materials are first to be collected: they are black chalk, † Italian and French, a little white, and some very fine black composition, on which is stamped "*Conté à Paris.*" Our tools are merely a knife to cut the points, and a port-crayon to hold the pencil. The chalks are generally kept on cotton or bran —for neatness we may keep the chalks in a little wooden box, as they soil every thing they touch.

Any common drawing paper will do for beginners; and for rubbing out, a little bit of bread

which

---

* The method I recommend is that pursued in the Academy at Paris, from a member of which I learnt, during a residence in France for instruction.

† The chalk is sold by the ounce, and is cheap; but boxes complete are to be had for 10s. 6d. and upwards.

which has not touched any grease should be provided. When the chalk is fixed in the port-crayon, the end is to be laid on the finger, and cut from the point, to prevent its breaking.

Working. The learner should be placed in such a manner, as that the light may fall upon the paper from the left side, and if the room has but one window it is preferable.

The paper is to be placed immediately before the pupil, and the copy perpendicular; for if it be slanting, the bottom of the copy must necessarily be nearer to the eye than the top, and the objects will consequently take an oblong form: the port-crayon must be held a little farther from the point than the pen, and afterwards, for greater freedom, still farther.

The first to practise are lines, horizontal, perpendicular, and curved. After these ovals, the form of which a head takes.

To build a house without some assistance from scaffolding, could scarcely be done. The lines are then to figure-drawing what scaffolding is to the builder.

On no account should the learner practise any feature less in size than the life; doing so would cramp the hand and depress the genius.

Having considered these directions, and prepared accordingly, we may give the young artist the eye marked No. 6, to copy. She will begin by making a horizontal line, — then two per-

After the preparation lines must be raised the object.

K　　　　　pendicular

Drawing.

Figures.

pendicular ones, these will direct the width of the eye, and the situation of the pupil; the eye-ball is then sketched, and the curves for the lids; afterwards the brow. So far is the first sketch, which should be examined with the copy, and the faults pointed out and corrected. When all this is done (and sketching should be as light as a hair stroke), we must take a pinch of bread, and slightly pass it across the drawing, until the remains can scarcely be seen; then the student will proceed to putting the sketch clear and dis-tinct, *au net*, as the French call it. Thus it is to be passed over again, in a bold, correct out-line: strong where there is strength, and deli-

Every sketch should be nearly ef-faced, and then put fair.

cately where it is to be light. It is wonderful to see the difference this new dress makes to the same object, and the practice of putting fair should invariably be persisted in, let the piece be what it may; for what can be a greater en-couragement to take pains in the shadowing, than to see a clear, perfect, and distinct outline? Besides this advantage, it teaches exactness, and amazingly strengthens the touch.

The features are taken separately.

The profile eyes are succeeded by full ones; and those by three quarter, looking up and down: the nose, in different positions; then pro-file and front mouths; and afterwards the whole profile.

To every one of these there must be some support and guide. Every head takes an oval form.

form. In this oval we must draw three lines: first across the centre from the crown for the eyes; in the third quarter for the nostrils; the remaining part to the lowest point is to be divided for the mouth and chin: thus, from the crown of the oval or head to the pupil of the eye is two quarters, from the crown to the nostril three, from the crown to the beginning of the chin three and a half, and to the bottom of the oval or chin four complete quarters. We are now to draw a curve line, which may seem like, or actually be, the side of an oval. The height of the ear falls between the eyebrow and nostril.

It may be thought that all this scaffold of lines is hurtful to the drawing. It is not, however, in the least; because they are sketched at first so very faintly, that they are effaced on the first application of bread, together with the faults, and great part of the roughness in the sketch; and as the poles are removed upon finishing the outside of an edifice, and are no more wanted, so is it with drawing; the foundation lines are effaced when they are no longer useful, but the artist, as I before said, must leave the piece clear, and give it a free outline.

Next to the single features of the face in all manner of positions, are to be made ears. They, as well as other parts in drawing, should be sketched square and bold, to give a grand and commanding

K 2 manding

manding style in handling the pencil. Ears may have a few locks curling round them for practice in hair; this should be at first wild, extremely curled, and in large divisions. Every future habit depends upon first impressions. If we give long lank hair, or even a little waved, our pupils will try to copy, and make tails like that of a peruke, and the stiffness they so contract will never be worn off. A luxuriance of style in young people is easily restrained, but a frigid, reserved, mean one, can seldom be made to spread into generous redundancy. Thus, if the beautiful woodbine throw her tender arms round the supporting tree, and sometimes through excessive gratitude pour forth too wild a multitude of sweet scented blossoms, we find it easy to prune with gentleness some and to restrain others; but how are we to act with the box, which, although in its own country a noble spreading tree, is yet, by our treatment, soil, and climate, a degenerate grovelling stump?

Shadow. There are three ways of shading. First, by hatching, where soft lines slant over one another; not in the least at right angles, like a cross, but rather like very oblong diamonds. The second by dotting, or undistinguishable hatching. The third by rubbing with a bit of rolled wash leather dipped in chalk-dust, called stumping.

Of these three, the first is the only true way

to

to form a bold style. Vast practice will be necessary before any thing be observed approaching to perfection. Notwithstanding which, we must not be backward in giving encouragement by praise :—" It is very well for the time, and I find you are improving : take courage, persevere, I see you will one day be clever," &c.

Hatching is begun finer than a hair, the line thickens by degrees, and gradually lessens. These regular strokes are done one way, and then they are slanted over by others. As the grain of the flesh seems to turn different ways, according to the swells and hollows, we must be particular in observing that the hatching curves this way or that, to humour the inclination of nature.

The second kind of shadow is done by the chalk pencil, but it properly belongs to miniature painting, in which it is most beautiful. Dots form the shade, thick or light; or a sort of rubbing or grazing of the paper by the pencil is practised, according to the object it describes.

The third is by means of leather and paper stumps. With these a little coloured or plain chalk dust is rubbed on. This is extremely soft and natural, especially upon brown paper, which is made for this purpose; the colour of the brown here forms the half tint, and the lights are thrown in by carmine, white, and red chalk, to

K 3   make

Drawing.

Figures.

No matter
what the sha-
dows, the
outline must
be fair and
distinct.

make the flesh tints; black for the dark shades;
red and black rubbed on paper, and the stump
drawn through it, will be a brown. But though
the shadows are made in these different styles,
there must always be one good outline for the
foundation, done either in pencil or chalk.

In the course of a few months, the learner
may have a regular profile, for which she must
draw an oval (bending it according to the atti-
tude of the copy), and make her lines as usual;
in small things, rubbing the scaffolding quite out
and the sketch nearly so, to be able to put it
fair; then will follow the shadow.

In sketching we generally begin by the princi-
pal points; in shading we do the same. Of a
figure, after the proportions are settled, the
principal is the head. Of a head, the principal
is the eye; this then is to be shaded first, then
the brow, the nose, and mouth. We mount up
to the forehead, and do that, the temple and
cheek, and ear. After these the hair: but silver
paper should be placed under the hand, to pre-
vent the rubbing, and the wrist must rest firm
upon a spot, for if it shuffle every thing finished
will be spoiled.

These quarter faces, full front, and heads in
all positions and in all views, should be studied
for one year at least, if we wish the young artist
to have strong principles. Never must the copy
be

First copies
should never
in figures be
less than na-
ture.

be less than nature. We may give old men,
young ones, infants, or females, but we should
have life only for our standard.

Every one knows that a face has some charac-
ter expressed in it. This we should always point
out to the learners. The features may be ex-
tremely like the copy, but the whole is insipid if
the character be wanting; and this is the diffi-
culty to conquer. I have seen two pictures ex- The great
point for
study is the
character ex-
pressed in a
figure.
tremely alike, and yet the character in one was
that of a bold pert woman, in the other a pure
and spotless angel. An eye might at first have
been deceived in these pictures, for resemblance
of features strikes instantly; but similarity of
character, or expression, requires study to dis-
cover, and then it seems to grow upon us, as if
the effect were hidden behind the painting, and
rose up gradually as it was searched for. These
reflections will lead us to observe how necessary
it is to be careful in every finishing touch, for
an interesting face may be rendered insipid by
one or two strokes. A placid eyebrow may be
made to frown by a curve near the nose, and a
smiling mouth may speak contempt by turning
down of the corners.

The passions in heads, by Le Brun, are a
very excellent kind of study for beginners; for
by them they are taught to regard with precision
little curvatures and particular marks.

Figures.

Figures. Females generally content them-
selves with copying. The sinews and vessels
they may draw as they see them; but if an im-
petuous genius will not be restrained, muscular
action in anatomy ought to be studied; I mean
by those, certainly, who are resolved to design.
In a general way, therefore, I should draw a
human figure of bone, and one of muscle, as an
introduction to the whole length, and merely to
give some connexion to the whole. These are
kept as references. It is not necessary to dwell
upon this introduction, nor to give a single ana-
tomical name; and if it were, I am very sure we
should all be puzzled to do so.

Now let me mark off and write down, by this
figure, the proportions. Seven heads and three
quarters for a woman, eight for a man.

From the crown of the head to the chin, one
head—(1).

From the chin to the centre across the breast,
one head—(2).

From the breast to the middle of the stomach,
one head—(3).

From the last point to the centre of the figure
or hip, one head—(4).

From the centre of the figure to the utmost
point of the knee bent, two heads—(6).

From the point of the knee to the utmost point
of the heel, two heads—(8).

The

The width of the figure is reckoned thus:—

From the tip of each middle finger, with the arms extended, is the height of the body.

The thumb is the length of the nose.

The hand is twice its breadth in length.

There are four lengths of the hand from the middle finger to the tip of the shoulder.

The length of the sole of the foot is reckoned the sixth part of the figure.

The great toe is the length of the nose.

These proportions are not always to be found in life. We must, however, have some guide to assist learners, and in giving them pieces to copy, we should ever be careful to select the most perfect. The Grecian and Roman are the only models of beauty upon which we should form young taste. The noble features, full of grace and expression, the dignified deportment, and easy and elegant flowing robes, are the finest studies to encourage or produce classic taste or judgment.

Hands and arms, feet and legs, are to be prac- tised separately, and then the bust; afterwards the whole figure, which should be sketched without vestment, that the proportions may be exact; the drapery, according to the copy, is then added.

As the beautiful disposition of the drapery is a matter of some importance in a picture, we should be careful to point out to the pupil where-

in

in any fault exists.   Nature or truth is our guide. Mantles, or robes, floating in the breeze, always play in graceful negligence; every fold is unconstrained, and yet connected; garments that are heavy in themselves, as satins and velvets, or that are not in action, seem to fall in large masses with tranquil arrangement and easy preponderance.

In making the back ground we must be careful of outlines in the principal objects or they will be lost. Some do the back ground first, which I think a pity; as, in this case, the outline cannot be altered, and it rarely happens that we might not improve as we shade the sketch.

Light minds
we may sup-
pose select
trifles for ad-
miration.
Let us teach our pupil to use their judgment when they examine a picture (as, indeed, they ought upon other occasions), and the foolish praises of ignorant people will not produce so great effect as they too often do. I have seen a young lady observe a charming figure in a noble painting, and after a pause, give a loud panegyric upon its ear-ring, and add, " What a pretty chair that is !" We should desire our pupils to observe the truth, the grandeur of the whole design, and then bid them take notice of the beauty, the harmony of the principal parts. What is to be expressed ?—Grief, hope, anger, joy, terror; behold how these passions are depicted. The head, the attitude, the drapery, all equally express the subject of the action. Then turn to

minor

minor objects : animals, even they partake of the
infection; nay, the very inanimate beings in the
scene adopt the prevailing character. Here then
we may gaze, whilst the eye, which wanders
over these touching graces, this affecting har-
mony, is at last dimmed in tears. Admiration is
too little to express our feelings. What is man,
that thou, God, art mindful of him! that Thou
shouldest endow him with such power!—yet he
must die. The hand that created these beautiful
images, the fine eye that sparkled as they rose
out of canvas, the great mind that throbbed
at the temple with the fervour of its lofty per-
ceptions, will soon, perhaps, have vanished to be
known no more.

Thus, profound admiration is rather a me-
lancholy than a clamorous feeling.

·When ornaments of dress accompany pictures
which our pupils copy, we should at first pay no
great attention to them. Young people are
often extremely anxious, I have observed, on
this point. We may, therefore, say, " Do that
wreath, or that pearl, as well as you can, but
keep in view the principal points; look to these;
never forget your subject. If it be a fine figure,
exert yourself to give dignity, simple grandeur,
ease, character, sentiment. The full and brilliant
eye, the open and generous forehead, the propor-
tioned and characteristic nose, the virtuous and
placid mouth, the rounded chin and oval cheek;
the luxuriant and waving ringlets; the arched

throat;

Drawing.

Figures.

Splendid mo-
numents of
art impress
the mind
with a thou-
sand affecting
ideas, that
are not to be
expressed by
language.

pose, to be put in its place, and the others will be soon added. The line of the horizon, which should be farther from the top than the bottom of a picture, is a nice matter, whether it consist in a ridge of mountains, a boundless plain, or an expanse of waters.

The pupil will do well to study for some time, at least a year, in black chalk or lead pencils, which are sold expressly for fine and large strokes : and several publishers have many progressive sets of lessons, in sketches, with instructions printed, some of which are extremely well spoken of.

Brutes.

Brutes.—Those who would draw landscapes must be able to copy animated nature. The ox chewing the cud ; the lamb cropping the herbage ; the shepherd's dog gazing on his master for orders ; and the shepherd himself leaning, perhaps, with folded arms on his crook, and listening with happy carelessness to the soft tinkling of his village bells. These must be thrown in the prospect to give it life, and quiet pastoral simplicity. The same objects in terror, confusion, or patient sufferance, will shew a war of elements or the ravages of man.

Flowers, fruit, &c.

Flowers, &c.—Shells, fruit, and flowers are very beautiful as paintings. They should be sketched with extreme delicacy, or the pencil will be observable when finished, which is a very great blemish.

Colours.—

Colours.—After the learner has studied some
time in plain black, she may proceed to using
colours, ground very fine, and mixed with gum
arabic and water, or with linseed, turpentine, or
other oils. The third sort of painting, in dis-
temper (or colours mixed with strong size), is
never attempted by young ladies, excepting when
they would ornament a floor to dance upon.
Oil painting is more durable than the other two,
and it is always more capable of improvement,
from the very circumstance of the colour being
ten, twenty, or thirty hours before it dries. For
grandeur and expression nothing can exceed it.

I see no reason why girls should not practise
in oils, rather than water, if they learn painting
as a charming amusement: but I should give
them the choice of either style.

We must not omit some general account of the
great masters in this fine art; it will lead to
some hints of the different schools which have
produced the beauties we so much admire. Pilk-
ington's Dictionary of Painters is a very interest-
ing work, and we might refer to it on the men-
tion of any celebrated name.

I have not spoken of the handmaid of drawing
(perspective), but as it is impossible to excel in
the first without some knowledge in the second,
and as it is a matter of importance to youth to
have a good guide, I refer them at once to the
little work of a friend expressly on this subject.

I saw

Drawing.
Landscapes.

I saw the plan of the book, and a few pages in manuscript: I thought very highly of both. The name of the author is Hayter; a beautiful miniature painter, and a very deserving man.

To be able to take a likeness, or a view, is a noble talent. After having studied some time, and being mistress of principles, and no inconsiderable degree of practice, the pupil may have a marble or plaster bust, or some article of furniture, or a little neighbouring scenery, to copy from various points of sight. Every picture in the same style will be different, yet possessing a family resemblance. Next to these is nature herself; and to attain perfection in imitating this, is the aim of every person who desires that his performances should amuse or instruct.

CHAPTER IX.

EXERCISES FOR THE MIND.

THE human heart is the servant of the mind. Be it then our care to train the latter, so that its influence may be not less lovely in virtue, than eminent in authority.

From the very infancy, this should be our grand object. The eye, the ear, the tongue,

are

are all active in amusing or giving impressions to the fancy, which at this tender age dances upon struggling reason, and effectually blinds her, if a kind friend do not interpose in behalf of the sufferer.

Exercises for the mind (in a general sense) should begin with the first dawn of reason. They do not then consist in long discourses, but in short, clear, lively, and chearful descriptions of every thing which a child should understand, expressed either by action or words. When it shews impatience, fretfulness, or perverseness, we are to look grave, rather than angry, and to express in the most easy and simple manner our sorrow for its naughtiness, and our determination not to submit to it; and when the little cherub has performed some act of forbearance or of opening virtue, we may smile, and embrace her, giving our reason why we do so.

The next duty is to encourage the everlasting questions, What is this? What is that? Bread, butter, milk, chair, table, coals, and a thousand other necessaries are in our sight every day, and we think nothing of them; but they are all matters of curiosity to children, and might be made very interesting subjects. I would not have children tiresome and selfish; a little girl well managed, will immediately be quiet when her mother says, " My dear, I am busy; I cannot talk to you now,"—or " you see, I am

speaking

Infancy.

speaking to this lady, and you should wait till I have quite done," would be quite sufficient.

But this is, as I have remarked, the especial, the important duty of the parent; and it cannot be observed too often, that the instruction of later years sinks into nothing, when compared with the good impressions that might be fixed during the first eight or ten years.

The exercises of which I would now particulary treat, consist of such as are proper for young ladies in the last four years of their education; I mean from the age of fourteen to that of eighteen. The design of them is to bring into

But other exercises are particularly applied to the last years of tutorage.

practice all the principles, rules, theory, that, during so many years, they have been endeavouring to retain. The drudgery of education is then over, and is followed by information and satisfaction. Knowledge, jealous of access, has hitherto shewed her avenues with difficulties; we surmounted them by industry. The gates of her superb museum are opened to us—we pass and enter the apartments of wonder as we think proper.

They may be of two sorts.

These exercises are of two sorts, by conversation and writing.

Conversation.

Conversation. I desire to unfold my subject, but words appear inadequate, as my thoughts are naturally crowded by it; for so many are the opportunities for the exercise of the mind in the conversations that may, and ought to arise between

tween a governess and her pupil, that it is extremely difficult to point out one—besides these, opportunities spring up so immediately from chance, that we can hardly calculate upon them.

Every thing in nature is magnificently great, or elegantly little—from the huge mass of fire that has from the creation poised the whole universe in its beam, to the diminutive insect which bursts into life at the dawn of day, is matured at noon, and dies of old age at night. Can we admire the work, and not adore the Maker? Can we look upon a mountain or a leaf; a planet or a fly; the firmament or a mite, and not remind our pupils of their Divine Creator? Impossible.

As the judgment ripens, the governess should frequently and chearfully explain subjects of religious worship, often very slightly understood. The festivals of the church; Easter, Palm Sunday, &c. the different saints, &c. their lives and deaths; the state of the Christian church in different ages and countries; the points wherein the established church differs from others, &c.

The next are subjects of morality. In the hour for needle work, or during recreation, the perceptress may chat upon any thing she pleases, and draw fine moral from particular incidents. The death of a playfellow, or acquaintance will afford an apportunity for dropping a few observations on the uncertainty of life, on which the

young

Conversation. young never reflect; the sight even of a beautiful and tender corpse where there is no danger of infection, is a very useful and impressive lesson. On the birth of an infant, she may reflect upon its helplessness, and the anxiety and affectionate care of its parents and friends. A good marriage is a time when we may mention the merit of the young lady, the tenderness of her father and mother; their satisfaction in her conduct, and the prudence of her behaviour and choice, in preferring good principles in her husband, to fortune; and her generous and delicate openings in the whole business with her revered parents. From these we may prophecy happiness.

A subject must indeed be barren which cannot afford one particle of reflection.

A disreputable and unauthorized marriage will induce us to observe how likely it is that sorrow may ensue; for any thing of this nature clandestinely begun, and hastily concluded, betrays a consciousness of something wrong, and is the cause of many a heart-rending pang to the parents, and of remorse to the parties themselves; to say the least of its evils. If a person be fond of talking scandal *to* us, we may assert that she would probably do the very same *of* us; for why should we be favoured by a tongue that spares neither sex nor age? But it is easier to conceive than to describe minutely those conversations from which benefit may be derived; if what I have hinted at be not sufficient for general application, further examples

would

would also be. useless; for in a word, whether *Conversation.*
religion, morality, nature, society, establish-
ments, all may be subjects for reflection. Sure-
ly it is not necessary for me to say, that such re-
flections are not to be dragged in, and strained
or pushed forward in every company and sea-
son? This would indeed be disgusting, and we
should be justly esteemed pedantic, selfish, and
dictatorial; but when the pupil and instructress
are quite by themselves, or with a particular
friend, who would take an interest in their con-
cerns, then they may converse with confidence
upon useful or pleasing matters.

I have somewhat touched upon this part of
education in other pages of this work. I trust
I may be pardoned the repetition; for its object
is one of great magnitude, and I could not well
omit a few words in this place. However, I have
now done with it, and proceed to

Written Exercises. The first of these is Eng- *English com-*
lish composition, which has been mentioned, yet *position.*
I must be permitted a few words more.

We give a young person an exercise to per-
form, and we explain and add the rules, which
she has besides learnt by heart. She inserts
both in her book, and continues to write rule
and example for many months, till we have rea-
son to conclude she is thoroughly grounded. We
may then try at composition from the same rules,
without referring to paper, but directly to the
memory.

memory. This is the kind of study I now desire to consider.

English Composition. The young lady has therto filled her paper with large margins rules, and pages of examples. Let us, at this period, give a larger book, and thus address her :—

" Your studies are now becoming extremel interesting. It is long since there appeared difficulty in remembering the principles; these, you perfectly understand. I give you now a larger book, and expect you will fill it in such a manner, from the theory impressed on your mind, that it may be pleasing to you as long as you live. Write one day a regular theme; another, an essay; afterwards a few verses, if you like, or a little anecdote, upon which you may make your reflections. You know that every event has a consequence, which is either good or bad; therefore do you write down any little particular that has happened within your own knowledge, and give your judgment upon it: but remember always to speak with gentleness where you cannot praise; for it may be, that one or two circumstances are unrevealed, which would lessen the harshness of appearances. Remember also, that it is sweeter, and more useful, to excite to goodness by speaking of virtue, than to represent vicious persons or actions by way of discountenancing vice."

On

On the appointed day in the week, the pupil *Composition.*
will write a regular subject. The governess
may give the proposition. The next week, a
theme, the next an essay, &c. thus :—

First week. Regular subject, for example;
" On fables and allegories." (*Walker.*)

Second week. A theme, as, " order is of uni-
versal importance." (*Walker.*)

Third week. An essay, as, " on generosity."
(*Walker.*)

Fourth week. Poetry.

Fifth week. Anecdote and moral.

Sixth week. Fable and reflections.

Poetry is a natural gift. I should always make
it a matter of choice; the pupil may attempt it,
or not, as she is inclined. If she desire to amuse
herself in this way, I am persuaded it will do no
harm, but probably good, for one reason; that
in this exercise of her fancy, taste, and judgment,
she will meet with very great difficulties before
she can have tolerable success, (for not even a
natural poet can write verses without exertion
and study) and that these difficulties will teach
her humility. We have no idea of the pains and
trouble attending works of art, until we our-
selves engage in them; and it is constantly re-
marked, that he whose knowledge is most super-
ficial, is most conceited upon it. The farther
we dive into profound truths, the more do we
                                    perceive

perceive our real ignorance, and the circumscribed boundary of our capacities. :

I apprehend that it is not the lovely talent for poesy, or indeed any other, for which we are ridiculed by men. A gentleman of liberal mind and accomplished manners, must be pleased to find in the woman he designs to marry, qualities which will be likely to render her a charming and engaging companion; but the perversion of these qualities is that which disgusts. There is a time for every thing, as we are told in scripture, and this is most true. If a female is even composing a hymn, when she ought to be attending to the calls of a parent, or to the management of her family, it is wrong; and the Almighty is in no respect pleased with the inconsistent offering: the parent is pained by his daughter's conduct, and the husband is out of humour with his wife and her poetry.　.　:　:　.　.

. By the same rule, it is not the time to bring quotations from some learned author, when the conversation turns upon family incidents. A lady must break down every fence, every medium, to be enabled to produce this witty display of hers; and after all, she gains nothing by the pretty impertinence. Gentlemen are not pleased at having their ears plucked by force, and are in no wise obliged by being regaled with the scraps of their own feast—and for ladies less

learned,

learned, they utterly despise the quotations, the quoted, and the quoter.

Let then the time for every thing be fully considered, and every thing of knowledge that is graceful will be beautiful in woman. In the disposition of her acquirements she will always put duty first, usefulness next, ornament last; and may we all never forget, how infinitely better it is to have good than shining qualities.

The first requisite in poetry is invention, the second is expression; its basis nature, and its true end, instruction.

This divine act is generally divided into blank verse and rhyme; and hence subdivided into many branches. We however call a subject a poem, which is not written directly in either of these, if the action be nobly conceived, finely ordered, and the whole ornamented with every figurative delicacy. Of this description are Telemachus, and the Death of Abel.

Of all poetry, the epic, or heroic, rises in pre-eminence. This is the action, or adventure of some great hero. Tragedy holds the second rank. The first is to form the manners, the other to instruct the passions; the first insinuates by a thousand little strokes of morality; the last admonishes by the awfulness of a just catastrophe.

Composition
Poetry.

An epic or heroic poem is the noblest work of human art. Tragedy ranks next.

L   After

After these, there are so many beautiful, yet inferior kinds, that I cannot ennumerate them.

Verses are lines made up of a particular number of long and short syllables, according to the measure. In some, a long and a short syllable will make a foot; consequently, if its line have five feet, there will be ten syllables; and this would be the case in blank verse also.

Some verses may have in a line two feet, or four syllables, as :—

> " With ravish'd ears
> The monarch hears."   *Dryden.*

Three feet, or six syllables :—

> " The morning opes on high
> His universal eye."   *Smollett.*

Four feet, or eight syllables :—

> " Oh parent of each lovely muse,
> Thy spirit o'er my soul infuse."   *Warton.*

Five feet, or ten syllables, which is the heroic measure :—

> " No force can then resist, no flight can save,
> All sink alike, the fearful and the brave."
>   *Pope's Homer.*

The same number of feet in blank verse :—

> " Would Cæsar shew the greatness of his soul,
> Bid him employ his care for these my friends."
>   *Addison's Cato.*

Lines

Lines of six feet, or twelve syllables : these are called Alexandrines, and they are often used at the end of a verse to give pomp. As,

" To truth proclaims, her awful voice I hear,
With many a solemn pause, it slowly meets my
  ear."   *Mason.*

Other kinds of verse have several short, and one or more long syllables; I shall give a few examples.

Of three syllables :—

 " Fires that glow,
 Shrieks of woe."   *Pope.*

Of five syllables :—

 " Give the vengeance due
 To the valiant crew." *Dryden.*

Of seven syllables :—

 " While the birds unbounded fly,
 And with music fill the sky." *Dyer.*

Of nine syllables :—

 " Not a pine in my grove is there seen,
 But with tendrils of woodbine is bound,
 Not a beech's more beautiful green, &c."
       Shenstone.

Of eleven and nine syllables alternately :—

" The cup was all filled and the leaves were all
  wet,
And it seemed to a fanciful view,
To weep for the buds it had left with regret,
 On the flourishing bush where it grew."
       Cowper.

      I have

Composition.

Poetry.

I have mentioned but a few sorts, because I have dwelt, perhaps, too long upon the subject. I would not wish to make poets of young ladies, but merely shew the variety of poetical numbers, to which some attention is requisite before they can arrange their ideas. I have now only a few words to add upon expression.

In every composition the intrinsic merit of the work depends upon the justice and beauty of the thoughts : but great thoughts should be grandly expressed; not in laboured terms, long words, and monotonous phrases, but in the sweetness of primitive simplicity, or the grandeur of unaffected majesty. Nature, all powerful nature, is the mother of true eloquence. As the passions agitate by turns, so she varies in her look, her voice, her words. Truth is her support, but variety is her constant companion. Behold her in sorrow, her words are slow, heavy, languid and depressed; in joy, all are short, quick, rapid, words seem to fly in peals : but in excess of both, she is mute, or speaks in broken sentences. For sorrow then, we drag out the thought in the slow spondees; words that seem to lengthen as we pronounce them. For joy, the quick and lively dactyl, which is expressed instantly. For softness, the most flowing sounds that breathe all the smooth and tender influence of the vowels. For roughness, the jarring consonant, the rumbling growl of discordant words, and the

Words should be suited to the idea.

furious

furious hissing of aspirates clashing with savage
riot, or grating in sulky harshness.

Thus nature varies, and like her should be
our representation. Fine thoughts strike us
even in a rude dress; but clothed in suitable ex-
pression, sweetly arranged, divided into noble
periods, and supported by the superb and lofty
figures of rhetoric, they captivate, they enchant,
they transport us. We are the slaves of the
writer. He either elevates us to the clouds, and
lends us proudly gazing from the high arch on
little empires below, or he precipitates us, as
lead, to the thick centre of this terrestrial mass;
when, as we follow him through the deep laby-
rinths of nature's granary, he suddenly snatches
us forth, and behold we follow him, submissive
as lambs, as he mounts the proud back of the
celestial bull, and sings to the music of the
spheres! Man, pre-eminent man, this is thy
mark of honour, this thy power. Strength,
riches, dominion, what are ye compared to rea-
son, to speech! Oh man, supreme over ani-
mated nature, not in strength, not in activity,
not in courage, but in these two magnificent
gifts! Cultivate them, cherish them; thou shalt
transport the soul of thy fellow, and chain him
by thy power to virtue.

Second Exercise.—I must descend now to the
second kind of exercise for the mind. It is called
extracts from the arts and sciences.

For this we should have a pretty thick and
large sized copy-book—perhaps an account book.
In the first page is to be written "Contents."
In the second, the governess must rule six or
seven perpendicular lines, for the introduction,
or ground work, which is copied from the En-
cyclopedia, or Chambers's Dictionary. The ar-
ticle is "knowledge;" thus, knowledge "is
either" will go into the second margin, "ra
tional, consisting in the perfection of, &c." will
go into the third margin, and so on, till all the
grand sciences are mentioned, and dwindle into
the ramifications of petty arts. After this great
outline is finished, the pupil must have her book
ruled down the middle of a few pages, and be-
gin to write as in a dictionary, a concise mean-
ing of every term she has used. Thus the first
is "meteorology"—Dr. Johnson and the Ency-
clopedia will give short definitions of this. We
shall find between them, that "meteorology is
the doctrine or history of the air, and the at-
mosphere and its contents, as cloud, æther, fire,
vapour, &c." The next head in knowledge is
"hydrology, or the history of water; including
springs, rivers, &c." These are merely for a
little dictionary of the sciences, which will oc-
cupy only three or four pages. After it, we de-
sire a thorough explanation of the whole. The
pupil may choose any one of the arts or sciences,
we will say "mineralogy." She then searches

in

in the Encyclopedia for the article, reads a page
at a lesson, and then skims off (if I may be al-
lowed the expression) all the cream, the great
principles; digests these facts, and puts them in
her book in the form of a regular abridgment.
When mineralogy is quite finished, and its grand
divisions and particulars will only take five or
six pages, she takes some other science, and pro-
ceeds in the same manner.*

    This extracting is so important to the young,
that I rank it next to composition. It teaches
them to remember what they read, to arrange a
subject in the mind, to separate the valuable
from the dross, and to compress their ideas into
regularity: finally, it fixes great principles of
science, and gives an extensive view of the ge-
neral knowledge of man, and helps them to ex-
press themselves with precision and modesty.

    Third Exercise.—The third kind of exercise
is relating to history. A writing-book must be
kept on purpose for abridgments of history. I
would have, first, an introduction, briefly consi-
dering the most remarkable changes in states,
from the first period of them to those of our own
time. There is in Guthrie a very useful chapter
upon the origin of governments, and the progress

L 4   of

Marginal notes: Composition. Extracts. The heads of every science are to be collected. The advantages of enquiring into the sciences are very great. Historical writing. Third exercise, history.

* I always desire to have a few leaves at the end of the vo-
lume preserved, for drawing any little illustration from the plates
of the Encyclopedia.

Composition. of civilization; nearly the whole of this might be copied off. With this ground-work the pupil must take up a sort of chronological history, beginning with Adam, and naming the different heads of the sacred book, giving the dates, ages of persons, with the manner of their deaths, whether natural or violent, &c. This will be called the Jewish History. Then will follow the different empires, which are comprised in Profane History; the Christian will be next, and the Modern last.

Jewish, Profane, Christian, Modern Histories.

Under the title England this may serve as a specimen of the style of the chronological part.

HENRY III.

Year.

Succeeded his father in the tenth year of his age.

He was born October 1 1207
Began to reign October 19 1216
Died 1272

Reigned fifty-six years.

We may then mention, after the chronology, any particular and interesting events that happened during the reigns; and so continue, by degrees, taking every kingdom separately, till we rest at George the Third; and we may afterwards add great occurrences as they chance to happen.

Fourth

Fourth Exercise.—This exercise is on geogra-
phy.

As the learner has been some time in fixing
places, boundaries, and particulars of every de-
scription in her mind, we must now adopt a plan
to bring them into practice. For this purpose
I require an imaginary tour. The young tra-
veller may choose her place of destination : she
may set out to Calcutta across continents ; or she
may visit the Cape of Good Hope, and wind her
track through the varied climes of the Great
Russian Empire, the Mounts of Caucasus, the
sacred plains of Palestine, the burning sands of
Egypt and Nubia, the regions of Ethiopia, and
the wilds of Caffraria ; or she may take passage
to Del Fuego, and cross over the straits into the
new world, which she may traverse or ascend to
the very source of the impetuous Missisippi. She
may confine her searches to the lovely Isles of
Britain ; or she may cross kingdoms to weep on
the tomb of an Achilles, a Cato, or a Virgil.—
Charming haunts of virtue and the graces ! May
the recollection of her bright records dilate her
young heart with sweet feelings of admiration,
and excite in it a desire for all that is affectingly
heroic or sublimely great.

These tours must be written however with
care. The best and largest maps, the first au-
thorities only, are to be consulted. As many

principles

principles are to be called into action, we are to proceed slowly. The heads are to be collected and written in the title page. History, curiosities, edifices, &c. &c. are to be kept in view, and every thing worthy of note should be mentioned. The scale at the bottom of the map will be a guide as to miles; but we are to remember that the miles of all countries are variable as to length. An Irish mile is longer than an English one, a Russian is shorter; therefore, when a reckoning is made, it should be according to the measurement of the particular country, calculated into that of our own, &c. In some parts there are only mules; in some they travel very slowly, perhaps not thirty miles per day. Now we must search out all these peculiarities, for it would be most ridiculous to say, we travelled over the Alps, as we might in England, at the rate of one hundred miles in one day; in short, every thing must be considered, and the gazetteer will always help us out. By way of interesting more, the tour may be in the form of letters, and wound up in a little narrative, in the style of a regular journal. When we set foot upon a new kingdom, such as Italy, I like the general produce and particulars of the country to be given in a pretty long description; after this, the different towns are mentioned distinctly as we travel through them, and in every one of note we should

remain

remain long enough to examine all the striking features and curiosities. This tour may be continued one day in every week.

Other exercises are for foreign languages. They are, *sous dicté*, and translations of English into other tongues, or of those into English. For *sous dicté*, the preceptress takes a French or Italian book, and at, any page reads a dozen lines, stopping at every eighth or tenth word. As fast as she reads the pupils write down on the slate the words from the sound of them, and correct them afterwards themselves by the book, the instructress shewing in what respect they have erred. The exercises in foreign languages have been mentioned in the regular study of them.

Such are the principal writing exercises I recommend to bring theory into practice. That all are practicable I am persuaded, because for years I myself have rejoiced in their good effects; yet, with all their utility, I will maintain that they are inferior to conversation—oral explanation solves in one instant the problem of whole pages. Study then is good, conversation is better; but an equal share of both is the perfection of education.

     CHAP-

CHAPTER X.

BOOKS FOR YOUNG PERSONS.

THE choice of books for youth is a matter of
such difficulty and importance, that one cannot
consider it too seriously.

The vast in-
crease of chil-
dren's books.

Formerly elementary books were so scarce,
that education was often absolutely at a stand
for the want of first principles. In our time the
shelves of booksellers are bending under the
weight of various productions; and it is found
necessary to establish libraries for the exclusive
reception of volumes dedicated to children.

In the course of the last century, but more
particularly towards the close, it seemed deter-
mined that the youth of both sexes merited
equal attention in their education. The noble
mental qualities of women were not to be con-
fined to the calculation of flour for pastry, or the
considerations of silks in the embroidery of a
chair cover; they were to employ their energies
in ranging through science, or in observing art.

The faculties
of women
judged wor-
thy of cul-
ture;

The grave parts of study were to temper their
exquisite sensibility; the noble part, to inspire
their generous bosoms with lofty and virtuous
sentiments; the profound parts to rein in the
proud efforts of their rich and luxuriant imagi-
nations;

Introduction.

nations; and the refined parrs to add to their
native dignity and gracefulness of carriage and
behaviour.

Such were the proposed advantages, besides
others. A being so lovely in acquirement, it was
expected, would be found to possess exemplary
piety and sound principles. Who can survey the
wonderous and beautiful works of creation and
not feel, impressively feel, the power, the exist-
ence of a God? and if a God, how great, how
good, how magnificent!

It followed then, that woman, thus educated,
would feel the delights of knowledge herself;
and, as pleasure must be divided to be enjoyed,
she would be anxious to share all she possessed
with those whom she most loved. Hence the
charms of her society with the lord of her affec-
tions, arising in the cultivation of a sensible mind,
and the modesty and submission only to be ex-
pected from the truly meritorious. But the chil-
dren? Children who are to be dependent in a
striking manner upon her, during many, or at
least several, years of their lives; these would, to
an incalculable degree, profit by her instructions
so well digested and so tenderly bestowed.

that they might be the pride of the husband, the hope of the child.

The usefulness of the proposal was determin-
ed; how to act upon it was the consideration.

Books were judged the first means. A few
men of talents stepped honourably and generous-
ly forward in this great cause. One stripped
science

The generous stepped forward and caressed science into the espousal of the cause.

science of her frowns, and cut an easy path to her abode; another threw the sublime works of the ancients into English simplicity, and condescended to add reflections upon the method of studying them. Another wrote upon the formation of female character; and others prepared for the chaste eye of innocence different lovely pictures of nature and art.

The shock of every revolution is more or less rude, according to the magnitude of objects attained, or the insignificance of matters subverted. The brain totally unprepared from infancy for these changes, grew giddy on its new possession; and vanity, for want of ballast, floated uppermost. Men became disgusted with the sight, who did not reflect upon causes; and learning in women was every where ridiculed and insulted. A celebrated writer, or student, dreaded to sit next a woman of education, for fear of being annoyed with hazardous quotations, or enthralled in a web of figurative eloquence; and for a plain man, he felt himself insupportably little under the triumphs of a female adversary. The man of virtue beheld with disdain that such learning restrained not the licentiousness of morals; and the man of intrigue gloried in publishing the new conquests which intoxicated vanity held out to his acceptance.

Parties strengthened to crush the new order of things. The theatre, the court, the preacher, the

the essayist,—all bodies conspired to reassume the right of pre-eminent faculties of mind. But woman held fast what, it was plain, was considered of some value to retain. *Introduction.*

Man sickened with disgust, and raised an arm to snatch back the gift.

In the height of the struggle a few mercenary or ignorant men resolved to take their advantage. They wrote in haste, and in ignorance, upon various subjects. The works were eagerly published by the booksellers; and were purchased with avidity by women, now become mothers, who showered this trash upon their children, determined that they should hereafter be living obstacles to the reversion of the newly acquired privileges.

But the female was alarmed, and securd her right in her offspring.

Women too were jealous of not sailing down this publishing stream. One wrote a pitiful novel, and called it a tale for youth; some joined in partnership, and produced a work for schools; and one jumbled a mass of letters together, and called the thing a Memoria Technica. What have not these wretched scribes attempted! The shops filled, shelves groaned, windows flamed like harlequins' dresses with the daubs that were to illustrate passages of these hopeful productions. Pens, ink, paper and figures were put in requisition. The brains of some did all they could do; and when they were spun out, the happy plan was adopted of putting the old woman into the mill to be ground young again, and forthwith came the innocent, chaste, the love-making

Writers, as they call themselves, for youth then rushed in a body to the shrine of interest;

and the town was overwhelmed to add to their lucre.

Introduction.

making old Mothers Goose and Shipton in high heeled shoes, yellow gowns, and frizzled wigs. Others started every thing in dissections; maps, kings, and queens were to be all pasted on wood and cut to pieces. Chronology was to be taught by a tetotum; and the rules of arithmetic by cutting a pasteboard lion, bear, or magpie through the middle, and joining it again. A few of these possessed ingenuity, but by far the greater part was gaudy glitter without use.

Virtue and genius were next overpowered by fashion and mercenaries.

Not even the revered names of Trimmer, Gregory, Aikin, Barbauld, Edgworth, Day, Murray, Chapone, More, Hamilton, Goldsmith, Johnson, Wakefield, Fordyce, Perceval, which have all adorned a page for youth, could intimidate these writers into silence.

The rage for buying a copy of every thing at the juvenile libraries, was found to extend through all the parts of education. In music, every old jig, whether Italian, Scotch, or French, was to have a new name, to be set in a new key, to be trimmed up with variations, and to have a flourishing engraving of laurel round the author's name. New and languishing words were composed to old songs; and a couple of naked cupids, throwing darts at each other, were thought so pretty a frontispiece to a young lady's music book that a purchaser was certain. Professors of music, whose noble talents were an ornament to the age in which they lived, condescended

scended to fall in with the madness of the day.
Their compositions suddenly assumed a lighter
appearance, and were to be distinguished by the
most frivolous titles. Sure of selling, professors
wrote in haste. One woman they thought would
not have fewer books, fewer pieces of music than
another; consequently, if one could be attract-
ed all would. The prettiest airs then went by
a soft foreign appellation.—" *Les petits Riens*,"
or " *Le Songe*," or " *Le Retour du Zéphir*;"
and even the most beautiful concertos were not
suffered to pass without being Cuckoos, or
Storms, or *Non plus ultras*.

In drawing, people started up to teach wood
painting, velvet painting, smoke of a candle
painting, tracing and window painting, &c. &c.
All these were sought for with eagerness, whilst
the noble principles of this fine art were ne-
glected.

All or no-
thing was the
motto for ac-
complish-
ments.

In dancing were the same extremes. Nothing
less than the opera steps, flourishes, flings, and
capers could be tolerated. In giving the last in-
structions to a fine young lady before her intro-
duction to her sovereign, the foreign waltz master
taught her the dance; and the young nobleman
or gentleman, whom she might afterwards meet
at a party, affectionately embraced and supported
her through the same.

Girls' seminaries, in particular, were all anx-
iety to be in the fashion. One of the most dis-.
tinguished

tinguished had a carriage suspended from the hall of attitude, to practise young ladies in mounting and descending the steps with grace. The dancing master superintended the important ceremony.

As ladies would learn of all things, Crispin thought his art too considerable in education to be neglected; he accordingly advertised to give ladies lessons in shoemaking, and proposed to sell his work-boxes complete, with awls, horn, cobler's wax, &c. &c. at a moderate price.

Yet, with all these, was to be trouble: women wished to know every thing and be spared the fatigue of learning. Accordingly one person made a musical instrument that could be thoroughly understood in six lessons; another advertised to give the most beautiful hand writing in eight; a third would make his pupils masters of languages in three months; and a fourth considered eight lessons sufficient to begin and finish the dancer; and to sum up the whole, an itinerant memory gentleman would teach every thing of art and science in four lessons.

The shortest path was esteemed the best; and he who professed to begin and complete an education in fewest lessons was most certain of employment.

Meanwhile, the most sensible and dignified writers, male and female, laboured hard to bring back the people to their senses. They wrote, argued, entreated. They told the parent, that nothing would be right, no education could attain its end, that was not begun and conducted upon principle; that it was not in the number of

accomplishments,

accomplishments, the depth of erudition, the *Introduction.* profusion of publications, that real and substantial advantage could be derived; but in attention to the unfolding of reason, and in the employment of every help to stamp virtuous impressions, and oppose every struggle of vice. These, they declared, were the grand objects; and that a knowledge in every science, a practice in every art, so far from being of the first consequence to a young lady, were mere matters of amusement or ornament; that she would never be respected for any thing but the purity and piety of her disposition, the modesty and affability of her manners, and the practice of duties inseparably connected with female tenderness, submission, and patience. Upon this foundation they agreed that sound learning upon generous systems, and accomplishments consistent with feminine dignity and grace, would add a lustre to rank, and would command the admiration and esteem of country, friends and dependants.

These works upon education were read (how Truth saw the folly of the day and expressed her disdain should it be otherwise?) and reprinted; and reprinted and read. Passages were quoted, yet impressions seemed on the surface: but truth spoke; she could not be entirely resisted. A few parents, by degrees, turned over Tom Thumb and Cinderalla, to inquire if the bookseller had no work, written expressly, that was fit for infant minds—

Introduction.

She was
heard, but
with reluct-
ance.

minds—something in the way of instruction. Au-
thors flourished in with their prose and rhyme
productions. The publisher shook his head.—
" I am afraid, Sir or Madam, that I must decline
the work. These things, somehow, don't take
now, as they used; I have suffered greatly by
losses in them; however you may leave your
production; I will look it over, and send you an
answer."*

Authors con-
tinued to
write, but put
a guard on
the title page.

In infants' books then the public taste is some-
what improved; yet people still buy hundreds
of volumes, under the most specious titles, which
contain much that has no moral tendency what-
ever; and some are neither calculated to in-
struct nor to be understood by persons of tender
years.

Let us now consider the subject in another
light.

Reading.

The power of
a book is su-
preme.

Of all the different branches of study, none is
more important than reading; of all the agents
in education, none are more powerful than
books. A book may be the ruin of innocence;
the prop of virtue; the comfort of the weak, the
terror of the strong; the polisher of a mind, or
the

---

* A bookseller, whom I know, was applied to by a gentleman
who had some juvenile poetry to dispose of. " I am sorry I cannot
treat with you, said he, I am plagued to death with works much
inferior to yours. I have on my hands no less than thirty manu-
scripts of the kind which can never be printed."

the depraver of a heart. A book is either the best treasure, or the greatest evil, in the worldly possessions of infancy, childhood, or adolescence.

As this vast power is lodged in books, let us, who preside over the education of young people, distribute them with carelessness at our peril.

Of all instructions, that which is conveyed through fictitious writing may be the most doubtful and dangerous. The professions of the introduction, the simplicity of the title, the glare of some of the plates, and the rash recommendation of an injudicious person, all conspire to throw people off their guard. The work is bought and presented to the child, who reads, remembers and imitates. In general these stories are a play upon the passions, enveloped in a glitter, which dazzles the imagination. Of instruction there is alas none, unless it be in that it were more honourable to be deficient in. This supposes the language understood, which it very often is not; therefore, to say the very best of such works, they create a disgust (the happy alternative) for all reading, or they disgust for every sort but that.

A book is not really instructive without every separate part be built upon a principle, and that these principles be all subjected and conducive to one great end.—This end is truth; either scientific, moral, or religious. The truth so finely supported

Essentials to children's books, are splendid, moral and natural languages.

supported by minor truths, all pointing to their great object, may be together called the moral.

2dly. The language should be natural, clear, open, and unaffected. The stronger the truth we advance, the less does it need embellishment. But as the husbandman, after the laborious duty of the day, feels a soft delight in adorning with wild sweets his own enclosure, in like manner, he, who has advanced strong truths, may rest awhile (still maintaining his honest character) and give pastime to his imagination.

Examination
of some few
children's
books in mo-
ral and lan-
guage.

Tried by these two rules, three parts of the number of books that are printed for youth (I presume not to go further) are immoral or unintelligible.

We are now to examine how far some of the books, written professedly for the young, are, first, comprehensible from their natural and easy language. Secondly, how much they are likely to amuse from their innocent cheerfulness and simple style of subject. Thirdly, how deep will be impressions of generosity, magnanimity, justice, humanity, delicacy, truth or piety, from the beautiful chastity of the sentiments, and the striking, yet endearing point of every reflection to some principle in religion or virtue.

No. I. Natural and easy language.
In Mavor's Spelling Book, the learned doctor
desires

desires that this, and other sentences of the like nature, may be learnt before the age of ten.

" Agriculture, the most useful and important of all pursuits, teaches the nature of soils and their proper adaptation and management for the production of food for man and beast."

I should be glad to know how a child, under ten years, would explain the words pursuits, nature, soils, adaptation, production; as for ideas, he would have none on the subject.

" Poetry is a speaking picture, representing real or fictitious events, by a succession of mental imagery, generally delivered in measured numbers. It at once refines the heart and elevates the soul."

" Chemistry is the science which explains the constituent principles of bodies, the results of their various combinations, and the laws by which these combinations are effected."

" Chronology teaches the method of computing time and distinguishing its parts, so as to determine what period has elapsed since any memorable event."

These sentences are equally as unintelligent to an infant mind as the preceding. With respect to poetry, I presume, every sort is not implied when we speak of refinement of the heart. We may surely say, that poetry, with every other work of taste, *ought* to refine the heart; but, that it *does*, is, I think, going far from truth.

The

The same universal compiler in his biography
says

Exam. V.   "A fatality attends the best concerted plans
of some able men, while a mediocrity of talents,
without energy, and almost without effort, not
unfrequently carries away the prize."—(Nepos,
p. 347.)

Exam. VI.   " To select the brightest luminaries from the
literary constellation which has gilded the British
horizon, is both a difficult and an invidious task."
—(Page 291.)

Be it remembered, these fine speeches are not
for men and women, but written expressly for
children; and adapted, as the title page says,
" to young capacities."

Neither of the sentences would be at all under-
stood by a child. She of course stops, if she
wishes to know what she reads about. The
meaning of one is to be, I suppose, expressed
thus : " Why some people are lucky, and some
are unlucky. So, if you are to be lucky, it mat-
ters not whether you exert yourself or not, you
will gain whatever you wish; and, if you are to
be unlucky, you need not try to be great or
clever, for you will never succeed." An useful
reflection ! ! !

As for *horizon*, and *constellations*, and *gilding*,
and the *invidious task*, I do not know how we
should proceed, especially as the child most pro-
bably has not yet gone through any *astronomical*
task;

task; and for gilding, she only recollects that the picture frames and pier glasses, in the drawing room, are said to be gilt.

" The First Catechism for Children, to ·be learnt at an early age." In the first page the tutor says, " Let me hear you count ten. One, two, three, four, five, &c." This is the first lesson. The second is upon the names of the days in the week, and then upon the months of the year. Behold! sixty duodecimo pages beyond, there are these questions and answers.

" *Q.* What is thunder?

A. The report of a stream of electric fire.

Q. What is lightning?

A. The flash of light occasioned by the same electric fluid.

Q. What occasions the tides?

A. The attraction of the moon and sun."

An infant must have made a wonderful progress from not knowing how to count ten to understanding such sentences as these. In the same book, page 39, there is a strange want of delicacy. I remember last year a lady requested me to hear her little girl's lesson. The child brought her book, hesitated, and looked confounded. I asked why she waited; she said, she did not like to learn that bit. I examined it, and quietly said " Why?" She coloured, and stammered " It is so nasty." I was much pleased

M　　　　　　　　　with

with this delicacy, and instantly turned over the leaf.

The subject was this:

" *Q.* What is beef?

A. The flesh of *dead* oxen or cows.

Q. What is mutton?

A. The flesh of *dead* sheep.

Q. What is veal?

A. The flesh of *dead* calves.

Q. What is pork?

A. The flesh of *dead* pigs," &c. &c.

" *Pictures for the Youthful Mind.*"

" The labourers in this work are mostly poor Irishmen, and are great *setters* both of *stones* and *potatoes*: it must, however, be acknowledged that one is not quite so quick in growth as the other. These men are content to *pave* their way to an honest livelihood; and find, by *laying down* their employment, a sufficiency to produce the necessaries of life."

This miserable pun is meant to amuse a child, who would not understand it; and, if she did, it could be of no advantage; for a pun is, at best, a poor apology for wit—at instruction it never aims.

No. II.

No. II.   Innocent Cheerfulness and Simplicity of
Subject.

*"A melancholy Song."**

" Trip upon trenchers,
  And dance upon dishes :
My mother sent me for some bawm, some bawm ;
  She bid me tread lightly,
  And come again quickly,
For fear the young men should do me some harm.
  Yet didn't you see,
  Yet didn't you see,
What naughty tricks they put upon me ?
  They broke my pitcher,
    They spilt my water,
  And huft my mother,
    And chid her daughter,
And kiss'd my sister instead of me."

   "Song III. *Of Man by Nature.*"

   " From God he's a backslider ;
   Of ways he loves the wider ;
   With wickedness a sider ;
   More venom than a spider.

   In sin he's a confider ;
   A make-bate and divider ·
   Blind reason is his guider ;
   The devil is his rider."

                  M 2   " Song

* Juvenile Songster, p. 39.

Marginalia:

Juvenile Books.

Innocence, cheerfulness, and simplicity of subject.

Example I.

Example II.

" SONG XIII. *Come kiss me.*"

Example III.
" O ! mistress mine, where are you running :
O stay and hear your true love's coming,
   That can sing both high and low.
Trip no farther, pretty sweeting ;
Journeys end in lovers meeting,
   Every wise man's son doth know.

What is love ? 'tis not hereafter :
Present mirth hath present laughter ;
   What's to come is still unsure ;
In decay there lies no plenty :
Then come kiss me sweet and twenty ;
   Youth's a stuff will not endure."

———

" The *Sleeping Beauty in the Wood* (with
other instructive and interesting Stories) de-
signed to promote good Humour and proper
Conduct. A new Edition."

Of this " *interesting*" and " *instructive*" book
for children, I shall only give a specimen in the
moral to the first story.

Example IV.
" *The Sleeping Beauty.* &c.—Moral."

" To get a husband rich, genteel, and gay,
Of humour sweet, some time to stay,
   Is natural enough, 'tis true ;
But then to wait a hundred years,
And all that while asleep, appears
   A thing entirely new.

Now

Now at this time of day,
  Not one of all the sex we see
  To sleep with such profound tranquillity.
But yet this fable seems to let us know,
  That very often Hymen's blisses sweet,
  Altho' some tedious obstacles they meet,
Which makes us for them a long while to stay,
Are not less happy for approaching slow;
  And that we nothing lose by such delay,
  But warm'd by Nature's ambient fires,
  The sex so ardently aspires
Of this blest state the sacred joy t'embrace,
  And with such earnest heart pursue'em;
  I've not the will, I must confess,
  Nor yet the power, nor fine address,
To preach this moral to 'em."

"Tales of the Hermitage."—(Innocent language!) Example V.
  "In less than five minutes Mrs. Roper re-
entered, followed by the jeweller and the crier,
and a voice half choaked with rage, exclaimed,
  " 'You vile, wicked, ungrateful hussy! is this
the way you requite my poor sister's kindness?
What! rob her of the most valuable thing she
possessed on earth; and then, with the art and
hypocrisy of an old offender, pretend to be going
out to inquire after the very thing you knew you
had first stolen, and then sold! But I see
through your tricks, you baggage, I do. You
was fearful your countenance would betray your
guilt,

guilt, and you wished to get out of the room to hide it. But where is the guinea you received from Mr. Martin? Give that to me, this moment, abandoned, wicked hussy.'"

No. III.   The Point of every Reflection to some Principle in Religion or Virtue.

The point of the different sentiments in a book to some object in religion or virtue.

I appeal to any person of sense, but particularly to parents, whether descriptions of balls, routs, satire, and ogling, are subjects to lay before the innocent eye of infancy; yet how few little books are not wholly composed of them! Let us take one of the most celebrated, and impartially consider its merits and its title to a place on the study shelf. " *The Peacock at Home*" lies before me. I open it, at the first page, and read:

Example I.

" The butterfly's ball, and the grasshopper's feast,
Excited the *spleen* of the birds and the beast."

The child runs up to me, with the book in her hand, and says, " What does this mean, ' excited the spleen of the birds and the beasts?' " Can I say spleen is ill-nature or anger, or shall I explain envy or malice ; and then add, " Why, the beasts had heard of the feast that these little animals had enjoyed, and they felt quite envious, or malicious, or angry, that others besides themselves should be amused." I must either give this answer, and excite the indignation of the child,

child, or I must tell an untruth and put an-
other meaning upon it, or I must be silent. So
then, this is the foundation of the story—spleen.
Let us proceed.

The beetle and the fly were the principal de-
scribers of their gaieties, and as they " humm'd
and buzz'd" the accounts,

" The quadrupeds listen'd with sullen displeasure,
And the tenants of air were enrag'd beyond measure."

A fine occasion, truly, for sullenness and anger
beyond measure. If a child be sulky, or fall into
a passion on a more trying vexation, she will, at
least, have an authority in the very books we give
to form her young mind; and if we do *not* give
them with the idea of improvement, for what
purpose then, I would ask? Is a child to read
for the sake of reading? If we think so, he or
she will not. No infant will pore over a book
unless there be in it something to interest the
noble and generous feelings of her little honest
heart; or, without there be something in it that
rouses a spark of ill-nature, ridicule, vanity, or
satire. If she cannot understand the sentences,
she throws the book down, is tired, and evi-
dently disgusted with reading altogether; but
if she likes the book, and continues it, she is
either ennobled or she is tainted.

The peacock is indignant, and, stretching his
tail, cries—   .   .   .   .

" Shall we, like *domestic* inelegant fowls,
As unpolish'd as geese, and as stupid as owls,
Sit tamely at home, humdrum with our spouses,
While crickets and butterflies open their houses ?
Shall such mean little insects pretend to the fashion ?
Cousin turkey-cock, well may you be in a passion."

  * * * * * * *

" So a fête I will give, and my taste I'll display,
And send out my cards for Saint Valentine's day."

It may be fashionable for a female not to sit
with her spouse; but it is not, I apprehend, a
very good lesson to inculcate. The idea is pretty
of sending out the cards on Saint Valentine's
Day, especially as the child will not forget to
enquire concerning it, and may be told many a
pretty nonsense that is committed through its
license. Pigeons are sent with invitations to this
rout. The turtle dove, the only wise animal
mentioned, sends an excuse, because she prefers
the society of her family ; for which she is derided
by the title of " nest loving." The three next
lines are sweetly simple !

" Dame Partlett lay-in, as did good Mrs. Goose ;
The Turkey, poor soul ! was confined to the rip,
For all her young brood had just fail'd with the pip."

The sensation that is caused amongst all such
as intend to accept the invitation, shews a fine
emulation in the noble art of dress—" Pruning
of coats," " ruffling of feathers," " polishing of
        bills,"

Juvenile
Books.
—

bills," " oiling of pinions," and such practising
in whistling, chirping, and such " clearance of
throats," of those that expected to exhibit, as
cannot but be a lesson not easily forgotten. The
taylor is very busy in' making clothes for the
young beaux.

" While the Halcyon bent over the streamlet to view
How pretty she looked in her boddice of blue !"

A picture for vanity. Love, of course, must
be admitted : one of the company is dressed

" In silver and black, like a fair pensive maid
Who mourns for her love !"

The hero of the tale, among other amiable
traits in his character, possesses that of never
forgiving an offence, though not immediately
done to himself. He will not invite the daw :

" As the Peacock kept up his progenitor's quarrel,
Which Æsop relates, about cast-off apparel."

This is a truly Christian principle ; and the
sentiment that follows is finely calculated for a
child's improvement :

" For birds are like men in their contests together,
And in questions of right, can dispute for a feather."

The opening of the ball, and the praise of the
waltz, shew infinite taste. The party at cards,
and especially

" The birds past their prime, o'er whose heads it was
        fated,
Should pass many Valentines, yet be unmated,

Look'd on, and remark'd that the prudent and sage
Were quite overlook'd in this frivolous age,
When birds scarce pen-feather'd were brought to a rout,
Forward chits! from the egg-shell but newly come out,
That in their youthful days they ne'er witness'd such
   frisking;
And how wrong! in the Greenfinch to flirt with the
  sisken.
So thought Lady Mackaw, and her friend Cockatoo;
And the Raven foretold that, ' No good could ensue.'
They censur'd the Bantam for strutting and crowing
In those vile pantaloons, which he fancied look'd know-
   ing;
And a want of decorum caus'd many demurs
Against the Game Chicken for coming in spurs"—

are *innocent, friendly, instructive* observations,
and shew *extreme delicacy!*

 The dance is succeeded by the supper, which
is described in all the pretty jargon of an epi-
cure and his cook. " Wasps *à la sauce piquante,*"
and " flies *en compôte*"—" Worms and frogs *en
friture,*" &c. The party scramble for seats, eat
their fill, and go home. And thus ends this
poem, *written for children*, sold at all the juve-
nile libraries, and in possession of half the chil-
dren of respectability in England. Let us now
enquire

 What is the moral?—It has none.

 What are the principles?—They are decidedly
bad.

         What

What then is its intention ?—I suppose we must answer, to teach the names of a few birds.

How ? Is this all? Cannot I leave the mention of birds to a more advanced age ? Shall I sacrifice my little cherub's truth, delicacy, innocence, every principle of candour and generosity, by such pernicious sentiments, to the knowledge of names of birds, of animated nature, of science itself?—Never. Moulder into dust my library. Thou, knowledge, be ignorance; but let my child be innocent and uncorrupted.

There are sequels upon sequel to this celebrated tale, all upon the same plan. The following paragraph is on the cover of one of them :

" It is unnecessary for the publisher to say any thing more of the above little productions, than that they have been purchased with avidity, and read with satisfaction, by persons in all ranks of life."

" Dame Hubbard and her Dog," " The Life and Adventures of Dame Trot and her Cat," and other stories of the kind—what do they contain of useful ? In what respect is the child's heart mended, or her ideas enlarged by the reading of them ? And if this be unanswerable, let us ask wherein her mind has not suffered by such trash ? How can a mind so filled relish any thing hereafter but novels, and those of the most extravagant kind ? What is " Grandmama, or the Christening not at Home," but a fine lady representation

sentation of a novel, and the ridicule of filial
piety.

"*Grandmama, &c.*"

Example II. A little girl is supposed to give an account of
the birth and christening of a little brother.
One would imagine her tender heart pouring
forth sentiments of joy, in the most artless de-
scription and language; on the contrary, no lan-
guage is less simple and less childish. The first
part begins with describing spring, and the child
drags in a pun:

" The crows coarsely caa, claiming part in the season,
Cabal like conspirators brooding *high trees-on.*"

She then proceeds to say, that the young heir
is born, the knocker tied up, enquiries sent in,
&c. &c. In the mean time her grandmother
she pertly describes " wriggling and quav'ring,"
and " so important grown,"

" She determin'd to have all proceedings her own ;
Such injunctions to one, and such cautions to t'other,
As if such a scene there had ne'er been another."

Half a dozen tradespeople are sent for to
furnish different articles of dress minutely pour-
trayed. A rich dress for the infant trimmed with
Valenciennes lace, &c.; a white sarsnet robe,
vandyked with lace, for the mother, and

" A delicate mob with vandyke round the face," &c.

Ottoman silk, and curly flaxen wig, for the old
grandmother. The wig thus mentioned:

"Well

" Well Tête'em, now make me a smart wig that's flaxen,
A spring wig I mean, no stiff powder'd caxen;
Light and airy throughout, no expense I will spare,
So its quite *comme il faut*, and *a je ne sçais quoi air.*"

This is a specimen of the whole poem. Is it the style of a child? If a child should really address us in such a manner, ought we not to check her flippancy? But the sentiments: are they natural? are they those of innocence and duty? —No. They may do in a novel, but they are disgusting in an infant's mouth. What has childhood to do with satire? Oh rash and presumptuous authors! are you fearful that children, youth, adults, should not soon enough learn this modish phraseology, these ungenerous [sentiments? Are you fearful that children should be too innocent, too natural? How do you suppose your writings are to benefit the young? What end have you? Where are the morals you inculcate? Becoming be your language, if your talents be not great; let innocence and truth, let these at least be the beauties of your sentiments. If a great book be a great evil, many little ones are, alas! profound calamities; for impressions of satire, ridicule, and ill-nature, or of disgust, frivolity and levity are made, that can never be erased, and which are the origin of every species of wickedness and the source of every woe.

Many prose fictions are as faulty as those in rhyme.

rhyme. It would be an endless task to give specimens of all. The celebrated " *Tales of the Hermitage*," (already alluded to) translated into Italian, by V. Peretti, are, I think, in this number. Every tale is a little novel in its names, descriptions, incidents, language. One is partly founded upon the worn-out subject of an illegitimate child being found in a basket, and brought up by a lady : the real mother, however, appears and gives her story, and dies, as usual. She was a Chinese, whose beauty had attracted an English sailor, who persuaded her to put on a man's dress, and come with him to England. She accordingly accompanied him, " and the unfortunate girl quitted her country, home, and friends, for an ungrateful and abandonned seducer, who soon after the ship was paid off, entered on board another bound for the East Indies, leaving her," &c. &c.

" *The Looking Glass*" is a book much used by children. In it are several exceptionable stories. In that called William and Amelia, there is a succession of fraud and coquettry the most striking. William is an orphan in the house of Amelia's father. They are both children, but are described as lovers. The boy affronts the young lady by giving a fine apple to a female friend of hers. Amelia is in a high jealous fit, and commands him to leave her in disdain ; nor will she forgive him until he begs pardon on his knees.

The

The hero refuses, piqued in his turn; but, after various manœuvres and deceitful tricks, he offers her a fine peach, falls on his knee in the arbour where she is reclined; and she bids him rise; when he assures her she is mistaken in supposing he loves another better than herself, &c. &c.

But I hasten to quit the subject. Willingly would I have resigned it to other hands—yet it was a duty. Parents, governesses, henceforth tremble to give a book, a leaf, a line to your children, your pupils, without having yourselves examined its sentiments, its moral, and its language.

CHAPTER XI.

LIST OF STUDIES.

THESE are arranged for three young persons, being a difficult number for one governess. As I must make a distinction, I shall suppose Ellen sixteen years of age, and Ann fifteen; these two may follow nearly the same course of study: the youngest, Susan, has a separate list, as she is but ten years. By these I propose to clear up any confusion of ages and particular system that may have appeared.

To

To be in the study by seven o'clock.

To half past seven;

Scripture reading ....ten minutes.

Preludes, Ellen ....ten minutes.

Preludes, Ann ....ten minutes.

to eight;

Ellen has her lesson from the } half an hour.
preceptress (new lesson) .... }

to half past eight;

Ann has her new lesson.......half an hour.

N. B.   Whilst one is at the piano-forte the other is getting her exercises on the slate, or her lessons.

Susan is preparing her lessons, and slate exercise, &c. &c.

to nine;

The governess hears lessons, or } half an hour.
corrects the exercises .... }

to ten;

Breakfast and recreation ......one hour.

to eleven;

Ellen practises her old lessons
on the piano, taking every one
by turns as it is marked on the } one hour.
card......................

Ann writes in her copy-book whatever has been corrected on the slate, and finishes other little exercises that are marked.

Susan reads English and French with the maps, and translates with her governess.

to twelve;

Ann practises her pieces on } one hour.
the piano .... }

Ellen writes from her slate into her copy-book and finishes any other exercise.

Susan may run about a little for recreation.

Ellen

Ellen and Ann read English (three quarters) and French (one quarter) together, with maps .... } one hour.

Drawing or dancing for Ellen and Ann.

Susan has her lesson of music from the governess, who divides her time with her and her sisters } one hour.

Dinner, recreation, or needle work, according to the family arrangement' .... } one hour.

Walk, Gaultier's Game, or recreation .... } three hours.

Monday—(Ellen and Ann).

Scripture reading, one chapter.
Preludes.

Exercises of music (on time) one line.
English exercises (Murray) half a page.
Translation (English to French) a page.

Lessons.
French dialogues.
Geography.
English orthography.
English grammar.

Reading.

Weekly.

Reading.

Geography with maps, three quarters of an hour.
French, one quarter of an hour.
Music lesson, half an hour.
Practice, one hour.
Drawing, one hour.

Tuesday.

Scripture reading (one chapter).
Preludes.

Theme writing, &c. (English composition).
Historical writing (one page).
Parsing (half a page.)

Lessons.

French vocabulary.
French verbs.
French grammar.

Reading.

History (maps), three quarters of an hour.
French, quarter of an hour.

Music lesson, half an hour.
Practice, one hour.

N. B. The theme is difficult to do: I have not given an equivalent for drawing on this day.

Wednesday.

Wednesday.

Scripture reading.
Preludes.

Geographical tour, two pages.
French grammatical exercises, half a page.

Lessons.
Geography.
French poetry.
Orthography.
French dialogues.

Reading.

History, three quarters of an hour.
French, quarter of an hour.

Music lesson, half an hour.
Practice, one hour.
Drawing, one hour.

Thursday.

Scripture reading.
Preludes.

French grammatical exercises, half a page.
English or French letter (alternate weeks).
Synonimising (six or eight lines).

Lessons.

Weekly.

Lessons.

Mrs. Trimmer's historical abridgments.
Ten or twelve lines of a celebrated oration to teach pronunciation.
English grammar.

Reading.

Biography, miscellany, or periodical paper.
Italian reading.

Music lesson, half an hour.

Practice, one hour.

On this day the pupils read separately. The studies are easy to give opportunity for the attendance of a master, or for cyphering.

Friday.

Scripture reading.
Preludes.

Translation, French to English, one page.
Translation, Italian, one page.
Thorough bass writing, one line.
Terrestrial globe.

Lessons.

Weekly.

Le sons.
Italian verbs.
Italian grammar.
Italian dialogues.
Italian vocabulary.

Reading.

Poetry (with Mythological Dictionary, separately).

French.

Music lesson, half an hour.
Practise, one hour.
Singing, one hour.

————————

Saturday.

Scripture reading.
Preludes.

Extracts, two pages.
Sous dicté, ten lines.
Celestial globe.

Lessons.
English poetry.
Watts's Scripture
Questions.
Arithmetical tables.
French verbs.

Reading.

Reading.

History.

Astronomy, or the wonders of nature and art.

Music lesson, half an hour.

Practise, one hour. Duets.

Drawing, one hour.

Sunday.

Scripture reading.

Verses (two or three), or collect.

Text writing (from the sermon).

Church catechism.

Two or three pages of sacred history (to read).

Such are the weekly studies of my own pupils. They have a copy of this list, and so clear is every different duty in their minds, that they are never, by any chance, at a loss. Every thing is finished by three o'clock; the books, maps, &c. in order, and the study completely arranged. Every pupil has plenty to attend to, and yet not too much. Whatever it may be, she is expected to do her best; and she well knows that the more pains she takes the sooner she will finish her occupation, and more certain will be her enjoyments afterwards.

Little Susan must have a list also, for we cannot give her the studies that her sisters have.

Monday

Weekly.

Monday.

Scripture reading.
Preludes.

French exercises, three lines.
Exercise, music.
Music lesson.
Writing.

Reading.

History, with maps.
French and translation.

Lessons. Geography. English spelling from an easy reading book.

Tuesday.

Scripture reading.
Preludes.

Reading music, one line.
Writing exercise.
Music lesson.
Parsing, (from Barbauld.)

Reading.

Geography, with maps.
French and translation.

Les. Vocabulary. French erbs. English spelling.

Wednesday.

Scripture reading.
Preludes.

French

Weekly.

French translation (fable), four lines.

Cyphering.
Music lesson.
Exercise of music.

Reading.

History, with maps.
French and translation.

Lessons.
French dialogues.
English grammar.
Vocabulary

Thursday.

Scripture reading.
Preludes.

Writing.
Cyphering.
Music lesson.
French exercise.

Reading.

Geography, with maps.
French and translation.

Lessons.
Geography.
French &c.
English spelling.

Friday.

Scripture reading,
Preludes.

Music lesson.
Exercise writing.
Reading music.
Globe.

Lessons.
French dialogues.
English grammar.
English spelli &c.

Reading.

Reading.

History, with maps.
French and translation.

――――

Saturday.

Scripture reading.
Preludes.

Music lesson.
Translation.
Parsing.
Globe, celestial (names).

Reading.

Poetry.
Useful arts and sciences, as Mrs. Trimmer's
Introduction, &c.

Lessons. | Poetry or oration a few lines). Geography. French spelling. Tables.

――――

Sunday is the same as for the elders.

――――

N   CHAPTER

CHAPTER XII.

ADDRESS TO YOUNG LADIES BETWEEN THE AGES OF SIXTEEN AND TWENTY.

Dear Girls,

Permit me, with the zeal of an affectionate friend and the truth of a faithful guardian, to hold an unreserved conference with you. I will not long detain you; I ask but half an hour; then return to the innocent pursuits of your happy age.

Lovely beings, designed for immortality ! little perhaps, do you reflect how soon, how very soon, that rosy and dimpled cheek will fade, that sparkling eye grow dim, and those tender and flexible limbs be clogged with infirmity : yet it must be so.

Look not sad. Why should you fear? Are you not young? Surely then you are innocent! 'Tis only for the guilty to tremble : for those who lead unprincipled lives; who break the commands of the Almighty; who strive not to please him. These only need shudder at the separation of the soul from the body.

Be you cheerful then : I would not depress

the

the charming sprightliness of your age. Think
me not a gloomy person too advanced in life to
remember the gaiety of youth; so far from it,
scarcely five years more have passed over my
head than have gone by the eldest amongst you :
but shall I say too, that during ten years I have
made it my study and my pleasure to instruct the
young? Shall I .... No; I will add
nothing to influence your minds. Judge me by
my sentiments. See whether in telling you what
little imperfections you should avoid, to be ad-
mired, loved, respected, to be really happy; see
whether I tell you true.—I will stand acquitted
or condemned by your own hearts and the voice
that whispers and colours the cheek of every one
amongst you.

My design is to treat of points connected with
female character—I mean particularly with that
of the young.

I shall divide character into two parts; prin-
ciples and manners. A principle is, I apprehend,
a strong and fixed determination to do whatever
is right; which is so firmly established in our
minds, that we need not wait one moment to
decide whether we ought to injure ourselves
and do right, or to enrich or gratify ourselves,
and commit a wrong act. If we can hesitate in
such a cause, we have not steady or good prin-
ciples.

Character.
Principles.

By

Manners.   By manners I mean the influence of these principles upon the action and language. Thus, to explain myself better, I may say, the principles are the strong roots of a tree; the actions are the trunk and branches, for they are even nearer to principles than language; finally, the millions of leaves fluttering on all sides, are the words we utter, which are of different sizes, tints, ages, and value.

But the manners I wish to make my consideration, as I have elsewhere noticed principles. Suffer me then to lead your attention to these, and we may together be enabled to relieve many a beautiful tree of leaves that are blighted, misshapen, or withered.

I shall treat my subject in six divisions. The manners of young ladies

In the study;

In the park, or street;

In the drawing room, and at meals;

In public, including visiting;

In the church;

In the drawing room and chamber.

I. *In the Study.*

No. 1. Study.   The study is the chief residence of pupil and preceptress. Some of you have resigned this part of the house to your younger sisters; others have

have still one or two years to fulfil its duties and conform to its rules. Perhaps you are wishing for the time to be elapsed. Believe me these are not the least happy of your days. You shake your heads, and smile in unbelief. Well, I am silent : you shall judge.

Now let us consider the duties of the study, and permit me to mention a few errors committed by some young ladies ; after which you shall ask your own ingenuous feelings, whether you have not at any time fallen, from thoughtfulness or caprice, into the same improprieties. If you have, I will forgive you ; I promise you the pardon of your kind and affectionate governess ; she will fold you to her bosom, and you shall tell her you will offend, you will pain her no more. For many and severe, perhaps, have been her trials. She has not, you know, many enjoyments. See how she is separated from her friends. Have any of you been sent from father, mother, sisters, home, and been surrounded by strangers ? Did you not feel very sorrowful; although you were making a visit, and expected to return soon ? Now your governess is, perhaps, many miles from her home, and has no hope of seeing her friends for months, or even years. She was a stranger to you all ; and you to her ; yet she attached herself to you, and turned all her wishes and thoughts towards your improve-

ment,

Manners.
Study.

The obliga-
tions of pupil
and precep-
tress are mu-
tual.

ment, happiness and welfare. All the day she
is considering how she can be of service to you;
and how she may best teach you to be wise and
good. Surely for all this you make a return of
attention, obedience and affection? Surely you
are anxious to do all she wishes you; and you
try, by every little kindness, to make her happy?
Indeed this is a duty particularly incumbent
on you. I knew several young women who
have been educated by a governess, who are
now from misfortunes obliged to be one them-
selves. I do not mean to say, that they lost their
fortune from their unkind behaviour; it pleased
God to take riches from them, either as a rebuke
to one, or a trial to all. Let us not then incur
His displeasure in any way, for fear of meeting
with a severer punishment than loss of property,
for with Him nothing is impossible.

Yet how naughty in this respect have I seen
some children; and, I think, particularly so at
their studies. You say, that is a difficult task?
—It is so. I know it is very hard work; and very
trying to the patience too; to toil or persevere,
during several hours, at studies which we can-
not understand; but we know that every thing
has an end, and an end there will be to our ig-
norance, it is to be hoped, some day or other.
Then what pleasure, what satisfaction! to under-
stand this or that, so as to find entertainment

                                                    from

from it. No more close study in dictionaries;
no copy-writing, no verb conjugating: all is
smooth and pleasant. We can take up a foreign
book and read, or we can open a music book and
play, &c. Is not this agreeable? Indeed I think
so, and certainly worth a little attention. And,
in truth, when we come to consider the matter
further, you may be well satisfied with your lot.
Let us look around us in every state. The King:
How are we taught by history, that those kings
are most happy in the government of the people
entrusted to their care, who have had the best
and wisest education. Kings must have then an
infinity of study; nobles, who are to be the ser-
vants and advisers of monarchs, are also obliged
to study hard; gentlemen also have a share in
the administration, either largely in senate or
office, or locally in the magistracy or corpora-
tion; tradesmen must work hard during an ap-
prenticeship of seven years, before they are con-
sidered capable of undertaking a business; and
a peasant's life is one continued round of activity
and labour. The females of the different ranks
are also obliged to be employed: no one is sent
into the world to be idle; every one has his task,
and a very pleasant one I think yours, to learn of
history, morality, every thing that can make you
good and charming women.

Now when a governess is endeavouring to give
this instruction to her pupil, and is anxiously ex-

N 4
plaining

Manners.

Study.

1. It is very disrespectful to shew weariness or other mark of inattention whilst any one is speaking.

plaining some point, is it not very provoking to see the young lady open her mouth, rub her eyes and yawn, as much as to say, " I don't wish to hear it," or walk away before she has heard all that is said, or look impatient, or else, just as the governess begins, say, " Oh yes, I know." Supposing even she do know, can it hurt her to hear it again? May she not find the circumstances differently and more clearly stated, and perhaps be entertained by some other observation quite new to her? There is a rudeness in this behaviour so extremely disgusting to an instructress, that, if it is often repeated, she cannot help feeling less and less of interest in her pupil's improvement; whereas the child who listens to her, and is grateful for attentions, shewing a desire to be taught, asking questions, and waiting for the answers, is certain of being in the end most loved and attended to, as she certainly will be the most clever.

2. Submission to reproof is also requisite.

But it is not enough to be obedient to instruction, girls must be submissive to reproof. They are young and giddy, and require the observance of some judicious person to turn them gently aside from numberless errors, and to lead them to the path of goodness and the graces. Young people have no idea of the dangers into which their inexperience might lead them; and when once we have quitted the right path, who can tell what may not be our danger? Besides, if they will

will not listen to admonition from teachers, nei-
ther will they to that of the parent who places
the teacher over the child; and if the parent be
neglected, we well know that neither the pulpit
nor commandments will avail any thing, so close-
ly is one duty attached to another. The young
lady who can resent the mild expostulation of her
governess by a haughty toss of the head, a pert
answer, a retreat from the room, slamming the
door after her, or by a sullen silence, is weaken-
ing the regard of a faithful friend, and preparing
inexpressible vexation to herself and family, from
her self-willed perverse temper, to say nothing of
the level on which she places herself by her lan-
guage and conduct, possibly below every servant
in her father's house. But, by way of excusing
herself, she says to any one who will listen to
her complaints, "My governess is so cross!"
Now let us imagine that she even was reproved
hastily, are no allowances to be made for a per-
son whose temper is tried from morning till
night, from week to month, and from year to
year? Has not this person to watch over one,
two or three children of different ages; to teach
them many things which they do not understand;
to hear them lessons which they scarcely learn;
to give them advice which they often disregard;
to tell them of matters which they immediately
forget; to remind them of duties which they
hardly hear; to shew them things which they

scarcely see? Has she not in the study at the
same time perhaps the forgetful, the perverse,
the giddy, the stupid, the peevish, the idle?
Indeed she might have all these in one child,
(though I hope such a subject is not very com-
mon,) yet she might have, and I am sure with
such a pupil and everlasting companion we need
not wonder if she were to be a little hasty; and
in such a case does a young lady make her more
comfortable; does she soothe her care and soften
her anxiety by sharply or improperly replying?
—No, indeed: but mild behaviour and gentle re-
spect would do so instantly. " I am very sorry,
I know it was wrong; I will endeavour to be
more careful;" or something of this kind has
an instantaneous effect in disarming anger.
There is something inexpressibly lovely in the
dear girl's disposition who can thus own herself
in the wrong, and be desirous of putting an end
at once to our uneasiness. So true is the saying
of Solomon, that " A soft answer turneth away
wrath." I am supposing, however, all this time
that the governess really is somewhat " cross;"
but it is only for argument's sake, for indeed I
have heard children call many a person " cross"
who have been a little grave, and some even that
were in the height of pleasantry and good hu-
mour.

There is another thing very tiresome to a go-
verness. I cannot call it a reproof, but a simple
command,

command, entirely for the advantage of the pupil, but which is often disobeyed. I mean relating to little habits. " Hold up your head, my dear; sit straight; turn out your feet; take your elbows from the table ; do not put your fingers in your mouth; or cross your feet," &c. All these have to be mentioned, perhaps twenty times in an hour, and are instantly forgotten. Surely young people should reflect upon the figure they will make in society, if they grow up with every awkwardness which their governess labours so hard to correct in them. A man, or woman, who has contracted any extraordinary or ill-bred habit, is immediately noticed for it on his, or her, entrance into life; and the many accomplishments they possess are not sufficient always to make the world insensible to their failings. I think it a pity, but so it is; and youth should be, therefore, greatly obliged to any person who will prevent any unpleasing habits from taking root in them; for some years hence no person will take the liberty or trouble of reminding them of faults, and they will be laughed at without knowing for why. Some girls are kicking off their shoes at the piano forte; playing with a bit of string whilst they say their lessons; or biting their nails as they learn them; with many more habits equally silly or bad. I knew a young woman who could never read without wetting her finger and rubbing it up and down on the margin of the

N 6   leaf;

leaf; she was fond of taking beautiful books from her father's magnificent library, and owing to this disagreeable habit, the finest and most valuable works were often rubbed into holes down the sides, and completely disfigured; yet she was unconscious of what she was doing. Every body knows the story of the gentleman, who, whilst he was publicly speaking, twisted a bit of packthread round his finger; if he dropped it he was silent, he could not utter another word; and of my own knowledge I may mention three gentlemen of family, fortune and education, who have all an unfortunate trick, whilst they are speaking: one says, when he meets a friend, " how do you do? What? what? Very fine weather. What? what?" Yet, I dare say, he knows not that he has the custom of saying this word at the end of every sentence. Ill habits are very soon acquired; and, if the friends and teachers are not very vigilant, young people copy or get them, and keep them during life.

The manner of expressing yourselves should be also particularly attended to as well as your pronunciation. How would it sound at your own table if you should say, " Will you take a little *air?*" for hare. " Do you ride on *orseback?*" for horseback. Very flagrant breaches of grammar you will not make, yet I have heard young ladies extremely well versed in grammar, say, for want of being admonished, " It was *me*," for I. "You

and

and *me* did that;" " *Him* and *us* went together,"
instead of " You and I;" " He and we," &c.
A very little observation would completely fix a
good habit of expressing your thoughts, and it is
surely worth while to feel at ease when we speak
in company. Now that I am upon the subject of
bad habits, let me advise you never to descend
to a mysterious secret behaviour that I have ob-
served in some young ladies. At first they do
not mean any thing, perhaps; but in time they
contract a thoughtful, significant, mysterious
manner, that is the very reverse of what should be
expected from the young, who are always sup-
posed to be artless, ingenuous and innocent. If
the servant brings in a note or letter, there is a
whisper concerning the person that left it; the
young heads are put together, and the paper is
scrambled into the pocket. The governess turns
round : " What are you doing?"—" Nothing" is
the immediate answer. " What are you talking
about ?"—" Nothing," all answer at once.—
" Why, have you not something from the ser-
vant?"—" Oh, it is nothing, but a note."
The governess replies, " then a note is some-
thing; why did you not say so at once, that the
servant brought you a note?" No more is said;
nods, winks and whispers go round, whilst the
foolish children think they are very like grown-
up ladies, I suppose; although they are like ill-
bred and ungrateful pupils. What secrets (I de-
test

Manners.
Study.

5. Whisper-
ing.

Manners.
Study.

test the very word), what secrets can girls have with girls? It must be something very discreditable if the preceptress and kind adviser may not be acquainted with it: but in truth it is not so: an invitation to tea, or a message about a doll, is often important enough to turn into a mystery; and these girls think themselves very clever if they can so manage it. But let me tell them this uncandid and reserved manner is very ill calculated to gain the tender confidence and interest of their preceptress. If they wish her to love them, they must be open, sincere, and frank; they must give their confidence, and she will treat them not as children, but as companions and dear friends. Besides, what unhappiness may they not be saved by an unreserved communication with the parent and instructress!

6. Neatness
indispensa-
ble.

I have a word or two more respecting manners in the study, and shall then finish. I am always extremely pleased to see this room in nice order, because we are led to think, that, where there is regularity in one respect there may be in all. In the very hours of study many books and slates, &c. are scattered over the tables, a little confusion there will be; but, immediately after things are done with, they should be put in order with expedition and cheerfulness; and if there is, as there ought to be, a place for every one, the room may be very soon cleared. Some girls take turns for this employment; but the better

way

way is to let her who may have finished first clear away.

Be good, and be attentive and industrious then in the study; and remember one thing which Mr. Walker says, " That the influence of a good education is so strong upon the countenance that it compensates for want of beauty: it gives sweetness, elegance, intelligence to the countenance, and a dignity to the expression that without it can never be acquired."

Be respectful and obedient to your governess; you will thereby gain her affection and zeal; and you will be admired by your acquaintances for the good understanding that subsists between you. Where there is a mutual regard there must surely be some merit and endearing quality on both sides.

II. *In the Park or Street.*

When the hour of recreation comes the preceptress gives the signal, and you prepare for a walk. Now I think ten minutes, at most, a very handsome allowance for putting on a spencer, tying a bonnet, and clasping the strong shoes; yet many young ladies do not scruple to waste twice that time in getting themselves ready, whilst their governess is waiting for them. This is a sad loitering custom to acquire; it is as easy to do a thing with alacrity, if we so habituate ourselves,

Manners. Study.

Mutual affection always supposes merit on both sides.

Error 1. Wasting time in dress.

Manners.
Park, &c.
ourselves, as to be slow; and it makes a vast
difference in the course of the week. At last,
however, after having been hastened by one or
two messages, the hall door is opened, and the
whole party imbibes with joy the pure and re-
freshing breath of heaven.

When I meet a group of this kind, I always
observe how it is disposed. Girls who love their
governess claim each an arm, and lock their
own within hers, whilst all chat familiarly toge-
ther; such are conversing, probably, on little
innocent, cheerful, or instructive matters.—The
2. Style of
walking.
next party is perhaps different. The young la-
dies have sometimes their arm within that of the
governess; sometimes, as the whim seizes them,
they walk coldly by her side. They see a friend,
stop, brighten up, express much pleasure in the
meeting, shake hands affectionately, and part.
Now the humour changes: they seize each an
arm of their governess, and begin with " What
a frightful bonnet Miss or Lady —— wears!
She is a very awkward girl; I wonder where
she is going to, dressed in such a way, &c. &c."
The preceptress makes an observation in favour
of the acquaintance; the young ladies are dis-
pleased, and withdraw their hands again.—In
the third party, the young ladies walk arm in
arm before the preceptress, and leave her to fol-
low them.

Happy

Happy and charming girls of the first, long
may you, by the amiable docility and gratitude
of your affectionate hearts, delight your precep-
tress, and gain the regard of all who know you.
Go on through your bright career. Examine all
that is lovely in nature; notice all that may be
curious in art. Enjoy the sprightliness, the
gaiety, the freedom of youth, yet be ever ready
to listen with respect to the prudence, the saga-
city, the temperance of age.—For the young la-
dies of the third-party I blush. Let me hasten
to consider those of the second. I am afraid
these are rather frivolously disposed. A very
little matter will win their affections, so a very
trifling one will lower the friend in their estima-
tion. They are very fond of noticing every thing
that is worn by persons of their own and other
families, and are sure to observe when such and
such acquaintance have new bonnets, new pe-
lisses, and new frocks. If they meet a friend
very fashionably dressed, they run, and leave
the governess standing alone, in their haste to
salute her; if she be shabby, they are satisfied
with a nod, and " How d'ye do?"

This unaccountable determination of many
young persons to regulate their respect and af-
fection by the dress or appearance of others, de-
serves a particular consideration and caution.
It is a dangerous propensity, and argues a very
weak mind; nay, I had almost said an ill-na-
                                    tured

(margin notes) Manners. Park, &c: 3. Judging too hastily by dress or appearance.

tured one. It however proceeds, sometimes, from thoughtlessness; and where this is really the case, a hint of the impropriety may be sufficient. For the use of such young ladies, I have obtained a copy of a letter written by a governess, whom I very well know. It seems she observed a disposition of this kind in her own pupils towards herself, and thereupon addressed them as follows:—

" MY DEAR CHILDREN,

" As the events of to-day's walk have
" produced on my mind a train of ideas, I can-
" not be satisfied until I have laid them before
" you, especially as I foresee consequences which
" render my subject the more necessary.

" It is not without infinite pain I however ob-
" serve, that I find you consider yourselves at
" liberty to criticise, and perhaps ridicule, the
" dress of that person, who is making it the
" ambition of her wishes to form the hearts and
" minds of her pupils to every thing that will
" render them most engaging, amiable, and
" happy.

" In doing this, you are not perhaps aware
" how greatly you lower yourselves. I hope,
" when you permit yourselves to be guided by
" the colour of a pelisse—of a shawl—of the form
" of a cap—of the length of a gown, &c. I trust
" at such a time you are influenced by the whim
" of

of the moment. This, at best, is caprice. If
I do not pronounce it to be so, I must call it
by the harsher title of illiberality and little-
ness of mind, to which I hope you are stran-
gers.

" Now suppose a person were really to dress
' most ridiculously. Do you think that any
' rude criticism of yours, and particularly im-
' mediately before his face, would produce an
' alteration? do you not rather imagine that he
' would feel nothing but indignation, and sup-
' pose himself insulted? Besides, do you con-
' sider your own taste the standard of propriety?
' May not any one differ from you in opinion?
' A person who makes a fool of himself by his
' fantastic appearance, will neither care for pity
' nor reproach; for if he is his own master he
' feels his right to act as he pleases, and will do
' so, if he live not in a country where the co-
' lour and other matters in dress are not
' regulated by the laws, as they are in China.
' What is the good you think to offer me, in
' marking your disapprobation of my dress?
' None. Long have I been my own mistress
' in this respect, and accountable to no one.
' You cannot imagine that I shall alter my
' plans now, and refer to you for the dress I
' am to wear.

" In short, dress is the last thing by which we
" are to judge of a person. *Neatness and nicety*
" are

" are desirable in all stations, and elegance in
" some; but all who are neat are not good, and
" we well know that all who are untidy or ec-
" centric in their dress are not bad characters:
" so as there is no possibility of determining by
" dress, let us only consider our own in mode-
" ration, and leave others to judge and act ac-
" cording to their choice. Conversation is in-
" deed frivolous when it turns upon such trifles,
" and it may be ill-natured, when it is connected
" with the persons themselves. You should
" look to the mind, the virtues, the disposition.
" These are what my eye is bent upon in you;
" even for accomplishments I care nothing, when
" put in competition with the heart. What will
" signify all the learning in the world, if you
" are wanting in generosity, in kindness, in
" good-nature? Besides, believe me, a satirical
" person is never loved. You may attract at-
" tention, you may be laughed at; but if you
" allow this odious habit to strengthen, you will
" not gain one real friend: all your acquaint-
" ances will say when they quit you, "my turn
" will come next," for why should one be spared
" more than another? If then the Almighty,
" who never regards features nor dress, has
" given you amiable dispositions, do not tarnish
" them by this ungrateful and unfriendly pro-
" pensity; for, by degrees, no tie will be too
" sacred for your raillery.

" As

" As for myself, you well know that my si-
" tuation in life does not require me to be dressed
" in embroideries, &c. If I were a lady of
" rank, paying visits and giving audience, I
" might dress in an expensive manner; but as I
" am simply engaged in the education of youth,
" my time is wholly passed in a study, amongst
" books, pens, and ink, my mornings entirely
" dedicated to my pupils, and my evenings chief-
" ly to myself, I consider it unnecessary and un-
" profitable to waste money (which my young
" friends, I should think, would rather wish me
" to save, that I might enjoy it after the fatigues
" of my profession are over). Besides, as every
" one has a different fancy, I might not be able
" even if I tried, to please all, therefore I dress
" to please myself, (I hope not inconsistently
" with my station in life); and as I do not know
" who should control me in this respect, I shall
" continue to do so.

" I have written this letter in haste, and part-
" ly in the dusk. I hope it will make the im-
" pression I wish. My desire is to see you rise
" superior to the trifling part of your sex, and,
" above all, to those who are pleased only in
" finding fault with others."

This remonstrance, I dare say, had great
weight with the young ladies, who I understood
were well disposed, but, as it must appear,
thoughtless, even to disrespect.

In

In the streets of a town, young women of all ranks cannot be too particular in their deportment. Loud talking, laughing, stopping to look at shops, gazing after people, staring at passing carriages; all these are improper. There is a modest dignity which is the only kind of manner to acquire and maintain; if a female walk with a friend in a street, she may talk little and softly, yet it is better to be reserved. We can say at home all we wish.

Even in her own carriage, a young lady should be reserved, her attitude always modest, easy and unaffected. How ill it looks to see young ladies in an open landau, laughing violently, throwing themselves backwards, or turning on one side, pointing to any one passing, or talking with vehemence amongst themselves. May this never be your case. May no eye gaze with surprise upon you, and then glance upon the armorial bearings and liveries, to set a mark upon you to the discredit of yourselves and family. Rather, may every eye behold you with respect, and every tongue mention you with honour.

III. *In the Drawing-Room, and at Meals:*

Released from the labour of the day, you hasten with light hearts to the drawing-room. There you meet your parents; happy girls who

possess

possess such treasures; and you who do not, have still a kind relative, or guardian, to whom you owe the overflowings of your grateful and tender hearts.

But how shall I open my subject? How shall I lead your young minds to the touching considerations of filial duty? How shall I be able to particularise one, when all are so numerous yet delicate, so closely linked and so endearing?

The father who clasps your hand in his, and looks up to heaven with a moistened eye, to beg a blessing upon you; the mother who leans over him to press you to her fond heart, and gazes with delight upon every feature of your innocent countenance, that offers the softened image of the faithful companion and husband of her youth. These, my engaging friends, are the objects for your early hopes, and tenderest concern. How tender have they been of you! Who but parents would have shewn such lively joy on your birth? Who would have endured like them the anxieties, the fatigues, the uneasiness, the sleepless nights, the watchings of your infant days. Who besides, would have trembled for every pallid tint of your little cheek, and have been fluttering in joy for every symptom of health and vivacity? Whose hearts, besides their's, throbbed in a tumult of hope at the bright promise of your opening faculties? Who has for so many years deprived himself of pleasures

sures

sures for your sake, and of conveniences for your
comfort; or whose purse besides that of your fa-
ther, is open to all your wants, wishes, advan-
tage, and even superfluities? Who but your
parents look upon the innocent beauty of your
forming stature, and pray with earnest solicitude,
that the God who made you so lovely, will enno-
ble you in virtue, and smile on you hereafter in
immortal bliss? But I should never finish were
I to enumerate, or rather try to enumerate,
the obligations you are under to the authors of
your existence. Be then obedient, be dutiful, be
kind, be virtuous, be good; you will raise them
to the utmost pinnacle of human felicity, and
make their aged hearts to beat with joy.

These are the dear friends whom you visit im-
mediately after your studies are finished. I con-
clude you take meals with them when there are
no strangers; consequently, dress yourselves
neatly to appear in the dining-room, as they
would wish you, and as becomes your age and
quality. Your parents give you the history of
the morning. Such and such persons have called,
and have given interesting news of a friend, or
relation, observes your mama. Your father tells
you what people he met in his walks, whom you
know; of the kind inquiries they made after his
family. If he is of the Lords or Commons House
of Parliament, or in an official situation, he tells
you with the sparkling eye of independence, and
the

the noble grandeur of a man who breathes but
for his king, his laws, and his beloved country,
that our brave countrymen have bled in our de-
fence, and are blushing under laurels and victory.
He gives you the Extraordinary Gazette that
you may have the pleasure of reading what it
contains; or he tells you of the interesting speech
of your Sovereign from his throne, that your
young heart may be animated with loyalty in
hearing of his solicitude for his people's welfare;
for however improper it may be in a young lady
to express political opinions in public, and to
join in controversy, yet every female should be
encouraged in a generous glory of the happiness
and honour of her country. And of what a
country am I now speaking! Oh! England,
England, loveliest of empires, fairest of queens,
sister of grace and virtue, parent of science, and
guardian of the arts; long mayest thou be loved
by men, emulated by monarchs, and cherished
by thy God!

Pardon this digression. I cannot speak un-
moved of my country; the subject is far too in-
teresting to pass it over without one humble
offering to its merit.

These conversations at last cease: you are re-
quested, with a smile, to shew any little per-
formance of the morning. You accordingly leave
the room to collect drawings, translations, com-
positions, &c. and you return with them. The

o

parents

parents examine by turns: with a blush of plea-
sure your mother says, " extremely well, es-
pecially in this part." Your father looks at that
part, smiles, pats your shoulder, and says,
" Go on, child, and improve." Now, my charm-
ing friends, this is the critical moment. Did you
write *that* part; did you compose or translate it
yourself, without assistance? I see the flush of
virtue colouring that fair forehead, she is re-
minding you of duty, of honour, of principle,
of justice. Be generous, speak. Do you de-

1. I et us re-
ject with ho-
nest contempt
the praise we
do not de-
serve.

serve that praise? No. " Mama, dear father,
I did not that; my governess, or my master,
helped me there." " Oh child of my affection,"
exclaims your father, " justly I may glory in
thy virtue. The writer of that line, and the
painter of that head, deserve our praise; but
the beauty of thy virtuous act, commands our
love and our esteem; happy we with such a child,
happy child with such principles!"

But I ask again. " Did you that part?"
" Yes." Enjoy then the praise you have earn-
ed; it is your due. Consider now the satisfac-
tion of your mind; see the fruits of attention
and perseverance: go on then and prosper.

. The dinner is not yet ready. You will not
surely sit idle. Have you no little employment?
netting, sewing of muslin, or any light work,
or fancy-stitch? No lady should be unhandy
with her needle. " Oh," you say, " dinner
                                              will

will be ready in ten minutes, it is not worth while to take out my work." I answer, indeed it is. That " not being worth while," has often made an idle person. Your cooks may not be punctual to the minute, and you may have fifteen instead of ten; but allowing only the last mentioned, what may not be done in the sixth part of an hour? A heathen philosopher has said, that we all complain of the shortness of time, yet we do not know how to employ half of our portion. I think it should rather seem, that we will not employ it, for we all know of things that ought to be done, but we are not in the humour, or, as we please to express it, " it is not worth while" to do them: consequently many an hour is wasted.

At last, the butler announces the dinner. You rise, I suppose, and wait till your parents and governess have passed. You follow to the dining-room, and take your seat at the table. The master of the house, or chaplain, repeats a few words of thanks to the Almighty, who has provided so bounteously, the family bow with grateful humility as he finishes, and then cheerfully prepare to partake of the repast.

At meals, young people should be careful to accustom themselves to every delicacy of behaviour. There is nothing graceful in eating, and it is possible to give extreme offence to a neighbour, by awkward, or incorrect habits.

Drawing-room.

2. Never to allow of the expression " not worth while."

3. At meals.

o 2 Making

Manners
Drawing-
room.

Making the elbows square; holding the bones with the finger; making a noise in eating; not wiping the mouth after drinking; picking the teeth; making a noise with the finger glasses,— many others which are troublesome or indelicate in a young lady. The great point is to be correct in private, that we may not find ourselves uneasy upon other occasions.

At these private dinners it sometimes happens that your father has introduced a person whom he wishes to honour, and whom he esteems. This person has abilities; he has merit; but 4. Kind attention to inferiors. rank or fortune he has none. By chance, or by the kind nod of your parent, this person is placed next to you. What is your conduct towards him? Are you anxious to relieve his little embarrassment? Do you speak with becoming simplicity and propriety upon some general topic that will induce him to feel ease in your generous goodnature? Do you offer to serve him to the dish before you? Amiable girl, your kindness shall not be forgotten.

The cloth is withdrawn. Conversation is familiar: you are sparkling in vivacity and health: your parents listen with pleasure to your remarks: but remember, that a piece of wit may pain a hearer. Reflect well upon the subject 5. When the heart is light we should be careful not to be brilliant at the expense of good-nature. you mention, and if you know it, never introduce one that can be disagreeable to the feelings of those around you. Do not speak ill of the absent,

absent, especially if you call them *friends*. Mi-
micry is a most dangerous talent. People laugh
at a mimic, but he is always dreaded as an ill-
natured person, or at least as a satirical one.

In the height of your charming spirit, some-
thing is said by a parent or the preceptress, that
displeases you. You are offended: nay, be not
so: nothing unkind was meant, why should you
be so very particular? Are you sure that you
never utter a word which differs from the opinion
of others? This is scarcely possible, therefore
be not hasty to suppose offence offered, when, in
reality, none is meant. Surely you did not push
your chair further, by way of discovering your
vexation: how simple!

I do not like to hear young ladies use set phrases:
—" I am giving you an infinity of trouble," or,
" I am going to ask you a very impertinent ques-
tion," &c. These are accompanied with a smile
of self complacency, and always put one in
mind of the French proverb: " we blame our-
selves but to gain praise." If the question be
really impertinent, why is it asked? and if it be
not impertinent, why say so? I know a lady
who often calls herself Dame Blunt, as an ex-
cuse for any little indecorum; but surely, a rude
thing is not to be made pleasant, by this manner
of apology, or self blame.

In the evening, you are generally desired by
your mama to play or sing; and any wish of

her's

her's· is no doubt immediately, and cheerfully complied with.· This is one end of your· accomplishments.   The amusement of yourself and friends.   May the graces and the virtues put the last finish to your education.! ·

IV. *In Public, including Visiting.*

Young ladies just quitting the study, and introduced at once to balls, parties, or exhibitions, are the objects of my present. solicitude.· ·

I have hitherto pointed out matters of caution : let me have now the inexpressible pleasure of opening my subject with a description of manners worthy of imitation.

The generous girl to whom I would allude, was shortly after I first knew her, introduced to company, as is customary at the age of eighteen. I had frequent and good opportunities of observing the way in which she was received by the world, and whether from intimates or strangers; proud or servile; dependants or equals; I found she had the esteem, or, if I may so express it, the good word of all. Those who knew not of her noble virtues, were prepossessed by the sweetness of her air, and the ease and simplicity of her language. Such as were acquainted with, and valued these in her, were also charmed by the variety and depth of her knowledge, and the number and brilliancy of her accomplishments.

How

How then did it happen that this young lady was so universally respected by relations, acquaintances, and inferiors? For this one reason, that in her intercourse with the world she thought only of others; but that in retirement, and in considering imperfections she thought only of herself. This is the true means of appearing, and of actually being amiable.

The disinterestedness of this charming girl was natural and unconstrained. Whether with two or three friends, or with a large party, she invariably maintained her character. At table not a particle would she have of any nicety, but instantly refused when invited to accept it, without she observed that every one had partaken. Were friends to be accommodated with beds in the house, her room was the first to be resigned. Was any plan proposed for a charitable purpose: her's was the first purse to be undrawn, or the first hand in eagerness to carry it into execution. Were several to be conveyed in her carriage to any place, her anxiety was to put herself only in the most inconvenient part of the vehicle. But all these are slight marks of disinterestedness compared to her behaviour in public: I mean by public balls, or other descriptions of parties, and the theatre.

It is surprising to see the pains some young women take to be noticed, or to gain admiration in an assembly; or, as I shall call it, in

public.

Manners.

Public.

Excessive eagerness after admiration defeats its own end.

public. But their very anxiety defeats its purpose. Where applause is so ardently coveted, it is seldom obtained, because the means employed are evidently discreditable. The motive too is a false one. If our aim be to please a higher power than that of man, there runs through all our actions a noble ease, a graceful negligence, as to admiration, which at the moment we seem careless of praise, most forcibly excites it; and which, whilst we are conferring the most trivial favour, seems to treble its value. Virtue is so lovely in every shape, that those who will not be at the trouble of acting immediately from her principles, notwithstanding, sometimes imitate her at a distance; and sometimes the artifice is not discovered. Thus, that amiable behaviour of which I have spoken above, will be practised by persons who do not act from sound, steady principles, but it will shew itself upon particular occasions only; whereas the benevolence, the universal charity, which was the strong characteristic of the young person I first mentioned, was founded upon a noble motive, and was of course fixed and unchangeable. Permit me to exemplify what I have here endeavoured to advance.

Those who only act a good character are always in danger of being betrayed either by speech or gestures.

A young lady with her mother enters a crouded drawing-room: the blush of modesty overspreads her cheek as she bows to those whom she knows, and as she receives the compliments of the lady of
the

the mansion. She takes her seat (not far perhaps
from her parent;) between two or three girls,
neighbours or acquaintances, whose rank in life
is vastly inferior to her's. She is very free how-
ever with them, and offers to adjust the hair or
frock that is disordered, of one. This young
lady is then modest, friendly, and without pride.
So far appearances are in her favour. But let us
give time to observe the steadiness of her con-
duct, and we shall judge whether she acts from
principle. No one can long sustain an assumed
character.

I see then a group of females approach : they
are of high birth and fashion. These nod or
speak to our young lady, and gaze immediately
upon her companions, as if to inquire who they
are.

Behold! she slides further and further, and
rises ; passes her arm through that of the nearest
of the young party, and walks away with them.
One of these says, " what odd girls were you
talking to ?" She replies, " oh, they live near
us in the country, so one must be civil, you
know, but they are extremely awkward, *poor
things,* and they dress so horridly,—but *I am
very sorry* for them. Yet you can't conceive how
pleased they are to be noticed by people like us ;
do let us all go up, and speak to them just to see."

*I. Caressing
but to ridi-
cule.*

Young woman, thy virtue is indeed assumed.
Thy virtue is shallow and capricious : thou hast

the

the lip of honey, and the tongue of a scorpion.
Thou soothest with one hand, whilst with the
other thou aimest a dart. Unhappy she whose
confidence is won by thy caress, and whose re-
putation is wounded by thy blow.

How unlike to such a character was the gene-
rous girl I have alluded to, in the beginning of
this division! Delicate in exciting a confidential
intimacy, if the person did not gain upon her es-
teem, yet studious to consult the feelings of all;
was she firm to every attachment, silent as death
where all must blame, full of life and energy
where praise could be bestowed.

When any one is praising another, I have seen
young persons grow tired, or dull: perhaps
make a very careless answer, or none at all, as
if the perfections of any one else could lessen
their own good qualities. We may praise a particu-
lar person, but we do not say, she alone is lovely
or virtuous; this would be presumption indeed.

But let us not mistake flattery for praise; for
it is an odious practice to acquire. We may con-
sider a person wrong or foolish in his conduct,
although we need not make our opinions public;
but it is shameful to persuade him to believe what
we do not credit ourselves, merely to gain some
advantage from him; for what other motive can
we have? Thus let us think all we say, but
not say all that we may think. Young persons
should always recollect, how much opinions are

altered

altered by particular circumstances.. They are
sometimes unmercifully severe upon a person
who has changed an opinion, without suffering
themselves to reflect upon the causes. A gen-
tleman may say he is partial to late dinner hours.
A year afterwards, he may declare that he likes
to dine early, and does so. We are not to be
startled at this change of sentiment, but endea-
vour to form some reason for his excuse. Per-
haps he dined early by chance, or by the order of
a physician during several months, and found so
much benefit and satisfaction, that he was in-
duced to keep earlier hours, to which he is more
and more attached. I grant this gentleman
should give his reasons for the contradiction; we
might have the noble pleasure of hearing him
say, that he had changed a bad habit for a, good
one; which is, in other words, owning ourselves
to be wiser than we were. For those who change
from good to bad, they at least deserve our
pity.

When a person is spoken of advantageously,.
we should not permit ourselves to doubt what, the
speaker says, without we have great cause for.
doing so. We should only feel uneasy when we
hear one spoken ill of; or doubtful when we are
praised ourselves

Some young ladies are extremely fond of talk-
ing and of giving what they call, "all the news."
If they live in the country, all the families in the

vicinity

Manners.

Public.

Those who
change opi-
nions for the
better, are to
be respected.

3. Fondness
for receiving
and giving
news.

vicinity of five miles are talked over; every particular circumstance that can be collected and magnified is made into an event worthy of relating. Only consider how ungenerous must be some of the representations, and how untrue! The same thoughtless females are very fond of whispers; they will gather round their acquaintances at a party, and entrust them with half a dozen secrets. " Don't mention what I am going to say." " No, no," is incautiously answered; then follows a very insignificant, perhaps unkind anecdote. The young ladies forget a promise so carelessly given, and the circumstance is blazed abroad.

Let me advise you then, to give no encouragement to young persons who find an interest in speaking unkindly of their acquaintances. The faults of others we must see, but let them be to us as warnings, not matters of derision. If some persons meet with not more mercy from God than they themselves shew, how hard will be their lot !

A few girls are particularly desirous of shining in company, and of saying smart things. This is a dangerous temptation which should be resisted. Any remark of wiser heads, any idea of another, they pass off as their own. This is unjust at the best, and does not procure credit either, for it is possible that some person

may

may know the person, or writing, in which the sentiment or act originated; at any rate, we do not lessen our real merit by giving the authorities; on the contrary, there is shewn a generosity, and a soul above false praise, that gains infinitely upon the heart of every auditor.

Upon the last part of this subject, I shall but slightly touch. It relates to your behaviour in company, consisting equally of ladies and gentlemen of all ages.

Now in such an assembly, I imagine the action to be the test of truth. We judge much from the words, but from action more. The action is then the great consideration of those who would study the human character. There are light dissipated persons of the other sex, who watch every careless action (of which the female thinks nothing perhaps) and who form opinions much to her discredit. A prudent young woman will pause, therefore, on words, before she utters them to men, and will regulate her action by unconstrained dignity.

But what do I say, she will regulate her actions? I should rather have maintained, that she should regulate the mind, for this is the principle which urges to action.

Now a truly modest woman has an air of ease in all her movement; she feels her heart sound, her mind calm, her senses under the controul of reason and religion; and action and language are
with

with her, but one. Truth unites them. But this cannot be with the giddy and frivolous. She may persuade herself that she has a pure and delicate mind, but conscience whispers now and then, that she is not so dignified as she ought to be. Accordingly she is fearful that this derangement should be visible in company, and hence arises the evident opposition between language and action. She says the most harmless, nay, insignificant things, whilst her action is not harmless. Soon, too soon, do her enemies percieve the failing, and assume a freedom, at once un-

generous and degrading. But the impertinences playfully uttered by them, are so witty, although they may be " rather saucy, or rather free, I could not help laughing," I have heard from such a young person. Alas, my friends, there is no wit in a sentence, or expression, that draws the blood with such violence into your cheek, forehead and throat; it could not have been any thing of a very innocent kind, that should thus force nature to shew her displeasure. " But there is no harm in laughing." Yes, there is. The crimson laugh shews, that however you think your duty obliges you to give no encouragement to such conversation, yet your taste is gratified, and you indulge it. Consequently, it may be supposed, that duty is irksome to you, and that you would never hesitate to trample upon it, if inclination urged. This may seem a hard conclusion,

but

but it is, I apprehend, very just; for if the young are not startled at the first appearance of vice, what is to prevent them from proceeding to crimes? No one, it is said, is wicked all at once; but becomes so, step by step; the first steps, then, ought to be shunned with unceasing care.

But it never hardly happens that an impropriety is uttered directly to a correct female. There is such truth, innocence, virtue, in her very appearance, that no unworthy tongue dares assail her ear. Every man feels a respect and an awe in the company of a virtuous and lovely woman; and every one, whether of generous or mean mind, is disposed to pay respect, where respect is really deserved. This is not an homage to females, but to virtue. But who can wonder that the young woman is lightly mentioned, when she permits herself to be embraced in a waltz; or to be surrounded by gay licentious men, whom she suffers by her laugh and speech, to repeat impertinent ideas, or anecdotes; while she herself is lolling across a sofa, her feet crossed, her arms negligently spread abroad, or playing over her fan; and whilst her dress, so light, so thin, so exposed, bespeaks her want of delicacy, and her carelessness? All these little circumstances separated, seem trifles, but together they say a vast deal.

I shall now go a degree further.—It is possible that

Manners.
——
Public.

7. The con-
sequences are
always
gloomy,
sometimes
dreadful, of
clandestine
attachments.

that some of you may be addressed by gentle-
men of family and fortune; but if you hope for
comfort or happiness in your marriage, permit
no clandestine attachments. Every man of ho-
nour and integrity is rejoiced to be allowed an
application to the parents or guardian, and the
steady refusal of a young lady to listen to him,
until he has appealed to them, is a certain proof
of her good principles, the test of his worth, and
is a sure means of heightening his respect and
affection, provided his pretensions are well
grounded. But if he hesitate and make any ex-
cuse, no matter what, rely upon it, he is con-
scious of something wrong.

Retreat instantly; you have not a moment to
lose. Virtue impels you. See him no more, but
upon the conditions named. If you carry on a
secret correspondence, you are distracted by a
thousand fears, distresses, terrors; if you marry
clandestinely, you wring the hearts of your pa-
rents, even if they pardon you; you are unhap-
py in having broken through sacred duties; you
dread retribution in your own children: finally,
you are certain of more or less of your husband's
contempt and suspicion; for you have lowered
yourself in his eyes; you have failed once, and
you may perhaps again. But you trampled on
your duty for his sake? He does not even con-
sider himself obliged by it. Is it in the nature
of the human heart to love what is wrong? No;

one

one of the strongest native principles which God
has planted in our breasts, is to love and ad-
mire goodness, and to feel an antipathy to vice.
Whatever he might once assert, then, it is out
of the nature of things, it is impossible, that he
should have more regard on account of your de-
scending to a wrong act merely for him. But it
is nonsense to say for him, it is as much to please
yourself.

May you all then be prudent, and may you be
rewarded, whether you marry, or remain single
to support the declining age of those who have
watched over your infancy, and led you up to
honour.

V. *In the Church.*

This most important subject is connected with
all that is truly valuable, religion.

I take it for granted that you all go to some
place of worship at least once every Sunday,
and that you are never prevented from doing so,
but by illness.

When the clergyman reads with an audible
voice the lessons, every young person should
have her Bible, a small pocket size, ready to
accompany him; for if she is not reading, her
attention may be distracted by different objects.

Young people should particularly avoid going
into church after the service is begun; did they
know

Church.

1. Coming
too late.

Manners.
Church.
know how degraded they appear in every eye
that is turned upon them, they would not dis-
grace themselves a second time. Those who are
too indolent or indifferent to the sacred duties of
the church had better stay at home than disturb
those who are engaged in devotion, by entering

2. Sitting
during the
prayers.
at an improper time. Neither should any ex-
cept infirm persons presume to sit during the
time of our fine prayers and litany being read,

3. Not join-
ing in the
singing.
which ought to be said on our knees. It is also
the duty of every person to stand up and join in
the psalms: some young people reply I cannot
sing well, but if our hearts are properly im-
pressed with devotion, we feel a sacred pleasure
in raising our voice to the Almighty, who re-
gards not the tone of voice, but the sincerity of
our hearts.

After repeating the short prayer at the conclu-
sion of the sermon in profound silence, the organ
strikes up with a sacred composition, the people
rise in a body; some press towards the doors—
others wait until their carriages can draw up—
while some, without appearing to reflect upon

4. Talking
after the ser-
vice;
what they have just heard, are seen nodding
across the pews, talking, or considering different
smart dresses. How indecorous, in the very
church: surely people might wait and salute
their acquaintance out of the church: but if this

5. Or doing
so during it.
is incorrect, what is to be said of those who
whisper, nod, and examine the fashions during
the

the service. As for the impropriety of laugh-
ing, jesting, and lolling in careless postures, I
trust it is too striking to need any comment, and
I hope such instances are very rare.

Persons of condition, at least those who pos-
sess a carriage, are handed to it; the vehicles
drive away. In a great town, few people are
known to each other at church. The remarks
are of course general. But in a country place
the matter may be otherwise.

If it be true, as is asserted, that those in the
country are fifty years behind the metropolis in
civilization, we might expect, or at least hope,
they were superior in the native virtues of the
soul. Yet how often there may we lament over
want of generosity and fellow feeling. Some
young ladies, I fear, are no sooner seated in
their carriages, after quitting the public service
of the Almighty, than they begin to utter un-
kind observations on persons whom they know
(and indeed they know by sight every body in
the church), and to some of whom they happen
not to be partial, for partialities and dislikes
run sometimes high amongst a few, and espe-
cially in a small town or village. One had a
wrong bonnet, another was too fine, &c. With
such females not even the sacred character of the
clergyman himself is untouched. He read too
fast or too slow, or he did not take breath at the
proper time, or he was a person who did not
                                        practice

practice what he taught, or some other insinuation is given, to the disadvantage of one or another.

7. Criticising
the parson.

Now supposing the clergyman to be faulty in some respects, (and who is not?) is it becoming to mention the imperfections of others, when we should be most intent upon our own? Besides, it is most ungracious at this particular time; he has at any rate been endeavouring to set our duty before us in the strongest light, and we should feel grateful for his zeal. Whether his heart be convinced of the extent of his responsibility as a steward and a minister of heaven, is a point fully known only to his God. Let the hearers all look to themselves.

In what I have said I hope not to be misunderstood. Persons who are wholly fixed to one secluded spot are certainly more likely to have confined ideas than those who have travelled. Yet it may be seen, that a mind is as narrow on its return from making a circuit as it was on the owner's setting out; and we may know persons of large generous souls, and ways of thinking and judging, who have lived in one retired place during life, and who possess the finest feelings of humanity. Every thing depends upon the manner in which youth are brought up; and if they are liberally instructed, if they are taught to do in every respect as they would be done by, and practise the duties connected with this precept,

cept, it signifies very little where they live, or how much they may have travelled from home.

VI. *In the Dressing-room and Chamber.*

When the clock gives the signal for rest, the young lady embraces her parents and proceeds to her apartment: perhaps she has a sister who shares her room—both enter, and the bell is rung for the waiting-woman.

Chamber, &c.

Now the occurrences of the day pass in view, all reserve in conversation is banished. Happy sisters who preserve a sincere and tender friendship. The servant enters, and, hastily closing the door, advances towards them with great familiarity. Do they not look coldly to check this freedom? No, they take no notice, but continue the conversation respecting some private matter that they have heard mentioned in the drawing-room. It is easily accounted for, how many particulars of families are spread through a neighbourhood, when a servant is thus allowed to hear every thing from imprudent children. When she wishes to listen she is quiet, but when every matter is exhausted of interest to her, when the sisters have declared their dislike to one person, their vexation on account of a second, their criticisms on a third, and their surmises on a fourth, the maid chuses to have her turn, and pertly says, "Well, ladies.

1. Encouraging the gossip of maid servants.

dies, what d'ye think I've heard to-night from Mr. Green the butler, and he had it for certain from Sir Harry's footman?" The young ladies instead of checking her idle tales, immediately exclaim, "What?" The maid, fond of her importance, shuffles and hesitates, and at last makes a very great favour of her news, (which she is all impatience to relate) and after "Well, ladies, you must not take any notice, for your mama, her ladyship I mean, wou'dn't like me to talk of such things," she begins some foolish or scandalous story, very likely false, of course against some one who happens not to be a favourite; and as it is well received, she soon produces another, equally witty and instructive.

That all this is really the case *sometimes* I am convinced of. And so dangerous are the consequences of the pernicious sentiments of many a lady's woman, that no inconvenience should be considered too great in order to avoid them. When girls are young, I should most earnestly recommend their sleeping in a large room with the governess, or in one immediately adjoining to hers. When they grow older, I do not see why two sisters might not assist each other in the dressing room. Two young ladies whom I know requested their mother to forbid the attendance of their maid at night, and I could not but commend their readiness to wait on each other; and I must add, with girls brought up

as

as they have been, no servant's chatter would
have found encouragement, though no girls have
less of pride : the truth is, that their taste is not
disposed for idle gossip; it has been more nobly
trained. They possess a mother who has faith-
fully discharged her trust from their birth to this
period, and she now feels the sweet rewards of
her unremitting care.

But let us consider whether by this intimacy
of the servant and mistress, there are any ad-
vantages opposed to all the bad effects.

It is an universal remark, that servants are,
especially in gentlemen's families, grown more
incorrect in their conduct, and more careless
than ever of the master's interest. Whether this
be true I cannot take upon me to say; but I do
think their manner (I still confine myself to fe-
males) is more disrespectful and familiar than it
was some years since. Does this proceed from
the advance upon their wages, or from the inti-
mate footing they often feel themselves upon ? I
do not know: but of this I am certain, that a
saucy disposition in a maid will not be improved
by the freedom of her mistress; nor will one of
any other sort be benefited by them: so true is
the proverb, that "familiarity breeds contempt."
The young lady who makes a companion of her
maid, is nevertheless surprised to witness her im-
pertinences when she is fretfully disposed, or
chuses to see them; the servant considers all
times

Manners.
Chamber, &c.

times alike, and is too high in consequence to make an apology: hence both are concerned in disputes, degrading to the one and offensive in the other. Separation is often the conclusion of the affray.

But sometimes ladies expect to gain the fidelity of their women by this condescension.

We may stand a chance of gaining the fidelity of domestics by attention to their comforts, anxiety for their welfare and happiness, regard for them during illness, a wish to promote chearfulness and harmony in themselves, readiness in giving them plain and honest advice upon occacasions, and by our willingness to reward their zeal and industry; also, by our concern to lend or distribute amongst them books, or other things, tending to afford innocent amusement, and to implant virtuous principles in their hearts.

Real fidelity
is only to be
purchased by
honest
means.

By doing all this, I imagine, if gratitude be not extinct, we must raise respect and an interest— surely fidelity cannot then be far off. But fidelity that cannot be thus created upon noble principles, never can be purchased by a mean and dishonourable familiarity.

It is scarcely necessary to notice to a British lady, that the first ornament of the person consists in a scrupulous delicacy with regard to its

Delicacy of
person the
diadem of
women.

neatness. The skin to have the freshness of the rose; hair to shine in glossy ringlets; teeth and mouth to be preserved lovely and in purity by application

application to the sparkling fountain after every
meal; the nails to shine in a clear small arch at
the tip of every finger;—an extreme attention
to these enchanting trifles has so much induced
foreigners to pronounce English women the most
lovely in the world: they naturally conclude
that outward purity is strongly indicative of in-
ternal innocence, and this idea gives a charm
that commands every thing of respect and admi-
ration.

After nicety of person is neatness of the ward-
robe. Every young lady should know how to
manage work, cut out, and order for herself,
that she may at least understand hereafter to
give proper directions to her woman; she should
be accustomed whilst very young to folding and
putting away every article of dress, and to the
preserving of every thing in order.

An hour should be appointed for rising, and
if possible for retiring to rest. A lady of qua-
lity, long after she was married, used, I remem-
ber, always to persevere in this custom as far
as she could, and if she staid even till the morn-
ing at a ball or party, she never made any dif-
ference, but rose after only two or three hours
sleep. This is a good plan if young ladies do
not stay out very late, otherwise it is impracti-
cable.

The time that is sometimes spent in talking,
after

Manners.
Chamber, &c.

Rising at a
stated hour is
very benefi-
cial.

after entering the dressing-room, might be very usefully employed.

What a beautiful sight have I beheld on opening the dressing-room door to wish a sweet girl good night. There she has been seated at her dressing table in a loose robe, her maid dismissed; herself, in the bloom of life, health, and beauty, like a tender rose just bursting upon public admiration and notice, unconscious of her illustrious rank, riches, and honours; lost to the world, and intent only on making a sweet interest with heaven; there she has sat, her arm supporting her head, and the long snuff of the taper shewing the earnestness of its mistress, whilst she herself has studied a beautiful and simple meditation, or the sacred precepts of the Bible! I have paused some moments to look upon so affecting a picture, till she has heard, started up, closed the book, and advanced to meet me. When all was quiet, she knelt down to offer up petitions for the protection of heaven, and then sought sweet repose.

When we reflect upon sleep, how entirely we are deprived of our faculties, how torpid, how quiet, how defenceless, we may surely acknowledge that it is indeed the image of death. The uses of sleep are many and invaluable. It is relaxation to the faculties; rest to the body; the soother of affliction, and quieter of passions.
Yet

Yet all this might have been effected some other . *Manners.* way by Omnipotence, if it had not pleased Him Chamber, &c. to give his creatures daily intimations of the great sleep in which we are for a time to fall, but after which we shall rise and put on robes of immortality. So by way of inducing us to live always prepared, the Redeemer has given us to understand that this night may be our last; that we may retire to rest in health this evening, yet awaken no more.

Let us all then, my charming friends, endeavour to arrange our accounts every day before we sleep, that we may not be afraid to pass into eternity before the next dawn; and may your innocent minds feel the hope that virtue and goodness can give. Be good on earth that you may rejoice and be blessed in heaven.   Adieu.

THE CONCLUSION.

SPECIMEN OF THE STYLE FOR CHARACTER
BOOKS ALLUDED TO IN CHAPTER I.*

September 1, *THURSDAY.*—Although you may be arrived at
800. an age when the commission of serious faults
cannot properly be expected, my dear Ellen, yet
I conceive much remains for your preceptress to
do, in order to strengthen your young mind in
every principle of virtue and goodness, which
may be there implanted by the lively and affec-
tionate zeal of your parents, particularly that of
your mama; for a young lady is more immedi-
ately under the guardianship of her mother than
of her other parent, provided she be so fortunate
as to possess him.

In pointing out to you the errors I may per-
ceive in your general conduct, I shall have one
object only in view,—your happiness; as in en-
deavouring to make you good and amiable, I am
trying to make you happy; for, rely upon it, vice
is

* To avoid every suspicion of personalities in the examples I
am about to give, I have mentioned names with which I was
never acquainted; general faults that are often observed in the
young; and a date of year in which I was myself in childhood.

is always attended with misery, even in this world: a wicked person is an unhappy one, let him appear ever so much to the contrary.

Be not offended if you sometimes see a little plainness in my memorandum. Your situation in life is an obstacle to your hearing of plain truths. Your equals will not be at the trouble, and your inferiors will never presume, to tell you that you have done wrong. After your parents, this is my duty to teach you to know yourself: an arduous undertaking for us both.

In two or three years you will be called upon by custom to take your rank in society; and whether or not, you may be under the roof of the dearest of friends, your anxious mother, you will be expected to act more upon your own free will than you do at present. That you may be prepared for such an important era of life, with firm principles and sound judgment, and charity for the failings of others by having studied your own, are my wishes when I thus lay my sentiments, I hope affectionately, although earnestly, before you.

And now, after so long a preface, which I will not suppose can have tired you, I must tell you that I was this morning very well satisfied with your attention to studies; and that I did not observe any thing in your behaviour to compel a remark, excepting the ungraceful manner in which you ate your custard-pudding, in order, I suppose,

suppose, to shew your brother how a pill was swallowed! Graceful actions are often indications of a refined and delicate mind, though many a rough sailor has had the finest and most humanized feelings.. At any rate, I should like to see you possessing elegance, if it need not be purchased at the expense of your sincerity and integrity.

Friday.—I have scarcely to find any fault of notice to-day, excepting with the argument you held with your mama. Surely, my dear, you must allow that it is more likely that that lady should know better what is pleasing to your papa than you can possibly do. Never attempt to talk your parents out of their opinion, it is extremely disrespectful, and makes you look almost undutiful, which, I am sure you are not; from several things trifling in themselves, perhaps, I have judged your heart to be affectionate, and, I trust, it will ever be so. Do not make grimaces, they have a vulgar appearance; pray leave off also that word " plague," which you have used several times to day—" What a plague is this and that." With your attention to studies I am perfectly satisfied. May you ever be attentive to well-meant advice, and may you always feel benefit from it! Adieu.

Saturday.—More grimaces! They really disfigure you amazingly; I trust you will leave off so foolish a trick. And now, my dear Ellen, I

hope

hope you have had a lesson (and I am glad it is
not a more serious one) upon jokes carried too
far. " An innocent little joke," you will say,
." we may have." There is danger in having
them at all. 'Tis true no bad effects may arise
from a little joke, but that little one may lead to
practise many serious and even fatal. In this
case you did not wish to inconvenience your
friend, but you recommended her to do what you
intended to joke upon; and in this there was a
kind of deception, although you did not consider
it so. By the smallest deception mutual confi-
dence is destroyed, at any rate lessened; and
suspicion and incredulity step in its place. I
hope, my dear, you understand me. I should
believe all you assert till I have discovered you in
an untruth, and then I should doubt your word.
I also trust you till you deceive me, and when
that may happen my dependence upon you va-
nishes; and this is the case with people in ge-
neral; in short it is the just punishment for any
species of vice. As for most practical jokes, they
are a composition of falsehood, illnature and
cruelty: they are acted in deceit; vex, or injure
the person acted upon; and by the success of the
plot excite the laughter or satisfaction of the in-
ventors. Never, my child, be concerned in tor-
turing your fellow creatures. Life is short;
employ it honourably; do what good you can :
you need not want for opportunity. .

I am

I am pleased to notice, that I was perfectly satisfied with your exertions in writing your theme; it was as well done as I could possibly expect. You are still young, and as you have so much time before you, and as I shall be ever ready to assist you with any instruction, I hope you will exert yourself, and let me see you perfectly prepared to meet the severe criticisms of the world: let it see you good, clever, and accomplished. . . .

Monday.—You have been anxiously expecting the arrival of this day, in the hope of having your character book. May it prove an useful monitor! At the riding-school to day I observed rather ungenteel behaviour, which was, I am well aware, caused by those rude girls to whom your seat was next. This shews you the force of example, and points out the necessity for care in the choice of an acquaintance. These young women will never be your companions any where but at that place; yet you yesterday appeared to be quite intimate. There is a quiet, easy, dignified manner, totally distinct from haughtiness, that you might assume to keep such forward people at a distance: but never confound this manner with pride, it would be a bad exchange for too much easiness of temper; and recollect, that it is extremely wrong to encourage a person to freedom, whilst at the same time you despise him for it: this is ungenerous and mean.

I

I have also to remonstrate upon what relates to
the hint given me by your mama, of certain habits
of controversy which you maintain now and then
with your sister. A disposition to argue and dispute
may be prejudicial to a young person for several
reasons. It creates an idea in the mind of a stran-
ger, that affection does not subsist in the family,
or at least among the children of it. It gives a fret-
ful, peevish turn to the temper, which in youth
cannot be too much guarded against, as it
" grows and strengthens with the growth," so
that at thirty a cross lady may be a peevish old
woman, for nothing *makes* age so much in a coun-
tenance as the influence of discontent and fretful-
ness; another reason is, that disputes are un-
pleasant and disrespectful to those who witness
them; and lastly, they are offensive to virtue and
religion.

Tuesday.—Well, my dear, I must expostulate
with you on the few harlequin tricks you per-
formed this afternoon; perhaps you intended
them for my amusement, for which I am obliged
to you; but I should have been more gratified
had you given me a few of your best Scotch or
Irish steps, or a game of battledore. I do not
conceive a young lady appears to advantage
when she is throwing her limbs into contorsions
and jumping like a rope dancer. I was sorry to
see you afterwards saunter about for half an hour

in

Conclusion.

in perfect idleness. Do you not know, that
" idleness is the source of all mischief?" If you
do not, you shall give me the satisfaction of see-
ing one of your best themes upon this proposition;
and the subject will, I hope, be deeply imprinted
on your mind. There is another little matter I
must notice.—I stood this afternoon some minutes
waiting for your determination upon, whether
you would walk with me, or accept of your
mama's offer of going with her in the carriage:
at last you resolved upon walking, and I went
into my room, put on my bonnet, &c. and came
down; I inquired for you, but you were no where
to be found. This I thought very incorrect. I
asked the butler if you had accompanied your
mama, and he replied that you had. Now a
country drive was very likely to be of service to
you, but you should have informed me that you
had given up the walking, of which I had not
the smallest idea. You say you told the servant
to acquaint me. Very likely, my dear; but you
know, I dare say, that servants sometimes forget
to give such messages. Suppose you had paid
me the compliment to come yourself to tell me,
that you regretted I had had the trouble of get-
ting ready, it would not have been more than I
might have a right to expect on such an occa-
sion, and you would not have been detained by it
two minutes. I do not wish any *formalities* from
you,

you, but that consideration which springs from real good-nature, which is sometimes called politeness; that kind feeling in the manners which spares uneasiness, and feels unhappy in having unintentionally caused it. This is what I desire in you, and to see it exercised on every occasion; then you will be esteemed (and deservedly so) good-natured, truly polite, or charitable; for these three words are nearly of the same signification. Good night!

Wednesday.—I am sorry to observe so much giddiness in your manner of writing; I really think you are anxious to do your exercises correctly, but you suffer your ideas to ramble from the point at which they should be fixed. You begin well, but when you have written a little your mind is taking a long journey, and your fingers scratch away without being attended to, consequently they do wrong, which the mind perceives directly upon her return home. Pray keep this good subject in better order. Indeed you are in general in a great hurry. Lord Chesterfield says, " A man may be in haste when there is a necessity for it, but never in a *hurry* (which you often are); for, if a thing is worth doing at all, it is worth doing well."

- With regard to your conduct to day I am much pleased with several points in it. They may appear insignificant when particularized, but toge-
ther

ther they are matters from which one may draw a good inference. I am fond of noticing good-ness of heart in a slight occasion. We are all ready enough to do our best when the world is gazing; but the character is best tried before one familiar friend; if it be then firm to its public principles, we may argue much in its favour.

Thursday.—I begin with requesting you to be very careful of giving decided answers. When I say, "Are you sure of such a thing?" you should never answer till you really are sure; otherwise I shall be apt to lose all dependence upon you, which I should be sorry to do. You are so very giddy that you will not give yourself time to think before you speak. I do not expect to see you grave and steady as an old woman, but I hope to see you collect yourself before you venture to say, with great emphasis, " Yes, indeed I am sure it is so." In the course of my instruction I am so fearful of leading you into error, that when I am even pretty sure of a circumstance, I say to you, " I cannot declare it for certain, you had better consult the book;" and have you not more confidence in me when I do this, than you would have if I were to be positive upon a matter of doubt? We are all imperfect creatures, and every one of us may, and does commit mistakes in judgment, memory, and perception; therefore you should never be *positive* upon any subject unless you are really certain;

and

and even then I would not advise you to be too
eagerly *positive,* for it is ill-bred and self-opiniated
to argue with your friends merely for the *plea-
sure* (if it be so) or hope of proving yourself dic-
tatorial. Your attention to me this evening
whilst I was speaking to you, and indeed your
anxiety upon any subject which can inform your
mind, are to me, my dear young friend, consi-
derations inexpressibly gratifying. How much
pleasure may I anticipate in conducting your
education! Nothing can be more agreeable to a
preceptress than to observe in her pupil a desire
for improvement. Depend upon it the more at-
tentive you may be, the more pleasure I shall
have in instructing you. Do you not feel amaze-
ment on contemplating the works of nature?
What are your reflections upon our evening's
conversation? What miraculous power but that
of God himself, could create such beings as we
have examined in our book of the microscopes?
The more you regard the works of your Creator,
the more you will ever see of his infinite wisdom.
What hand of man could form that wonderful
organ the eye? Could the most clever amongst
mortals even produce that little part for which
we searched, called the cornea? Could any one
below omnipotence frame and place over the eye
a moveable cover of fine delicate skin which
should be possessed of such soothing elastic
powers? Could any one of us even produce by
manufactures

Conclusion. manufactures the most simple leaf of the forest? Could we even form such a creature as the little troublesome fly that buzzes round our ears in the gaiety of his little merry heart? Not one of these apparent trifles can man perform. Let us then in grateful wonder offer praise to Him who has, in millions of ways, proved his own perfection in his perfect works; and his incalculable goodness in making all these works for the beauty, necessity, or comfort of man.

It were easy to produce many more examples for the character book, but I would not encroach on the reader's patience. May this specimen be considered not unworthy of attention; and may every preceptress who adopts her plan from it, be rewarded in the improvement of the child; in the full and perfect approbation of the parent; and in the proud satisfaction of mind, that ever results from success in honest exertion.

THE END.

Printed by Cox and Bayls,
Great Queen Street, Lincoln's-Inn-Fields, London.

NEW WORKS ON EDUCATION,

Forming most acceptable Presents for Youth of either Sex,

PRINTED FOR

H. COLBURN, 50, CONDUIT STREET, HANOVER-SQUARE.

——————

1. LES DELASSEMENS de LA JEUNESSE, Recueil de Contes, Historiettes Morales, &c. suivi de Pièces choisies de MONTAIGNE, PASCAL, LA BRUYERE, et VAUVENARGUES. 4 vol. 18mo. orné de douze jolies Gravures. Price 14s. bound.

2. CONSEILS A MA FILLE, ou Nouveaux Contes, par J. N. BOUILLY, Auteur des " Contes à ma Fille," 2d edition, improved and embellished with plates, price 6s. bound.
Do. in English.
" The amusing work of " *Contes à ma Fille*," so creditable to the author, is, in our opinion, *surpassed* by these Nouveaux Contes, which contain many instructive lessons conveyed in simple and expressive terms."—*Gent. Mag.*
" To the young French scholar we can particularly recommend this performance as exemplifying the elegant and easy turns of the language, and the peculiarities of the idiom."—*Crit. Review.*

3. PETITS ROMANS et CONTES MORAUX, par Madame DE GENLIS, 7 vols. 35s.

4. RECUEIL de NOUVELLES, par Madame DE MONTOLIEU, Auteur de Caroline de Litchfield, 3 vols. 12s.

5. BELISAIRE, par Madame DE GENLIS, 2d edition, 1 vol. 12mo Price 5s.
" The Belisaire of Madame de Genlis being exempt from those exceptionable passages which are to be met with in that of Marmontel, is strongly recommended, and has lately been adopted in preference for the use of schools and young people."

6. SAINCLAIR, ou la VICTIME des SCIENCES et des ARTS, par Madame DE GENLIS Price 3s.
" A delightful little tale, told with great simplicity, and conveying an excellent moral in the most pleasing form."—*Critical Review.*

7. LA BOTANIQUE HISTORIQUE et LITTÉRAIRE, suivie d'une Nouvelle intitulée les Fleurs ou les Artistes. Par Madame DE GENLIS, 2 vols. 12mo. Price 10s.

" These volumes are evidently the result of most extensive reading. The author, rejecting all scientific details on botany, has employed herself in collecting an historical account of every use which has been made of the different kinds of plants and vegetables, every custom, tradition, supposed medical or religious efficacy attributed to them, and every literary or other purpose to which they have been appropriated."—*Antijac. Review*, 1812.

8. COURS de LITTÉRATURE, Ancienne et Moderne, par Madame de STAEL HOLSTEIN. Précédé de Mémoires sur la Vie de l'Auteur. 2e édition. 2 tom. 21s.

9. FENELON, DE L'EXISTENCE DE DIEU. 1 vol. 12mo. 5s. 8vo. 10s.

10. MISCELLANEOUS QUESTIONS in HISTORY and CHRONOLOGY, for the Use of Schools. 3d edition, improved, 2s.

11. OBSERVATIONS ON WORKS OF FICTION, and particularly those for Children and Adolescence. 4s.

12. LAURA VALCHERET, a Tale for Adolescence, by the Author of the preceding. 5s.

13. CONDORCET'S sure and easy METHOD of LEARNING to CALCULATE. 3s. 6d.

ITALIAN LITERATURE.

14. IL LETTORE ITALICO, the Italian Reader; being a selection of Extracts from the most eminent Italian Writers, in prose and verse, beginning with SOAVE and ending with DANTE, with explanatory Notes, forming a series of progressive lessons, the study of which will enable the scholar to read and properly understand the works of each writer. By M. SANTAGNELLO, Master of Languages.

Also by the same eminent Professor,

15. A COMPENDIOUS and EASY GRAMMAR of the ITALIAN LANGUAGE, comprising a new and improved classification of the verbs, with appropriate dialogues, &c. 2d edition, improved. Price 7s. bound.

N. B. This Grammar, already adopted at several female seminaries of the first respectability, is admirably calculated, from the simplicity of its plan, to enable the scholar speedily to acquire a complete knowledge of this pleasing language.

16. ITALIAN EXERCISES; adapted to the Grammar, 1 vol. 12mo.

17. AN ITALIAN TRANSLATION of Madame COTTIN's admired Tale of ELIZABETH. By M. SANTAGNELLO.

Lightning Source UK Ltd.
Milton Keynes UK
UKOW01f1928010218
317233UK00011B/540/P